WHAT ARE WE DOING HERE?

MARILYNNE ROBINSON

McCLELLAND & STEWART

Library and Archives Canada Cataloguing in Publication data is available upon request

ISBN: 978-0-7710-7345-8
ebook ISBN: 978-0-7710-7346-5

Text design by Jonathan D. Lippincott
Jacket design by Strick&Williams
Jacket art by Samantha Hahn
Printed and bound in the USA

McClelland & Stewart,
a division of Penguin Random House Canada Limited,
a Penguin Random House Company
www.penguinrandomhouse.ca

1   2   3   4   5   22   21   20   19   18

Penguin
Random House
McCLELLAND & STEWART

James and Megan
Joseph and Katherine
Beatrice and Theodore

Nearest and Dearest

Contents

WHAT ARE WE DOING HERE?

Preface

This book is a collection mostly of lectures I have given in churches, seminaries, and universities over the last few years. Most of them reflect central preoccupations that are to my mind matters of urgency and that arise from the way we think now. I know it is conventional to say we Americans are radically divided, polarized. But this is not more true than its opposite—in essential ways we share false assumptions and flawed conclusions that are never effectively examined because they are indeed shared.

In great part this is the fault of our intellectual culture. It pains me to say this. These are people I identify with and have learned from and whom I wish I could admire wholeheartedly. The fact is, however, that much of what I have learned from them has amounted to my taking exception to a book or a lecture and then mulling over the reasons for my discontent with it. This is no doubt obvious from my earlier essays.

Here is an instance of the alarming like-mindedness that has emerged among us over the last few decades. Many teachers in the humanities have treated it as true that this country was always fundamentally capitalist, intending the word to mean more or less what they think Karl Marx intended by it. In

99.5 percent of cases they have never read a page of Marx, so they have no idea what he was describing. Capitalism in his time was largely the commerce between American cotton fields and British cotton factories, which generated great wealth on both sides, together with vast, nearly absolute poverty on both sides, among English workers and American slaves. It is true that slave labor was used in Northern states while they were under British law, which demonstrates that the use of it was economically viable there, too. Nevertheless, after the Revolution those states acted to ban it.

In the South cotton capitalism accelerated, inspiring dreams of Mexican and Central American conquest. The South was otherwise remarkably static. Little schooling or publishing went on there. It realized a fantasy of itself in a hastily contrived, clapped-together timeless order, the kind enjoyed by the moneyed in the Old World, many of whom bought their castles and furnished their chapels with profits from the slave trade. I have heard, more times than I can count, that capitalism was an American invention, and the basis of our "exceptionalism." Supposedly it was the North that was capitalist, able to bully the pastoral South because the North was greedy and aggressive, and industrialized. Marx neither said nor implied any such thing, certainly not in his essays about the Civil War. As he was well aware, Southern slavery was part of an industrial workforce whose great center was in England. Its tactics of exploitation were in the last degree greedy and aggressive. The great vision of the South was the spread of slavery and cotton all the way to California. Anyone who bothered to read Jefferson Davis would be clear on this point.

This nonsense is important first of all because it legitimizes rapacious capitalism as preeminently American, the source of our success, including those freedoms we acknowledge. And it describes a national character formed around the values associated with it, a generalization that has important interpretive consequences—everything that has happened in our history is to be understood in its essence as profit driven. Among liberals who subscribe to this notion, which they all do, since they tend to feel that we as a nation are gravely deficient in humility, this produces a slick, unreflecting cynicism. Among those whom we call conservatives, it produces an unembarrassed enthusiasm for self-interest, so long as the interest in question is their own. It encourages the kind of brutalist heroics celebrated in the pages of Ayn Rand. On left and right, such thinking makes the enlightened, humane development of American culture over centuries inauthentic. It is shocking how defenseless the protections of the environment, of the poor, and even of the rights of voters have been shown to be in recent years. No one defends these things as American, because the Left no more than the Right thinks of them as among our core values. The great engine of capitalism can mow them down, since they were derivative at best and in any case are proved to be inessential by the very fact that they are vulnerable and exceptional. Self-interest, on the other hand, is universal and constant—and was presumably the motive behind these institutions in the first place. True, it can take some tortuous reasoning to account for their original economic utility. But if a conclusion can be assumed to be true, there is no need to worry about arriving at it by means that might otherwise seem dubious.

The Left does not understand the thinking of the Right because it is standing too close to have a clear view of it. In important respects, the Left has nurtured and rationalized it, neglecting and distorting history in the process, therefore removing potential correctives. It is easy to tell a roomful of eighteen-year-olds that given time the efficiencies of capitalist free labor would have eliminated slavery. So the Invisible Hand would have been the real liberator, if the idealists had simply stepped back and let it do its work. Presumably this is the kind of thing President Donald J. Trump had in mind when he said the Civil War could and should have been avoided. He might have learned this from the Far Right, but it could equally well have come to him from more respectable sources. Again, nothing in the thinking or in the aspirations of Jefferson Davis suggests that he foresaw anything less than a vast expansion of slavery throughout the Americas. An unbridled South would have brought catastrophe far beyond our borders. Dare I mention the Mexican War? We can assume that abolitionists were naïve in failing to leave history in the ungentle hands of economic forces, or that they had mercenary interests greater than accommodation with the vast wealth generated by slavery. Or we can assume that they listened to the voices of the South and learned from them how very much was at stake. But why bother with context? Still, even after very many years, it sounds bold and provocative to flatten the historical landscape and to deal in moral equivalencies.

•

We have surrendered thought to ideology. Every question is for all purposes the same question, every answer the same answer. Why has anyone done anything? Self-interest. This is true of the whole species, but it is most emphatically true of Americans. Where in all this is wisdom, courage, generosity, personal dignity? To think in such terms is naïve. These qualities are merely apparent, never determinant. To say that we as a national community have benefited from them, that individuals have actually considered the general welfare from time to time and addressed it, acted in light of it, is to slide into shameless nationalism. The Right is more than happy to be excused from these ideals, standards that have, historically, been invoked in order to mitigate the uglier impulses, greed prominent among them. The Left cannot account for the civic virtues in theoretical or ideological terms and feels awkward speaking of them in religious terms. This is only truer because the Right has made religious language toxic by putting it to uses that offend generosity and dignity. Perhaps the worst thing about ideological thinking is that it implies a structure in and behind events, a history that is reiterative, with variations that cannot ultimately change the course of things and are therefore always trivial, no matter how much thought and labor goes into the making of them. The notion of an abiding sameness despite superficial differences can have consequences that are hilarious and awful, as when a roomful of professors, flown in from the corners of the world to share their thoughts, in all seriousness identify as wage slaves because they are dependent on their earnings. The other side of this is the permission given by the concept of class war to people on the right who consider themselves successful, therefore embattled. They can resist arguments for economic justice as if they were existential threats, the grumblings of resentment that, if acted on, would loot them of their trophies. In this country, at least, it is more temperament than circumstance that leads people to identify themselves with one side or the other. Meanwhile, actual American workers have no place in the conversation. If they identify with it at all, it is in their refusing to think of themselves as an exploited class, and in their readiness to identify with success and power. This is entirely understandable given the alternative, and given the memory, recent for many of them, of times when they could count on fairly compensated work, with everything this implies for personal latitude and social mobility.

It is no accident that Marxism and social Darwinism arose together, two tellers of one tale. It is not surprising that they have disgraced themselves in very similar ways. Their survival more than one hundred fifty years on is probably owed to the symmetry of their supposed opposition. Based on a single paradigm, they reinforce each other as legitimate modes of thought. So it is with our contemporary Left and Right. Between them we circle in a maelstrom of utter fatuousness.

I say this because I am too old to mince words. We have, in our supposed opposition, gone a long way toward making class real—that is, toward cheating people of opportunity. Historically, education has been the avenue by which Americans have had access to the range of possibilities that suit their gifts. We have put higher education farther out of reach of low-income people by cutting taxes and forcing tuitions to rise. And we attack public preparatory education. We make an issue about family background in terms of suitability for college, when in fact anyone who has paid a reasonable amount of attention in a decent high school will be fine in college. Unless he or she is working two jobs to pay for it, that is. I have taught for many years in a highly selective program that attracts students of every background. There is absolutely no evidence that those whose education would be called "elite" are at the slightest advantage. Our prejudices are impressing themselves on our institutions and therefore on the lives of all of us. The willingness to indulge in ideological thinking—that is, in thinking that by definition is not one's own, which is blind to experience and to the contradictions that arise when broader fields of knowledge are consulted—is a capitulation no one should ever make. It is a betrayal of our magnificent minds and of all the splendid resources our culture has prepared for their use.

WHAT ARE WE DOING HERE?

What Is Freedom of Conscience?

Director's Lecture at Neubauer Collegium for Culture and
Society at the University of Chicago: May 5, 2016

I assume that conscience is a human trait widespread enough to be generally characteristic, not originating in culture though inevitably modified by it. Guilt and shame, and dread at the thought of incurring them, are clearly associated with conscience, which grants them legitimacy and which they empower. Conversely, the belief that one's actions are endorsed by conscience can inspire a willingness to stand against custom or consensus in matters that might otherwise be considered wrong or shameful, for example, rebellion against the existing order.

The idea of conscience as we think of it is reflected in the Greek of the New Testament. It is to be found in Plato as self-awareness, a capacity for self-appraisal. In the Hebrew Bible it is pervasively present by implication, an aspect of human experience that must be assumed to be reflected in the writings of the apostle Paul and others. In Genesis a pagan king can appeal to the Lord on the basis of the integrity of his heart and the innocence of his hands, and learn that God has honored his innocence and integrity by preventing him from sinning unintentionally. The king's sense of himself, his concern to conform his conduct to the standard he brings to bear on it, which is a standard God acknowledges, is a kind of epitome of the concept of righteousness so central to the Hebrew Bible. That the king is a pagan, a Philistine, suggests that the Torah regards moral conscience as universal, at least among those who respect and cultivate it in themselves.

Beyond the capacity to appraise one's own actions and motives by a standard that seems, at least, to stand outside momentary impulse or longer-term self-interest and to tell against oneself, conscience is remarkably chimerical. An honor killing in one culture is an especially vicious crime in another. We have learned that effective imprisonment at forced labor of unwed mothers, or of young women deemed likely to stray, was practiced until a few decades ago in a Western country, Ireland, despite the many violations of human rights this entailed. One might expect it to have ended in any previous century, if consciences were burdened by it. Americans have just awakened to the fact that we have imprisoned a vast part of our own population with slight cause, stigmatizing them at best and depriving them of the possibility of a normal, fruitful life. Conscience can be slow to awake, even to abuses that are deeply contrary to declared values—for example, liberty and the pursuit of happiness. And if conscience is at peace with such things, if it rationalizes and endorses them, does it still possess an authority that justifies its expression, since acceptance is as much an act of conscience as resistance is? After all, in this country, where freedom means that a consensus permits the actions and policies of government unless recourse is had to demonstrations, recall, impeachment, legal action, or rejection by voters, we are normally reconciled to things we may not approve of. Conscience obliges us—always fewer of us, it seems—to respect the consequences of elections, without which democracy is no longer possible. It is not always easy to tell a slumbering conscience from one that is weighing consequences.

People who believe that an unconstrained capitalism will

yield the best of all possible worlds might earnestly regret the disruptions involved in it, the uncompensated losses suffered as a consequence of capital being withdrawn in one place to be invested in another, solely in the interest of its own aggrandizement. But how does one intervene in the inevitable? Cost-benefit analysis has swept the human sciences! It explains everything! Depending, of course, on highly particular definitions of both cost and benefit. I have never seen an estimate of the wealth lost when a town falls into ruin, nor any calculus of the wealth lost when a workforce is idled, over against the wealth created in consequence of these creations of poverty. What is the cost to the Chinese, who are never asked if the benefits of factory work outweigh the loss of clean air, drinkable water, and the health of their children? The fact that a loss is immeasurable is really not a reason for leaving it out of account. Impoverishment of populations on the basis of financial self-interest makes a joke of personal freedom. Yet we accept the legitimacy of economic theory that overrides our declared values. This is to say, the public conscience is not touched by grand-scale dispossessions because it is numbed by a dubious theory, and by the fact that real power, neither political nor legal nor inclined to notice politics or law except as illegitimate intrusions on its limitless prerogatives, has passed out of the public's control as they pass more and more deeply into its control.

•

Freedom and the sovereignty of individual conscience are ideas that in early American culture and in precursor movements in England and Europe arose together and informed each other in important ways. The great conflict in the Middle Ages, putting aside monarchical adventurism, baronial restiveness, and so on, was between dissident religious movements and the established church. The question at issue was whether or not people had a right to their own beliefs. In the thirteenth century, two

Crusades and an Inquisition were carried out in southern Europe against the large and influential movement called Catharism, or Albigensianism, that was associated with Languedoc but also was important in northern Italy. These people are still accused of strange doctrines and a world-hating cast of mind, as heretics have always been, but this was probably not true, of them at least, since they were associated with the troubadours and the courts of love, and since they were so deeply nonviolent that their prosecutors could distinguish them from others by a very simple test: Told to kill a chicken, a Cathar would refuse. They were defended by non-Cathars in the region in what became a protracted but effective war of extermination. These events established policy for the treatment of dissidents, also called heretics, in Europe for centuries.

It seems fair to wonder if even terrible suppression is not, over time, a stimulus and a preservative. Whether Catharism persisted despite it is a difficult question, since the word was sometimes used polemically, and since its texts were so thoroughly expunged and its reputation so blackened that it would be hard to identify traces of its influence in subsequent history. But dissidence persisted. John Wycliffe, the fourteenth-century Oxford professor whose theological writing spread throughout Europe and remained influential in England into the period of the Reformation, was exhumed from his grave and burned as a heretic. Those associated with his teaching, known as Lollards, were burned as well, again into the period of the Reformation. It must have been conscience that made them and so many others act as though they were free despite the drastic constraints placed on their freedom. Conscience appears throughout history in individuals and groups as a liberating compulsion, though the free act is so often fatal.

Through it all, freedom of thought and belief became a powerful cause in its own right. It had scriptural warrant, which mattered more as translation and printing made the Bible more widely accessible. In his Letter to the Romans, Paul says that whatever does not proceed from faith is sin. A marginal note in the 1560 Geneva Bible, the dissenters' Bible, says the word *faith* here is to be understood as meaning *conscience*. That is, according to Paul there are "matters indifferent." His examples are eating meat sacrificed to idols, drinking, observing holy days. Such things are neither right nor wrong in themselves, but occasions of sin for anyone who feels such things are sinful to be done or to be omitted. Hamlet, that conscience-burdened man, carries the point too far when he says, "There is nothing either good or bad, but thinking makes it so." The obligation to act consistently with one's conscience, which Paul intends as grounds for tolerance among Christians, had the effect of making the enforcement of religious conformity intolerable. It gave disputes about transubstantiation or auricular confession the highest seriousness for dissidents who could not accept these or any number of other doctrines and practices. Henry VIII, for all his supplanting of the pope, was fiercely determined to keep Catholic worship and teaching intact in the English church. He was just as happy to persecute Protestant dissidents as Catholics, so tensions continued and took on a more political character because the king's seizure of power was a political act.

The fact that I focus in this essay on the Anglo-American history with freedom of conscience reflects my own interests and limitations, not any assumption that these cultures were unique in engaging it or that they had a special gift for it. It emerged so potently among them as a fortunate consequence of accident and cataclysm, and of the courage and great learning that was characteristic of the period throughout Europe. Like all the loftiest ideals it has never been realized anywhere in a pure and final form.

Under Edward VI and his Protector, the Earl of Somerset, no one, Catholic or Protestant, was executed on grounds of religion. Edward (and/or Somerset) attempted to bring the English church into line with the Reformation on the Continent, changing Latin into English, ending priestly celibacy, replacing the altar with the Communion table, and removing icons from the churches and destroying them. Notably, they also more or less ended censorship and suppression of the press. Mary I, Edward's half sister and successor, reversed all this and launched on her notorious burning of Protestant leaders. Elizabeth I, less notoriously, executed Catholics, but as traitors, skirting the issue of religious persecution while subjecting them to a death much more horrendous than burning. The next regime that could claim to have executed no one on religious grounds was the Protectorate of Oliver Cromwell in the mid-seventeenth century. Cromwell was a dissident, a Puritan though with no role in any church, whose government seems in many ways a continuation of reforms begun by Edward VI. He gave England its first written constitution, a terse document outlining the form of government, with a paragraph ensuring freedom of religion—to everyone but Catholics.

To say that freedom of conscience had and is having a difficult birth would understate the matter radically. For all the turbulence of British religious history, its issues were delimited, in theory at least, by the fact that it was a tempest among Christians, who shared basic assumptions, however passionately they felt their differences. In his Letter to the Romans, Paul asks the new congregation, apparently divided by cultural and ethical differences between its pagan and Jewish members, "Who are you to judge another's servant? It is before his master that he stands or falls, and the Lord will make him stand." This is advice meant for members of a community of believers, people who accept servanthood as descriptive of their and their fellows' relationship to God, and who see this relationship as personal in the sense that God loves where he loves and compensates for his servants' failings by his grace. Ideally they have accepted a particular obedience, with origins in the Law of Moses, exemplified in the life and teachings of Christ. So much might the apostle see, or hope to see, in the early church. But history tells us that no great effort has ever been required to narrow the circle of those who should be seen as God's servants, whose errors would be made good by God's grace and therefore should not be judged. We all know the enormities that have made themselves presentable to the Christian conscience, often enough campaigns of violence against other Christians. Sects and denominations remember the injuries their ancestors suffered long centuries ago, and can become indignant at the thought of them. They might also remember injuries they inflicted, if the comforts of identity were not diluted a little by such ventures into honesty.

Here is another thing Paul says in the Letter to the Romans, still in the context of his thoughts on tolerance and the authority of conscience: "The faith you have, have as your own conviction before God." That is, do not judge fellow believers and do not offend them. It may be fair to wonder if this excellent advice has gone unheeded all these years because faith has tended to be a conviction shown to *men*, who, if we can trust Paul, are a good deal more fastidious than God.

•

I believe in the reality of conscience, having observed it in myself and others. I am a little surprised to find it disappearing before me as I write. Consider the word *conscientious*. It names a sensitivity to duty and obligation that is very widely felt, the basis of civilization, in all probability. We notice default because it is exceptional. We are all indebted to legions of strangers who show up to work every day and do what needs to be done. If they did not, presumably they would feel guilt or shame in some degree. They align their lives, more or less, with a standard internal to them, and are very worthy of respect in this regard. This fundamental respectability of people in the aggregate is the great resource of political democracy.

At the time of the English Civil Wars, Cromwell's formidable army of common men held formal debates to determine the kind of government that should replace the defeated monarchy. What an utterly extraordinary moment. Religious freedom, freedom of conscience, was of the first order of importance to them, dissenters that they were. After the Restoration their disputes and the habits and assumptions that surrounded them came to North America, especially to New England, where the population was already deeply sympathetic to Cromwell, and where he had helped sponsor a colony, Saybrook, in Connecticut. American political thought, which seems so uncannily mature in its earliest expressions, in fact had a long history behind it. The Commonwealth under Cromwell, for all its problems, functioned better, and let England thrive better, than under the royal governments that succeeded and followed it, until William of Orange intervened to end the dynastic incompetence. He landed an army large enough to make his arrival an invasion, if history had chosen to call it by that name. Cromwell's Commonwealth failed at his death because he had no appropriate successor. William of Orange followed him in establishing the primacy of Parliament.

So the thousands of refugees and immigrants who came to America, after the Cromwell years and the Restoration, had had the experience of watching or participating in the first modern revolution, and had seen government by a sovereign Parliament as well. And they had felt once again the force of religious oppression. It is customary to look to John Locke and Edmund Burke to find the sources of American political thought. Of course, Locke's family had been on the side of the Commonwealth and Cromwell in the Civil Wars, which is to say that affinity with his thought can have had as much or more to do with influences shared with him as with the impressiveness of his philosophy. One need not mention Diggers and Levelers, though there is no reason to dismiss them entirely from the less elegant strata of American opinion. And the English Leveler John Lilburne, an early seventeenth-century champion of liberty as a universal birthright, has been quoted in U.S. Supreme Court decisions and is credited with influencing the writing of the Fifth Amendment. No doubt such people had descendants here. As remarkable as the maturity of political thought in the colonies is the readiness with which at least a very significant part of the population accepted the rationale for revolution. This is consistent with the fact that it would have been the reenactment of a deep and defining cultural memory. The American Revolution has been treated by some historians as lacking sufficient provocation. The list of the king's offenses in the Declaration of Independence is not unimpressive. And the liberalizations that are supposed, by some Burkean process of amiable concession, to have brought England to a place that mooted the colonists' legitimate grievances are a little hard to discover.

Influence may have gone deeper still. Wycliffe based his theology and his social thought on the intrinsically sacred human person, just as Thomas Jefferson did his in the preamble to the Declaration. Lovely old ideals, redolent of Scripture, never realized, never discredited or forgotten, having their moment over against the corruptions of, say, plantation life. My theory would account for Jefferson's fluency and passion in expressing values that he had never lived by, that Wycliffe himself had never seen realized, except, perhaps, in the Pauline brotherhood of some furtive conventicle.

•

While I am on the subject. I find the giant lacuna in American historiography, the colonial side of the Interregnum particularly, so strange as to exceed in interest most subjects upon which learned attention has actually fallen. There are taboos in history, unspeakable opinions. Take, for example, the case of Winston Churchill, the greatest man of the twentieth century, according to a poll I saw recently of American opinion. Did his famous stand against Hitler really amount to more than waiting for the colonies and the United States to step in, as they had done so recently in the first twentieth-century war with Germany? Is it not condescending to tell people, whose maimed brothers were selling poppies in the streets, that though they might lose their sons, there would still be cakes and ale? Has anyone really read the Iron Curtain speech lately and pondered how many of the worst policies for dealing with the Soviet Union in the post-war period are set out in it? And this in 1946, when Russia had not yet had time to reckon its truly staggering losses? Has any-one read up on Churchill's social policies before the war, with their excruciating severities, to be suffered by those same classes who would fill the ranks of his armies? I know it is rude to raise questions about Churchill, and I think this is interest-ing, since we flatter ourselves that we are willing to question anything.

Conversely, it is somehow unrespectable to have an interest in Cromwell, who is stigmatized in a way that makes him a sort of latter-day Albigensian, a religious fanatic hostile to all of life's pleasures, and an autocrat besides. Stigma is a vast oubliette. Amazing things are hidden in it. Cromwell's importance to American history, therefore to the history of the modern West, should be beyond doubt. I know that he is of great interest to certain specialists. But their work has not brought him the kind of attention that would make him accepted as a factor in the cultural history of New England, let alone the world at large. The French Revolution was Cromwellian, with certain grue-some elaborations. The guillotine may actually have a kind of melancholy glamour that has helped put the Puritan Cromwell in the shade, historically speaking.

All this is relevant because it demonstrates the vulnerability of awareness to distortion and omission, not only in individual cases, a commonplace, and not only in the general population but in important fields of scholarship, where exquisite resources have been hoarded to make real and thorough inquiry as possible as such things ever are. I am eager to grant that there is a basic moral competence in people, which makes conscience meaningful. It is entirely consistent with my theology to believe that this capacity for moral self-awareness is the God-given basis for the freedom and respect we owe one another. Yet I hesitate to grant that there is an equivalent intellectual competence that would allow conscience to be appropriately directed. Worse, I am persuaded that seeming failures of insight and understanding are in fact willed, that an active historical or scholarly conscience would not tolerate them. After the Iron Curtain speech angry crowds surrounded Churchill's hotel in New York. Stalin was not alone in considering the speech a declaration of war—in 1946, for heaven's sake, before the ashes of the last war were cool. In the speech Churchill proposed the British Empire as de facto encirclement of the Soviet Union, urging Americans to sustain what Britain could not, for the advantage it would give us in a coming atomic conflict. From the side of wounded Russia, encirclement may have looked very like an iron curtain. While Churchill did not foresee all the worst consequences of the Cold War, he did help to make them inevitable.

Why bother to be fair after all these years? It might be a salubrious exercise that would make us better able to be fair in the future. Perhaps our great investment in the legend of Churchill's heroic wisdom helps us overlook the possibility that a little wisdom on our part might have helped to spare the world much grief and disaster, present and to come. To consider the possibility would be a significant act of conscience. All this suggests to me that freedom of conscience is more profoundly inhibited by prejudice and taboo, internalized by us all, than it is by laws and institutions. We can see that it is easily manipulated by subrational means, suggestion, and repetition. And it can be inappropriately invested, making us confident when we would be better served by doubt.

•

What do we lose when we ignore early American history and, to the extent that we notice it, mischaracterize it? The stigmatizing word that makes the North fall out of sight is *Puritanism*. The South seems to have been dominated by the plantation economy and chattel slavery that were typical of British and European colonies in the New World, and to have had no conspicuous peculiarities of thinking that came with New England's history of settlement. Of course this distinction is too sharply drawn. Distinctions between populations always are. And yet it has never ceased to be true that North and South are different cultures, and that their histories lie behind their differences. Because the relationship between New England and the Cromwell Revolution are not acknowledged or attended to, the meaning of Puritanism, British and American, has been vulnerable to distortion and trivialization. It is not a name the movement chose for itself, for one thing. In fact *Puritan* translates the Greek word *Cathar*, that other name for Albigensians. It is striking how similarly they are caricatured, as gloomy religious fanatics who hate life. Early New Englanders are sometimes said to have tried to establish a theocracy. If this were true, it would be hard to imagine how their arrangements could have been more theocratic than the papacy was at the time, or than an Anglicanism that enforced conformity of worship with penalties, including loss of basic civil rights—how it could be more theocratic than the European norm, that is. They were an unusually homogeneous group to begin with because they did emigrate on account of their religion. Later immigrants were on the losing side of a failed revolution that had become, over time, a struggle between religious factions. Cromwell wanted plain, russet-coated fellows in his army, God-fearing men, he said, because they were tough and brave and reliable. So his army became, in effect, Puritan.

In 1630, twelve years before the English Civil Wars began, John Winthrop famously called the colony he would help to establish at Massachusetts Bay a city on a hill whose success or failure would be known to the world. It would have the world's attention because it would be a radical community, an experiment, created by covenant among members whose bonds were hoped to be mutual charity—that is, compassion and love. There were already a few places in Europe where traditional rulers had been ousted, notably thriving little republics in Switzerland and the Low Countries. Persecution and exile had made Protestantism strongly aware of itself as an international movement. It made very extensive use of the technology of printing, strongly encouraged literacy, and had important intellectual centers such as Wittenberg and Cambridge.

Like Cathars and Cromwell, the American Puritans are assumed to have been particularly severe, but in an age when judicial mutilation was commonplace in England and Europe, and where capital crimes were innumerable, evidence I have seen suggests that the Puritans were in fact notably restrained. A scarlet letter, however regrettable in itself, is certainly to be preferred to slashed nostrils and cropped ears. I name this famous letter, fictional as I assume it is, because Hawthorne's novel has served as evidence of an appalling severity, when in historical context it would have been no such thing. *The Crucible* is about the McCarthy era, of course, but it is taught as a phenomenon that captures the essence of American Puritanism, when witch trials were carried on in Britain and Europe into the eighteenth century. All this should be too obvious to need saying, and yet these two works of fiction lie like a glacier on the history of

America's radical and progressive history, obscuring questions such as why, by the time of the writing of the Constitution, slavery could be described as an institution peculiar to the South, with enslaved populations allowed for in the representation of Southern states exclusively. Recently publicized evidence that slave labor was used in the colonial North demonstrates its economic viability in the North, and that under British law there were no limits to its use. And still in 1789 it could be treated as peculiar to the South.

This country is in a state of bewilderment that cries out for good history. How are we to account for liberating thoughts and movements, things that have gone well? What has been the thinking behind our great institutions? I have found little help in answering these questions. I hope for a day when I can immure myself in some fine archive and explore them for myself. Early American historiography is for the most part a toxic compound of cynicism and cliché, so false that it falsifies by implication the history of the Western world. To create a history answerable to the truth would be a gift of clarity, sanity, and purpose. The great freedom of conscience would be its liberation from our own cynicism, conventionalism, and narrowness of vision.

What Are We Doing Here?

The Liverpool Hope Hopkins Lecture, an Annual Public
Lecture, Hosted by the Department of English at
Liverpool Hope University: July 20, 2015

I have been reading lately about the rise of humanism in
Europe and Britain. The old scholars often described themselves as "ravished" by one of the books newly made available
to them by the press, perhaps also by translation. Their lives
were usually short, never comfortable. I think what it would
have been like to read by the light of an oil lamp, to write with
a goose quill. It used to seem to me that an unimaginable self-
discipline must account for their meticulous learnedness. I assumed that the rigors and austerities of their early training had
made their discomforts too familiar to be noticed. Now increasingly I think they were held to their work by a degree of
fascination, of sober delight, that we can no longer imagine.
John Milton said, As well kill a man as kill a good book. He
was arguing, unsuccessfully, against licensing, the suppression
or censoring of books before publication. This was usual in the
premodern and early modern world, of course. How many good
books were killed outright by these means we will never know,
even granting the labors of printers who defied the threat
of hair-raising punishments to publish unlicensed work, and
which others risked hair-raising penalties to own or to read. To
put books into English, the vulgar tongue, the language of the

masses, was once radical. Teaching literature written in English is a recent innovation, historically speaking, and was long regarded in the more renowned institutions as a lowering of standards. It is still the case in some countries that the work of living writers is excluded from the curriculum, perhaps a sign of lingering prejudice against the vernacular, against what people say and think now, in the always disparaged present. In America this scruple is gone and forgotten. Writers not yet dead, in many cases only emerging, are read and pondered, usually under a rubric of some kind that makes them representative of gender or ethnicity or region, therefore instances of some perspective or trend often of greater interest to the professor than to any of the writers. These categories, woman or black or immigrant, can be encumbrances from their point of view, obstacles to the reading of their work as something more than sociological data. If there are courses explicitly attentive to white men as a subgroup, I have never heard of any. Male and white is still the default where literature is concerned, in the academy, at least. This is not the fault of any of these men, and they should not be undervalued or misread on this account. But knowing what a book costs any writer, in years not least, I hope for the day when all good books can be read as speaking in as broad a voice, engaged with the Great Questions. However, I am too aware of the ragged beast history has been to fret over the fact that its manners are not perfect yet. I think it is most excellent that so many voices are being heard, and that the ongoing life of this endless human work is acknowledged in real time. This has supported the teaching of writing that is so widespread in American universities. These same living writers come into the universities to lecture and teach, as the great literary figures whose writing is consecrated by time could not do, even if they wished. This is in effect a system of patronage that leaves no one beholden, and that makes thousands of students aware that writers are not so unlike themselves, a valuable stimulus to aspiration.

All this works rather well. It has given me an interesting life, allowing me all the time a novel requires and every resource for following out the questions that arise as I work. I have enjoyed the company of young writers, and I have learned from them. I know that one is expected to bemoan the present time, to say something about decline and the loss of values. O tempora! O mores! But I find a great deal to respect.

•

That said, it is a familiar irony that prohibition and deprivation can make things potent and ravishing, and that plenty very often dulls our taste for them. There is a great deal of questioning now of the value of the humanities, those aptly named disciplines that make us consider what human beings have been, and are, and will be. Sometimes I think they should be renamed Big Data. These catastrophic wars that afflict so much of the world now surely bear more resemblance to the Hundred Years' War or the Thirty Years' War or the wars of Napoleon or the First World War than they do to any expectations we have had about how history would unfold in the modern period, otherwise known as those few decades we call postwar. We have thought we were being cynical when we insisted that people universally are motivated by self-interest. Would God it were true! Hamlet's rumination on the twenty thousand men going off to fight over a territory not large enough for them all to be buried in, going to their graves as if to their beds, shows a much sounder grasp of human behavior than this. It acknowledges a part of it that shows how absurdly optimistic our "cynicism" actually is. President Obama recently set off a kerfuffle among the press by saying that these firestorms of large-scale violence and destruction are not unique to Islamic culture or to the present time. This is simple fact, and it is also fair warning, if we hope to keep our own actions and reactions within something like civilized bounds. This would be one use of history. And here's another. We might stop persuading ourselves of the truth of notions that are flatly implausible in light of all we know, or could know if we cared to. Then we would be less confident in imposing our assumptions on behavior, including our own, that they cannot help us interpret. The aversion to history shelters some very important errors, and sometimes does so aggressively. A society is moving toward dangerous ground when loyalty to the truth is seen as disloyalty to some supposedly higher interest. How many times has history taught us this?

In the context of contemporary politics, someone who has a certain awareness of history—President Obama, for example—is expected to speak as if he did not. He is expected to have mastery of an artificial language, a language made up arbitrarily of the terms and references of a nonexistent world that is conjured out of prejudice and nostalgia and misinformation, as well as of fashion and slovenliness among the opinion makers. Any dialect becomes second nature to those who live among its speakers, and this one is pervasive in ordinary educated life. Anyone who has wandered now and then into the vast arcana of what we have been and done is prone to violating the dialect's strict and narrow usage, and will be corrected. I am not speaking here of the usual and obvious malefactors, the blowhards on the radio and on cable television. I am speaking of the mainstream media, therefore of the institutions that educate most people of influence in America, including journalists. Our great universities, with their vast resources, their exhaustive libraries, look like a humanist's dream. Certainly, with the collecting and archiving that has taken place in them over centuries, they could tell us much that we need to know. But there is pressure on them now to change fundamentally, to equip our young to be what the Fabians used to call "brain workers." They are to be skilled labor in the new economy, intellectually nimble enough to meet its needs, which we know will change constantly and unpredictably. I may simply have described the robots that will be better suited to this kind of existence, and with whom our optimized workers will no doubt be forced to compete, poor complex and distractible creatures that they will be still.

Why teach the humanities? Why study them? American universities are literally shaped around them and have been since their founding, yet the question is put in the bluntest form: What are they good for? If, for purposes of discussion, we date the beginning of the humanist movement to 1500, then historically speaking, the West has flourished materially as well as culturally in the period of their influence. You may have noticed that the United States is always in an existential struggle with an imagined competitor. It may have been the Cold War that instilled this habit in us. It may have been nineteenth-century nationalism, when America was coming of age and competition among the great powers of Europe drove world events. Whatever etiology is proposed for it, whatever excuse is made for it, however rhetorically useful it may be in certain contexts, the habit is deeply harmful, as it has been in Europe as well, when the competition involved the claiming and defending of colonies, as well as militarization that led to appalling war. The consequences of these things abide. We see and feel them every day. The standards that might seem to make societies commensurable are essentially meaningless, except when they are ominous. Insofar as we treat them as real, they mean that other considerations are put out of account. Who died in all those wars? The numbers lost assure us that there were artists and poets and mathematicians among them, and statesmen, though at best their circumstances may never have allowed them or us to realize their gifts. What was lost to those colonizations? The many regions of the world that bore the brunt of them struggle to discover a social order they can accept as legitimate and authoritative, with major consequences for the old colonizers and the whole world. Who loses in these economic competitions? Those who win, first of all, because the foot soldiers of those economies work too much for meager, even uncertain pay and are exposed to every insult this cheapening of fundamental value visits on the earth and the air. How many artists and scientists ought there to be among those vast legions? And among their threatened children? There is a genius for impoverishment always at work in the world. And it has its way, as if its proceedings were not only necessary but even sensible. Its rationale, its battle cry, is Competition.

A great irony is at work in our historical moment. We are being encouraged to abandon our most distinctive heritage— in the name of self-preservation. The logic seems to go like this: To be as strong as we need to be we must have a highly efficient economy. Society must be disciplined, stripped down, to achieve this efficiency and to make us all better foot soldiers. The alternative is decadence, the eclipse of our civilization by one with more fire in its belly. We are to be prepared to think very badly of our antagonist, whichever one seems to loom at a given moment. It is a convention of modern literature, and of the going-on of talking heads and public intellectuals, to project what are said to be emerging trends into a future in which cultural, intellectual, moral, and economic decline will have hit bottom, more or less. Somehow this kind of talk always seems brave and deep. The specifics concerning this abysmal future are vague—Britain will cease to be Britain, America will cease to be America, France will cease to be France, and so on, depending which country happens to be the focus of Spenglerian gloom. The oldest literature of radical pessimism can be read as prophecy. Of course these three societies have changed profoundly in the last hundred years, the last fifty years, and few with any knowledge of history would admit to regretting the change. What is being invoked is the notion of a precious and unnameable essence, second nature to some, in the marrow of their bones, in effect. By this view others, whether they will or no, cannot understand or value it, and therefore they are a threat. The definitions of *some* and *others* are unclear and shifting. In America, since we are an immigrant country, our "nativists" may be first- or second-generation Americans whose parents or grandparents were themselves considered suspect on these same grounds. It is almost as interesting as it is disheartening to learn that nativist rhetoric can have impact in a country where precious few can claim to be native in any ordinary sense. Our great experiment has yielded some valuable results, here a striking demonstration of the emptiness of such rhetoric, which is nevertheless loudly persistent in certain quarters in America, and which obviously continues to be influential in Britain and Europe.

Nativism is always aligned with an impulse or strategy to shape the culture with which it claims to have this privileged intimacy. It is urgently intent on identifying enemies and confronting them, and it is hostile to the point of loathing toward aspects of the society that are taken to show their influence. In other words, these lovers of country, these patriots, are wildly unhappy with the country they claim to love and are bent on remaking it to suit their own preferences, which they feel no need to justify or even fully articulate. Neither do they feel any need to answer the objections of those who see their shaping and their disciplining as mutilation.

What is at stake now, in this rather inchoate cluster of anxieties that animates so many of us, is the body of learning and thought we call the humanities. Their transformative emergence has historically specifiable origins in the English and European Renaissance, greatly expedited by the emergence of the printing press. At the time and for centuries afterward it amounted to very much more than the spread of knowledge, because it was understood as a powerful testimony to human capacities, human grandeur, the divine in the human. And it had the effect of awakening human capacities that would not otherwise have been imagined.

Alexis de Tocqueville, an early and classic interpreter of American civilization, published his great *Democracy in America*, in two volumes, in 1835 and 1840. He was interested in the new society for its implications for civilization in Europe, especially France. His treatment of it is equable and perceptive, though he does have his doubts. Speaking in his introduction of the effects of the spread of learning in the countries of the West, he says:

> From the moment when the exercise of intelligence had become a source of strength and wealth, each step in the development of science, each new area of knowledge, each fresh idea had to be viewed as a seed of power placed within people's grasp. Poetry, eloquence, memory, the beauty of wit, the fires of imagination, the depth of thought, all these gifts which heaven shares out by chance turned to the advantage of democracy and, even when they belonged to the enemies of democracy, they still promoted its cause by highlighting the natural grandeur of man. Its victories spread, therefore, alongside those of civilization and education. Literature was an arsenal open to all, where the weak and the poor could always find arms.

This passage provides a sense of what became newly available to respect and admiration as knowledge spread through the populace—poetry, eloquence, wit, imagination, depth of thought—where they would not have been seen or acknowledged in earlier generations. The old humanist joy in what people are still abides in Tocqueville, and he draws a humanist conclusion about the brilliance of people simply as such. Old Walt Whitman wrote, "I celebrate myself, and sing myself, / and what I assume you shall assume, / For every atom belonging to me as good belongs to you." Any excellence, while it is given by heaven, more or less at random from the world's perspective, is testimony to the fact that human beings are endowed with a capacity for excellence, whatever form it takes in any individual case. Their natural grandeur, which is overturning the old order, is not a matter of political or economic power, which, according to Tocqueville, is a consequence of the emergence of these gifts and secondary to them. The splendor of the gifts themselves, as they are liberated by new areas of knowledge, by fresh ideas, makes the case for democracy.

It is to be noted that these gifts are highly individual. There is no talk here of the folk or the masses, though the transformation of society Tocqueville describes has potential for a radical, progressive overturning. There is no suggestion that those who are rising can or should be shaped or led toward participation in a benign new order foreseen either by them or for them. The social order is forming itself around change brought about by these individual expressions of a collective grandeur. Tocqueville sees something like inspiration sweeping through the West as knowledge spreads and science advances. Crucially, there is no mention of competition, no implication of a hierarchy of abilities or gifts. Every excellence, every achievement enhances the general wealth of possibility for yet more excellence. And it is interesting to note that for Tocqueville there is no simple notion of utility. This awakening of minds and spirits is a sunlight that falls across the whole landscape of civilization. The questions being put to us now—What good are the humanities? Why are they at the center of our education?—might, for all history can tell us, be answered decisively by this vision of the effects of learning, which did take hold and flourish as the study of ancient poetry, philosophy and language, Scripture and theology, and of history itself by means of the printing press and the rise of vernacular languages, long before science and technology even began to come abreast of them.

Is Tocqueville describing something real? He stood at a place in the evolution of culture where there would be both a continuously new, because incremental, expansion of literacy and learning, and a vast population they had not yet touched. John Keats, briefly Tocqueville's contemporary, was moved by an Elizabethan translation of Homer: "Then felt I like some watcher of the skies / When a new planet swims into his ken." What was it that Keats took from this encounter? What "wild surmise"? Keats holds such a rarefied place in literature now that it is hard to believe he was once ridiculed as one of "the Cockney school of poetry." But his sonnet is expressing that old humanist privilege, of being "ravished" by a book, and of finding that it has a suggestive power far beyond its subject, a potency the affected mind itself might be years in realizing. I talked once with a cabdriver who had spent years in prison. He said he had no idea that the world was something he could be interested in. And then he read a book.

In the history of the West, for all its achievements, there is also a persisting impatience with the energy and originality of the mind. It can make us very poor servants of purposes that are not our own. A Benthamite panopticon would have radically reduced the varieties of experience that help to individuate us, in theory producing happiness in factory workers by preventing their having even a glimpse of the fact that there could be more to life. Censorship, lists of prohibited books, restrictions on travel, limits on rights of assembly all accomplish by more practicable means some part of the same exclusions, precluding the stimulus of new thought, new things to wonder about. The contemporary assault on the humanities has something of the same objective and would employ similar methods.

Workers, a category that seems to subsume us all except the idlest rich, should learn what they need to learn to be competitive in the new economy. All the rest is waste and distraction.

Competitive with whom? On what terms? To what end? With anyone whose vigor and good fortune allows them to prosper, apparently. With anyone who has done a clever thing we did not think of first. And will these competitors of ours be left to enjoy the miserable advantage of low wages and compromised health? And is there any particular reason to debase human life in order to produce more, faster, without reference to the worth of the product or to the value of the things sacrificed to its manufacture? Wouldn't most people, given an hour or two to reflect, consider this an intolerably trivial use to be put to, for them and their children? Life is brief and fragile, after all. Then what is this new economy whose demands we must always be ready to fill? We may assume it will be driven by innovation and by what are called market forces, which can be fads or speculation or chicanery. Oh, yes, rowdy old capitalism. Let it ply its music. Then again, in the all-consuming form proposed for it now, it is a little like those wars I mentioned earlier. It is equally inimical to poetry, eloquence, memory, the beauty of wit, the fires of imagination, the depth of thought. It is equally disinclined to reward gifts that cannot be turned to its uses. The urgency of war or crisis has been brought to bear on our civil institutions, which is to say, on the reserves and resources of civility we have created over many generations.

We in America are famous for our endless and costly election seasons. I think they are a good thing, all in all, even though as an Iowan I am subjected to the campaigning longer than most of my countrymen. There is a logic in exposing candidates to grueling scrutiny for months at a time. Once one of them is elected, he or she will have more control over public perceptions. But in the adversarial environment of primaries and

elections, things are revealed that are highly germane to the
question of a candidate's suitability for the presidency, which is
certainly the most intense and pressured office in the world.
Many of the candidates make themselves ridiculous, providing
valuable information to the electorate. The parties grope to
discover what is possible, what is needed or desired. Or, notoriously, they offer themselves as agents of certain interests of
friendly billionaires, which, we are to believe, align themselves
nicely with the public interest. None of this is truer for the fact
that it plays out in the press. We have no corner on foolish or
mercenary politicians. But we do give ourselves a good long
look at them, and weeding takes place. It is regrettable that all
the expense in time and money does not buy a more substantive
national conversation. Still, we find out what notions and attitudes are lurking in the minds of some of our politicians,
and what they hope will have the power to stir some part of
the populace.

One of our candidates has called for an attack on the "university cartel," by which he means our system of public higher
education. The phrase is startling, considering that these institutions are in effect great city-states, shaped by their regions
and histories, largely supported by their alumni, variously spe-
cialized around faculties that are attracted by distinctive areas
of excellence. Recently, despite their enormous contributions
to science and technology, they have been losing the support of
many state legislatures, first on the pretext of austerity, and
then on the grounds that they were properly understood as
burdens on the public rather than as public assets. As state financ-
ing fell, tuitions rose, involving many students in burden-
some debt. For generations people had, in effect, prepaid their
children's and grandchildren's tuition and underwritten the
quality of their education by paying taxes. Suddenly the legislatures decided to put the money to other uses, or to cut taxes,
and families were obliged to absorb much higher costs. For

this, blame has fallen on the universities. And since the new cost of university is weighed against potential earnings, students and families being so burdened, the humanities are under great pressure to justify their existence. As it happens, the Massachusetts Institute of Technology has a fine music school, and Rensselaer Polytechnic gives its students prizes for fiction and poetry. These schools might know something about nurturing the technical mind. But there is an impulse behind the recent assaults on great institutions that is historically expressed as social engineering. The ideal worker will not have a head full of poetry, say the neo-Benthamites. It is assumed, of course, that he or she will be potentially omnicompetent in service to the ever-changing needs and demands of the new economy—highly trained, that is, to acquire some undescribed skill set that will be proof against obsolescence. We await particulars. But the object is clear—to create a virtual army out of the general population who will compete successfully against whomever for whatever into an endless future, at profound cost to themselves. All this differs from military engagement in one great particular. The generals are always assumed to be free to abandon their armies and go over to the other side, if there is profit in it.

The United States is in many ways a grand experiment. Let us take Iowa as an example. What would early nineteenth-century settlers on the open prairie do first? Well, one of the first things they did was found a university, which is now about one hundred seventy years old. Agriculture became, as it remains, the basis of the state economy. How did the university develop in response to this small, agrarian population? It became, as it remains, a thriving and innovative center for the arts—theater, music, painting, and, of course, creative writing. The medical school and the professional schools are fine, as well. The sciences are very strong. But the arts are the signature of the place and have been for generations. Let us say that these old Iowans did not invest their resources and their youth as wisely as they might have. Or let us say that, the world lying open to them, they had the profound satisfaction of doing what they wanted to do, at a cost to themselves in mercenary terms, with immeasurable returns in humanist terms. Their university has been a great nurturer of American letters. If Tocqueville was right, it has nurtured a great deal more besides.

What are we doing here, we professors of English? Our project is often dismissed as elitist. That word has a new and novel sting in American politics. This is odd, in a period uncharacteristically dominated by political dynasties. Apparently the slur doesn't stick to those who show no sign of education or sophistication, no matter what their pedigree. Be that as it may. There is a fundamental slovenliness in much public discourse that can graft heterogeneous things together around a single word. There is justified alarm about the bizarre concentrations of wealth that have occurred globally, and the tiny fraction of the wealthiest one percent who have wildly disproportionate influence over the lives of the rest of us. They are called the elite, and so are those of us who encourage the kind of thinking that probably does make certain of the young less than ideal recruits to their armies of the employed. If there is a point where the two meanings overlap, it would be in the fact that the teaching we do is what in America we have always called liberal education, education appropriate to free people, very much including those old Iowans who left the university to return to the hamlet or the farm. Now, in a country richer than any they could have imagined, we are endlessly told we must cede that humane freedom to a very uncertain promise of employability. It seems most unlikely that any oligarch foresees this choice as being forced on his or her own children. I note here that these criticisms and pressures are not brought to bear on our private universities, though most or all of them receive

government money. Elitism in its classic sense is not being attacked but asserted and defended.

If I seem to have conceded an important point in saying
that the humanities do not prepare ideal helots, economically
speaking, I do not at all mean to imply that they are less than
ideal for preparing capable citizens, imaginative and innovative
contributors to a full and generous, and largely unmonetizable,
national life. America has known long enough how to be a
prosperous country, for all its deviations from the narrow path
of economic rationalism. Empirically speaking, these errancies
are highly compatible with our flourishing economically, if they
are not a cause of it, which is more than we can know. The
politicians who attack public higher education as too expensive
have made it so for electoral or ideological reasons and could
undo the harm with the stroke of a pen. They have created the
crisis to which they hope to bring their draconian solutions.

Neo-Benthamism stands or falls with our unquestioning
subservience to the notion of competition, which really comes
down to our dealing with the constant threat on the part of
these generals to abandon their armies and, of course, with their
demonstrated willingness to act on the threat. Does anyone who
cares for such things owe them those great and ancient pleasures of life—poetry, eloquence, memory, the fires of imagination, the depth of thought? Do the pressures created in the
larger world deprive us and the world of gifts the Chinese or
the Russians would bring to it? We know these cultures have
been rich and brilliant in ways that are no longer visible to us,
at least. If we do have this effect, is there one thing good about
it, for us or for them? If the vastness of the Russian imagination,
the elegance of the Chinese eye and hand, were present to us
to admire without invidious comparison, of them to us or us to
them, wouldn't the world be richer for us all?

If the rise of humanism was a sunrise, then in this present

time we are seeing an eclipse. I take it to be a merely transient gloom, because the work of those old scholars and translators and printers, the poets and philosophers they recovered and the poets and philosophers who came after them, the habit of literacy and the profound interest in the actual world and the present time, have all taken hold, more profoundly than we know. We have not lost them. We have only forgotten what they mean. We have forgotten to understand them for what they are, a spectacular demonstration of the capacities of the human mind, always renewed in our own experience, igniting possibilities no one could have foreseen. Tocqueville may be no more than conventional in speaking of them as "gifts which heaven shares out by chance." And it may be that the convention of ascribing our gifts to a divine source, a convention that comes down from the earliest humanists, gave him and them a language able to capture something our truncated philosophies cannot accommodate. I never hear the phrase "human grandeur," though many a planet has swum into my ken, though I know the rings of Saturn in detail. Step back and consider that, more or less hidden from sight, uniquely on this tiny planet there was a cache of old books and scrolls, testimonies to human thought, that when opened, opened the universe to us—six hundred years on, of course, which is not a heartbeat in cosmic time. An amazing tale, certainly. We deal in disparagement and feel it proves we are freer of illusion than earlier generations were. We are, as we have always been, dangerous creatures, the enemies of our own happiness. But the only help we have ever found for this, the only melioration, is in mutual reverence. God's grace comes to us unmerited, the theologians say. But the grace we could extend to one another we consider it best to withhold in very many cases, presumptively, or in the absence of what we consider true or sufficient merit (we being more particular than God), or because few gracious acts, if they really deserve the name, would stand up to cost-benefit analysis.

This is not the consequence of a new atheism or a systemic materialism that afflicts our age more than others. It is good old human meanness, which finds its terms and pretexts in every age. The best argument against human grandeur is the meagerness of our response to it, paradoxically enough.

Then how to recover the animating spirit of humanism? For one thing, it would help if we reclaimed, or simply borrowed, conceptual language that would allow us to acknowledge that some things are so brilliant they can be understood only as virtuosic acts of mind, thought in the pure enjoyment of itself, whether in making a poem or a scientific discovery, or just learning something it feels unaccountably good to know. There is an unworldliness in the experience, and in what it yields, that requires a larger understanding than our terse vocabularies of behavior and reward can capture. I have had students tell me that they had never heard the word *beautiful* applied to a piece of prose until they came to us at the workshop. Literature had been made a kind of data to illustrate, supposedly, some graceless theory that stood apart from it, and that would be shed in a year or two and replaced by something post- or neo- and in any case as gracelessly irrelevant to a work of language as whatever it displaced. I think this phenomenon is an effect of the utilitarian hostility to the humanities and to art, an attempt to repackage them, to give them some appearance of respectability. And yet the beautiful persists, and so do eloquence and depth of thought, and they belong to all of us because they are the most pregnant evidence we can have of what is possible in us.

Theology for This Moment

Honorary Lecture at the University of Lund, Sweden:

May 26, 2016

Moses tells us, Jesus tells us, that we are to love the Lord our God with all our heart, soul, mind, and strength. Theology should give us some beginning of an idea of what it might mean to satisfy this commandment. A first step, I propose, would be a step back from all other disciplines and categories, to invite a kind of awe at the entire phenomenon of Being that embraces disciplines and categories and error and aspiration and everything they touch, that embraces thought, and error, and the work the mind does in its sleep. Jesus, again quoting Moses, says another commandment is like this one, that we love our neighbor as ourselves. Our neighbor, like ourselves, is, objectively considered, a creature born out of the tremendous, potent workings of the cosmos since, as they say, time began. We are also to love our enemies, which would surely mean taking on that most difficult and humbling realization, that what they intend for evil, God, in the course of historic time, might well intend for good. We who live now have an overwhelming wealth of knowledge, for want of a better word, since we seem to have a great deal of difficulty absorbing the knowledge we amass. We actually have some capacity to describe the emergence of Being, and to read in very distant light some part of its vast, prehuman life. We have some insight into the brilliance of the trillion lives within our lives, the microbes and molecules that create us and sustain us. Brilliant voices wait in our books to speak in our minds, if we let them. There is a synthesis that is unique to theology, an acknowledgment that, in sacred matters, in this theater of God's glory we share with those strangers, our neighbors, love means awe, and awe means love.

A theology for our time would recover its old magisterial scale and confidence. It would address anything and any relation among things, and give the world a supple, inclusive language, far more adequate to what we know, less restricted in what we acknowledge, than any we have at present. For a long time we have treated systems and ideologies as if their terms were at last sufficient to reality, as if, in excluding all heterogeneous assumptions, of religion particularly, they offered a truer representation of the world.

These systems and ideologies, however we might embroider them, are in effect simple and simplifying—the invisible hand, the survival of the fittest, the dictatorship of the proletariat, superego, ego, and id. They are the antibiotics of the intellect, killing off a various ecology of reflection and experience in order to eliminate one or two troublesome ideas. What will replace that ecology is an open question, of course, and how potent, even to the point of pathology, the strains will be that survive the purge. My metaphor seems alarmist. I know that before we devoted ourselves to Darwinism and Marxism and Freudianism and capitalism it was theology that was meant to inhibit thought, and that these successor monisms modeled their claims on the old claims of religious orthodoxy. We human beings never can make a truly fresh start.

Nevertheless, a theology that would embrace rather than exclude would be a departure, not only from its own troublesome history but from the narrowness and aridity of the secular thinking that has displaced it. Theology has always employed language of a kind now isolated in the precincts of religion—"the beauty of holiness," "grace and peace"—phrases that evoke a particular experience, a synesthesia of thought and aesthetic response. From the point of view of objectivity as presently understood, beauty and holiness are excluded terms, and grace is as well. The accepted means of establishing what is real cannot acknowledge them. Yet the celebration of holiness in every form of art has shaped civilizations. Granting human proneness to error, it is naïve to imagine that it afflicts religion or anything else uniquely. It is the genius of science to have built this predisposition into its method, but this has not made science proof against the greater error involved in supposing that it is in fact the arbiter of reality.

Christian theology uniquely among the forms of Western thought need not proceed by exclusion. In the beginning God created the heavens and the earth. Christ was in the beginning with God and without him nothing was made that was made. The categorical blessing put on all that exists raises the problem of evil, certainly, but more important it asserts a very broad, unconditional reality, a givenness that in its fullness reflects divine intent. It is the tendency of all the systems and schools I have named to raise questions about the origins and even the reality of human selfhood. Specifically they challenge the moral self, that old wanderer through the trials and temptations of earthly life. Considering how they differ in their premises, it is striking how consistently they exclude personal agency, how deterministic they are. Yet we all experience the reality of moral choice continuously. A theology for our time would acknowledge this reality along with the entire complex of subjective experience—love, generosity, regret, and all their interactions—without a diminishing translation into veiled self-interest. It could create a conceptual space large enough to accommodate human dignity.

I have read too much history to have any impulse to ideal-
ize the past. Great pity and very great respect are owed to
all those generations who lived and died before us, not least
because they, through war and plague and famine, conferred a
precious heritage on us of art, language, music, and thought.
And they conferred as well a tremendous burden of festering
hostilities, vicious inequalities, and outright crimes that we
have had no great success in understanding or meliorating, that
we have in fact compounded. Those of us who, by accident of
birth, live long and enjoy relative peace and well-being know
well enough that humankind beyond our borders still struggles
under its ancient burdens, with their modern variants. How to
make moral sense of this is a question that has been pondered
earnestly for generations, yielding few unequivocal results.
Modern hospitals quickly become pest houses in the absence of
an infrastructure many countries find difficult to sustain. Traditional agriculture becomes a pool of cheap labor, exploited
until cheaper labor is found elsewhere and then abandoned to
the effects of social and cultural disruption. Ragtag armies
have ferocious weapons. The fluidity of modern societies and
the chaos of failed states expedite human trafficking.

The list is long, and we are implicated in it all, in ways both
obvious and subtle.

I offer this very dark view of the world not only in order to
pose the inevitable question—What is to be done?—but also to
respond to this question in terms that are now more or less
precluded by the practical urgency of these problems. The response I propose is that we preserve as we can the heritage we
have received and that we enlarge and enrich it for the sake
of coming generations. For a long time I assumed that this was
simply a thing civilizations did, a practical definition of the
word *civilization*. Now I see that wealthy countries are stepping
away from ancient commitments, to humanist education, first
of all. Humanists are the curators, in their own persons, of art,

language, music, and thought. The argument everywhere now is that the purpose of education should be the training of workers for the future economy. So the variety of learning offered should be curtailed and the richness of any student's education should be depleted, to produce globally a Benthamite uniformity of aspiration and competence, and a subservience to uses not of his or her choosing. Max Weber's iron cage is slamming shut.

Why this should be happening now, where it need not happen, in countries that could be called, by global standards, plenty rich enough; why it is considered prudent to alienate, starve, even amputate institutions that are riches in themselves and creators of wealth of every kind, I do not know. But the impulse is at work all over the West, inducing us to sell our birthright in exchange for a reward far less certain and sustaining than that famous pot of lentils.

In the West it was theology and its consequences that built these great institutions, and the ebbing away of theology that has made them seem to many to be anomalies, anachronisms, and burdens, as well. They were addressed to the many mysteries of human life on earth and to the knowledge of God. Their mission would seem to have been the very height of impracticality, if it were not so intrinsic a part of the emergence of the modern world.

•

Theology and religion are not synonyms. Either can exist without the other, and either is diminished in the absence of the other. I can speak only of Christianity, of course. It would be a great presumption on my part to seem to generalize, farther, at least, than to say that the highest intellectual and aesthetic achievements of every culture I know of seem to be associated with and addressed to their highest disciplines of religion, to their theology. The intentions that have created these institutions have made them stewards of defining cultural values, of conceptions of truth and definitions, by example, of beauty.

At this point I should clarify my terms. By religion I mean the individual and communal embrace of the particulars of a faith, or loyalty or affinity to it that might not involve thoroughgoing belief in every article of its creed, that might be or seem to be almost exclusively aesthetic, ethical, or social, but is in any case important to one's self-definition. Religion has a public character that can distract even the pious from its origins in the human intuition that reality is rooted in a profounder matrix of Being than sense and experience make known to us in the ordinary course of things. By theology I mean the attempt to realize in some degree the vastness and the atmospheres of this matrix of Being. Theology is the great architecture of thought and wonder that makes religious experience a house of many mansions, open to the soul's explorations, indeed, made to invite and to accommodate them.

One thing theology must do now is to reconsider and reject the kind of thinking that tends to devalue humankind, which is an influential tendency in modern culture, one that, not coincidentally, runs parallel to the decline of religion. This devaluing of the species in effect puts aside everything interesting about us as irrelevant to the question of our true nature. Objectively speaking, this is a remarkable project, itself a datum to be factored into a consideration of the many ways we are strange. A new theology should be open to recognizing our anomalous character, not least for the light it sheds on the precious and amazing lawfulness of the world, ourselves excepted.

There is a sentence from a translation of an Old English dream poem called "Pearl" that is especially pleasing to me. It says, "My soul by grace of God has fared / Adventuring where marvels be." The speaker of the poem is describing a dream encounter with a lost infant daughter as a young woman in paradise. For me the phrase has a more general application, to life on earth. The sheer plenitude of things a mortal encounters is a marvel in itself. There is not only religion, never able to escape doubt, its shadow. There is also feigned religion as well, and religion that has slipped into utter derangement. There is not only lofty and glorious theology but theology as grinding labor, engrossed in its own difficulty. Nothing human beings do or make is ever simply itself.

No other species than ours could be called earnest. This is our response to special difficulties that attend our singular nature. We are unique in the effort we spend on the problems of defining our purposes and then accomplishing them, as the materials we put into them—facts, thought, words—slip and change while we work. No other species could be called ambitious, determined to reshape the world beyond the modest sufficiency that satisfies the niche-finding and nest-building generality of creatures. Error could be thought of as an extravagance parsimonious nature denies to migratory butterflies but lavishes on us unstintingly. Out of this indeterminacy, this great latitude, and within it, we construct our minds and our civilizations. These are all things to be marveled at, certainly.

There is a persistent tendency in modern thought to deny the anomalous character of the human presence in the world. No other creature could aspire to contriving a scheme that would reconcile itself fully to a present understanding of nature, especially one clever enough to be continuously changing its understanding of nature. We are never more unique than in our long struggle to deny our exceptionalism. Though it seems very unscientific to ignore logical contradictions—for example, these attempts to reason away the capacity to reason— this effort is commonly called science and is deferred to as science by much of society, including stewards of its religious culture. By my lights this is altogether a phenomenon of that freedom to err that I have mentioned, a gravitationless space where ideas propagate and elaborate themselves free of the disciplines of reason properly so called. A major thrust of this school in recent years has been an argument against altruism, the capacity for generosity, for intentionally conferring benefit on another at cost to oneself. According to this theory, family enjoy what appears as generosity among its members because one instinctively protects those who share one's genetic makeup in the degree of their consanguinity. In other words, the benefit is to oneself because it insures one's genetic immortality—in some degree, for a while, since endogamy is genetically unwise and exogamy overwhelms any particular genetic heritage in fairly short order. Of course endogamy is practiced in some cultures and must have been the norm in a great many in premodern settings where physical and social mobility were sharply limited. If the theory of genetic "selfishness" has merit, then these pools of self-similarity ought to yield communities brimming with generosity and mutual devotion. This seems not to have been the case, however. The old tendency of the crowned heads of Europe to marry their cousins provides a formidable counterexample.

I will note here that the emotions whose reality is supposedly reasoned away by this school of thought are precisely those humankind are traditionally said to share with God. Christianity is, after all, the narrative of a cosmic altruism. "God is love" is an equation of meaningless terms if this interpretation of the emotions is granted.

Certainly the age of marvels has not passed and will not so long as humankind roams the earth. This school of thought that would disallow the testimony of our emotional experience as evidence of the nature of our motives uses brilliant machines to make the point that in response to certain stimuli certain regions of the brain light up, indicating increased activity. Among things in life that surprise, this would surely rank low. Nevertheless it is offered as evidence to support the assertion that our emotions are not what we take them to be, that our feelings are a sort of ruse, a strategy to conceal our true, selfish motives. Questions arise. What is this mysterious self that must be kept in the dark about its own baser impulses? How can it be fastidious about its ethical life when the impulses it conceals from itself are both natural and universal? This self looks to me like a rather robust survival of what was once called a soul, here offered as a fix for a theory that would otherwise be rejected out of hand. If its scruples are potent enough to shape the nervous system, how can they not be potent enough to shape behavior itself? All this is just an inelegant contrivance meant to excise humankind's moral qualities insofar as they cannot be reconciled to evolutionary theory. In another laboratory, perhaps associated with a mental hospital, the same brilliant machines scrutinize the brains of those who lack generosity and empathy, whom we call psychopaths, and who are taken to be organically injured or disabled, in any case abnormal, in that their behavior is unconstrained by these emotions the evolutionists consider to be actual enablers of self-interest. Is it more remarkable that we are all by nature psychopaths? Or that these theorists do not read each other's journals?

I mention all this simply to make the point that much influential thought is fundamentally incoherent, and no less influential for this fact. How we think about ourselves has everything to do with how we act toward one another. There are circumstances, we all know, in which ordinary people can become virtual psychopaths. If our feelings are meaningless and our actions are in essence all of one kind, our passage through this vale of tears can't mean much. To the extent that anyone takes this kind of thinking seriously, humanism will be unsustainable as an idea. It is entirely possible that the desire to put down the burden of moral responsibility is the source of these theories, and that they are a product of cultural demand rather than a subversion of cultural values. Surely, flimsy as they are, no one would subscribe to them who was not predisposed to share their conclusions. People speak of disillusionment. But discrediting the moral worth of people in general while discounting the capacity for empathy in oneself minimizes the meaning of crime and liberates the criminal, as in the case of the psychopath. It opens the way to profounder disillusionment. Finally, mercilessness has always come easily to human societies. The penumbra of indeterminacy, of potential choice, that always hovers can, as they say, quite suddenly decohere as brutality and resentment. To rationalize crude motives is one of the stranger projects of our period, in light of their continuing history of staggering cost.

A theology for our time would reintegrate Being. Our ways of understanding the world now, our systems and ideologies, have an authority for us that leads us to think of them as exhaustive accounts of reality rather than, at best, as instruments of understanding suited to particular uses. Scientific method is brilliantly successful at doing what it is meant to do, observing and describing the physical universe. The uses made of it reflect moral choices that cannot be derived from it. Inoculation has saved many lives. When the practice was new it was criticized on scientific grounds for burdening the race with lives that would better have been lost, eugenically speaking. What a human life is, how its value is to be reckoned, is a religious or philosophic question. Descartes for his purposes confirmed the truth content of his perceptions by assuring himself that God would not lie. A great deal is assumed here—notably that God sustains an active and honorable relation with human consciousness. This being the case, science is made possible by the intrinsic value of the individual in the divine scheme. Descartes need not establish this value by translating a theological statement into the terms of his method. To do so would be to undermine its foundation.

Scientific method does not, at any given moment, provide an all-sufficient test for the reality of everything. It knows what it has the means to know. Dark matter, overwhelmingly the greater part of the mass of the universe, was inferred and discerned as part of a recent series of insights into the nature of the universe. It seems to be radically different from the kind of matter to which we are accustomed. It will remain "dark," incomprehensible, until science decides what kinds of questions will be fruitful, what kinds of observations will be possible. Science is incremental—a few decades ago dark matter would have been impossible to conceive of. Science exploits accident and relishes surprise—the discovery that the universe is expanding at an accelerating rate, which was entirely unanticipated, opened the way to this radically new conception of the cosmos. Impressive as all this is, its greater meaning is that we can't know what we don't know, what we may never think to ask. It is an abuse of science to assume that the methods and terms of its understanding are ever sufficient or final. The understandings of human nature that have been proposed to us as scientific diminish us, even as science itself is amazed by our complexity, even as science itself is a demonstration of our brilliance. I notice that when archaeologists discover some anatomically prehuman creature, possibly a collateral ancestor though probably not, their descriptions generally begin with a sentence containing the phrase "surprisingly sophisticated." The rock-and-bone evidence of sophistication that remains after so many millennia indicates, usually, that they ornamented themselves, made tools, buried their dead, and cared for their aged and disabled. Why is the sophistication always a surprise? Presumably because a model of prehuman nature persists, unmodified by these discoveries. Again, I suppose the evolutionary model of human emergence discourages the thought that these creatures should share important traits with us, given the inadequacies of their prefrontal cortex. What can we do with the evidence of altruism, surely the right word for tending the frail in absolutely primitive conditions? Would anyone suggest that they also were deceived as to the true, selfish nature of their motives? We may have misunderstood many things because our own tale of origins cannot be reconciled with the fossil record. And this might be true because human evolution as we have imagined it has been one side in the antique battle between Darwinists and fundamentalists.

I have absolutely nothing to propose that would make sense of the fossil record, which seems to be more complicated by the day. But I do find it beautiful that whatever these creatures were, ornament pleased them, and they could be gentle and provident. A marvelous light falls over the beginning of things and over us also, inclined as we are to pick up a shapely stone or a pretty shell. None of this is at all incompatible with a profound sacredness of Being. Early Darwinism was virtually identical with racial theory, the races to be ranked, so it was thought, as stages in human development. Therefore the sophistication of these nonhumans continues to surprise. They are burdened by our prejudices. Surely it is much more scientific to relax the hold of old error and take it as true that the world is as wonderful in its mystery as any theology could hope to express, and that science, rather than impoverishing it of mystery, lavishes new marvels on us day by day.

Granting its power, it is not clear to me that this or any method should be made to function as a metaphysics. We cannot say that the stars were arrayed to instruct us in the glory of God, to dispose our minds to wonder, to make us feel our finitude within an order of Being for which millennia are more transient than a breath. This, for all we know, is the accidental consequence of the accidental emergence of the constellations, the fortuitous interaction of our unfathomable brains and senses with dazzling reality. In the beginning, it was a very remarkable atom that blossomed into a cosmos and is blossoming now in every thought anyone will think tomorrow, in the accelerating rush of space toward what no one knows. We must step back and acknowledge that any accounts of the initial moments that make the event seem straightforward and comprehensible are deeply wrong. Nothing else could be true, considering what it has yielded.

•

A new theology must begin from and always bear in mind the fact that there is something irreducibly thrilling about the universe, whatever account is made of it. I mention that primal particle, the mother of all accident, or so we are to assume, because it does integrate all Being, both potentially and in effect, now and through all futurity. Thought, language, emotion, culture, as surely as matter and energy, must derive from the initial moment that is now understood to have eventuated in the universe as we know it. What other origin could be proposed for them? If they evolved in some sense, they did so as they were prompted by the reality that contained them, one we can understand now as highly special. The complexity of ancient languages and of what we know of ancient thought discourages confidence that we are at the kind of straightforward advantage to them that evolution can be taken to imply. It would be theistic to say that the capacity for abstract thought, for example, was introduced into humankind by some external agent. This is not my style of theism, but others might find it an appropriate patch on a perceived unlikeness between the workings of the mind and what we call the material world. Let us say instead that this capacity must have arisen out of the transformations potential in that first particle and realized over time, consistently with these potentialities. Then, if this is the case, there is a profound, intrinsic relationship among all forms of Being. Within this universe there is no other or beyond, though there may be any number of modes of Being intrinsic to it that we are not aware of. (I have seen speculations that we feel the influence of other universes, and who can say finally that we do not?) Proceeding on conventional assumptions, we can, as a thought experiment, run time backward until all phenomena are folded again into that first particle.

I would expect accident to be invoked here, or the operations of the random. But the particle has made the rules. Quantum indeterminacy is mine, says the particle. And so are gravity and the speed of light. If we propose other universes, as many do now, we must assume differences among them that could well be radical. Our universe emerges consistently with constraints that we must assume are special to it, since slight difference would ramify through eons. So "accident" and "randomness" can only be thought of relative to our expectations. If they are hedged in by even this degree of particularity, then perhaps we need other names for and conceptions of the phenomena we take to be described by them. Quantum entanglement is haunting evidence that what we take to be true about space and time need not pertain even within our universe. How can any kind of determinism, even of accident and its consequences, be imagined if space and time are in any degree local and circumstantial? Perhaps they are a shared illusion—though anyone who has watched a cat calculate time and distance, then pounce, knows that they are not our illusion only.

The meaning of all this for the new theology is that we have estranged ourselves from Being by applying certain tests to determine the reality of things, tests that are themselves implicitly naïve or tendentious definitions of reality. Human consciousness has at least as great an impact on the planet as any force of nature, yet its existence is in doubt because science does not know how to describe it. If there were a lens that could capture the psychological or spiritual weather massing on this little globe, we all know it would show us very dark clouds. If climate change is worrisome, this brooding turn in our collective mood has the potential to exacerbate this and a thousand other problems, and to disgrace us as it does so.

Therefore, in conclusion, a theology for our time should

help us to know that Being is indeed the theater of God's glory, and that, within it, we have a terrible privilege, a capacity for profound error and grave harm. We might venture an answer to God's question, Where were you when I created—? We were there, potential and implicit and by the grace of God inevitable, more unstoppable than the sea, impervious as Leviathan, in that deep womb of time almost hearing the sons of God when they shouted for joy. And we are here, your still-forming child, still opening our eyes on a reality whose astonishments we can never exhaust.

The Sacred, the Human

The Truman G. Madsen Lecture on Eternal Man at the
Wheatley Institution at Brigham Young University:
September 17, 2016

Lately I have been reading Jonathan Edwards, and reading about him, for a lecture I will give in January. I have mentioned a number of times that many years ago my sense of reality was transformed by my reading a section of his treatise *The Great Christian Doctrine of Original Sin Defended*, more specifically, a footnote about the nature of moonlight. I was assigned to read Edwards in an undergraduate philosophy course. His treatise rescued me from the small and dreary determinisms that were offered to us as insight into human nature and motivation, then Freudianism and behaviorism. His argument is that there is nothing in Being that accounts for its persisting as itself from moment to moment. The constancy of moonlight is not intrinsic to it but is instead the effect of the continuous, continuously new reflection of sunlight. So with the apparent continuity of everything that exists, of existence itself. This is a perfectly sound insight from the point of view of physics. For Edwards it means that creation is constantly renewed as an act of God, who therefore remains free relative to his creation, within constraints he has set for himself, which preserve order, identity, and intelligibility. He is also therefore pervasively present and engrossed in it.

How long has the so-called rationalist side of this old and very central controversy argued that reality is a mechanism of sorts whose own workings are fully sufficient to account for its origins and evolution, its past, present, and future? Three centuries at a minimum. On this basis, religion has been marginalized as an unnecessary and implausible account of things that are properly within the boundless domain of science— including, emphatically, human nature and motivation. We know enough now about the infinitely small and the unfathomably vast, about the fine textures of Being and the torrents of galaxies and constellations that pour through the universe, to be, it would seem, beyond our long fascination with the mechanical and also beyond our antique habit of treating this anomalous biosphere as if it existed in isolation from the cosmos that contains it and of which it is made, or as if we could extrapolate from our quotidian knowledge of it to arrive at a fair description of reality as a whole. Determinism should be a little humbled by the fact that for a century causality itself has been seen to be a profound mystery, the old rules of sequence and locality not exhaustively descriptive.

Yet the disciplines that treat of the human psyche are determinist as ever. These days we are believed by many to be locked into perpetual cost-benefit analysis, unconsciously guided by a calculus of self-interest somehow negotiated at the level of the genome. The, shall we say, biomechanics of all this are never described, of course. It has the apparent advantage, for its exponents, of marginalizing the mind, in fact anything that has ever been called the psyche, not to mention the soul. So did phrenology, eugenics, Marxianism, Freudianism, behaviorism. We have no capacity for meaningful choice, so they all tell us.

Every one of these theories was powerful in its time, then passed into the kind of history we are always ready to forget. But the thing conserved out of all this, the thing always to be found within every new packaging, is a gimmick for asserting that we are not ourselves, that we are deceived, self-deceived, in the matter of our motives and experience. To annul the self as an intelligent moral actor is a terrible thing, objectively considered. It is literally the stuff of horror movies. Yet whatever form this notion takes in a given moment, the impulse is powerful and persuasive, and not just to sophomores. Having no more, perhaps less, empirical basis than belief in elves and fairies, a fairly recent appearance of this impulse under the term "the selfish gene" has enjoyed considerable authority. Its precursors have been embarrassed by scientific advances or have simply gone out of style, in either case demonstrating their lack of empirical basis. The selfish gene, a theory that does not even nod to the complexity and fluidity of the genome, will no doubt hang around until some new costume is found to dress up the old idea.

Behind the conception of reality as transparent and self-sustaining, and of the mind as a delusion that enables uncountenanced behavior whose sources are elsewhere—in the id, in the reptilian brain, in the genome—there are at their origins and in their propagation two intentions, which are undertaken as if to spread enlightenment, with something like the benign intent that moves Christians to send out missionaries. One purpose is to dispel belief in God, and the other is to dispel the soul as concept and as felt reality. I want to be very clear about two things before I proceed. First, in these strange times I do not want to be taken to suggest a conspiracy, a cabal, a sinister other, or an intent on anyone's part to undermine all we hold dear, etc., etc. This strain of thought, this scientism, has been active and influential in Europe and Britain for centuries, among those very cultures with whom we feel special affinity. Second, I believe instead that I am describing a deep and long-standing tendency in human and Western consciousness, one felt as persuasive, and as progressive and inevitable, by many religious people. As irrational, ill-informed, and unlovely as I find these theories, I know that many people take precisely the same view of religion, and often, to our disgrace, they have very good grounds. I know excellent people who take these theories to be true, and feel in good conscience that they owe them loyalty and belief because they are true. I know also that they are accepted as the only alternative on offer when the institutions of religion make themselves malicious or ridiculous. There are churches that uncritically accommodate themselves to these theories, so far as possible and farther—as they accommodated themselves in earlier generations to eugenics and racial science. And then there is the large segment of the population who know nothing about religion at all, except what they hear from its very loudest voices, and who are therefore, understandably, secularists.

So great is my respect for secular people that I wish they had a metaphysics worthy of them. I would be very interested to see a secularism based on contemporary science, though I grant the difficulty of deriving a metaphysics from anything as surpassingly dynamic and complex as the universe has proved to be at every scale, and as continuously open to reconception as our understanding of it must be. Of course positivism forbade metaphysics as a language and as a mode of thought, which amounted to radically narrowing the questions it would or could address while jettisoning a great part of Western tradition. An experience-based model of reality, which was proposed to take tradition's place, was inevitably smaller and simpler, friendlier to thinking that did not aspire to engage with ultimate things, or even, perhaps especially, with penultimate things, notably the human mind or soul. Experience, as the word is used in this context, does not include acknowledged mental experience, reasoning, or intuition, certainly not aesthetic response. I must assume, however, that these theories I mention answer to the sense of reality, that is, to the mental experience, of their exponents—are, intuitively plausible to them, affirmed inwardly. This response may be helped by the fact that what might seem most radical in them has actually been familiar for a very long time.

To illustrate this point I will quote a few passages from *Religion and Science*, published in 1935 by the Nobel Prize winner Bertrand Russell. His prize was in literature, but he speaks very confidently for science—a latitude I must grant him, since I do the same sort of thing. Russell says that though psychology is still at an early stage of development "something has been achieved, and much ancient error has been discarded. Much of this ancient error was associated with theology, either as cause or as effect." He follows the idea of the soul through Plato, Descartes, Kant, Hegel—and concludes that "within the realm of what can be known there is no room for the conception of substance, or for its modification in the form of subject and object. The primary facts which we can observe have no such dualism, and give no reason for regarding either 'things' or 'persons' as anything but collections of phenomena." He says that "psychology, in like manner, is finding it necessary to give up such concepts as 'perception' and 'consciousness,' because it is found that they are incapable of precision." Following the implications of science as he understands it, he offers this: "So long as it could be supposed that one 'perceives' things in the outer world, one could say that, in perception, one was 'conscious' of them. Now we can only say that we react to stimuli, and so do stones, though the stimuli to which they react are fewer. So far, therefore, as external 'perception' is concerned, the difference between us and a stone is only one of degree." Then this: "Memory, it may be said, is something distinctively 'mental,' but this again may be denied. Memory is a form of habit, and habit is characteristic of nervous tissue, though it may occur elsewhere, for example in a roll of paper which rolls itself up again if it is unwound." And finally, for science, "there does not seem to be such an entity as the soul or self." This is the always breaking news, always newly arrived at, always a conclusion compelled by the latest science, quaint as this science appears to us now when invoked by the earlier writers in this tradition. The patient didacticism is there from the beginning, the erudite exposure of the errors of religion, and, of course, the triumphant scientism. Whether contemporary exponents would mention stones or rolled paper in discussing human motivation or memory, I doubt. But the case Russell makes for the nonexistence of consciousness and the self is entirely up-to-date, if only in its conclusions. This might make him a man of foresight, a prophet—together with Hume and many others—or it may simply mean that these premises and conclusions never change, however profoundly the science upon which they make their claims for authority transforms itself. I believe the selfish gene is now making its way toward the museum of discredited notions, to crowd the dusty case already occupied by assorted homunculi—the blond beast, economic man, the evolutionary throwback, the dysgenic, the blank slate. Then what rough beast, its hour come round at last—no, it will be a beast whose claims to alarm are encouraged in the genteel environments in which it finds itself at home, a place always already prepared for it.

When we had no better access to the brain as an object than by mapping the contours of the skull to gauge the relative proportions of the lobe of veneration and the lobe of amicability, when early Darwinism could interpret unfavored traits as evidence of evolutionary primitivity or atavism, when Freud could offer his sketch of a three-chambered brain that would neatly accommodate the three contending personae of the Freudian self, when the gene and its functions seemed fixed and straightforward, then it would have been relatively understandable to insist on a reductionist model of the human self—relatively understandable, that is, as opposed to its persistence in the present, despite the insight we have now into the endless complexity of everything, from the subatomic to the intergalactic. The neurons and synapses in that brain are now reckoned in numbers that are literally astronomical. Elegant nature can hardly be imagined to have put such unfathomable complexity to such fundamentally simple work as these psychologies have posited for it. Edwards has a place in creation for things good in themselves. The spectacular brain would surely be one. But this is a theistic notion.

In general it is difficult to say what anything *is* without reference to what it *does*. We are surrounded on every side by the effects of the human brain on the material world, which are certainly as complex altogether as anything on earth after the biosphere. The arts, music, and philosophy are things of inexhaustible interest to human societies over centuries. Still, there are those who would account for all this brilliance and urgency as the effect of tiny increments of applied self-interest. And there are those who can be persuaded that this probably is the case. But the great truth, never taken into account, is that nothing is simple. Absolutely nothing. Mitosis in a cell seems to be about as complex as the Thirty Years' War, which is to say that complexity in both cases beggars description. There is absolutely no analog in reality as we now know it to support reductionism of the kind that offers a fundamental simplicity as the essential character of anything at all. Therefore this immutable core belief, which survives and flourishes when science has moved far past the point where either ignorance or incomprehension could seem to sustain it, is interesting as an artifact. Why is it conserved, and why is it, as it has been since its emergence, a powerful presence in the world of ideas, an effective rebuke to all acknowledgment of the profundity of the human mind and circumstance?

•

Edwards's synonym for a human being is "a moral agent." *Agent* means, of course, that one can act, and *moral* implies that one's actions are meaningful in a social as well as a cosmic context. To me this sounds like reality. His definition is, I think, empirically testable, at least in its worldly applications. Any newspaper could be entered in evidence. I have just begun his treatise *Freedom of the Will*, which I had not looked at since college. My memory and his reputation lead me to expect him to deny that the will is free, though his thinking is always vastly more nuanced than his reputation. In any case, in the degree that his argument is determinist, a defense of an ancient and troublesome element of Christian doctrine, it compares interestingly with these modernist theories I have described. Although they are often proposed as being more humane and rational than Christianity, often with special reference to the dread theological terms *election* and *predestination*, they are themselves so starkly determinist, so determinist in every iteration, that this is arguably their point. Then again it could be true that the limits any sane person feels on his or her meaningful freedom are real and narrow enough to make at least a tentative argument for determinism. This would have been truer of the generality of people in any previous century. Or, again, the same tacit argument could be made by the accidents and injustices anyone must be aware of in the ordinary course of life.

Be that as it may, it is interesting to note how consistently these theories diminish or dismiss the phenomenon of consciousness called the self, a given of experience if there is such a thing in this world. This is true even when the governing motive behind all behavior, as they understand it, is self-interest, which seems to me to imply alertness to the interests of an entity that satisfies for their purposes the definition of a self. While on the one hand they might insist they intend a radically reduced and deromanticized entity, on the other hand, the interests of a self beyond the level of subsistence are

highly circumstantial and particular, so the self can only be assumed to be complex, likewise whatever unnamed and undescribed mechanism it is that reckons its interest from one occasion
to the next. (I excuse phrenology on this point, since it did
grant to the brain lobes devoted to a number of amiable traits.)
Interestingly, Russell allows for the possibility of freedom, with
reference to the human will. What this could mean in the absence of self or consciousness I cannot fathom and he does not
explain—but those who argue as he does are too confident of
their thinking to check it for anomalies. For him freedom is
implied by quantum indeterminacy, reasonably enough. Elsewhere he says, "The belief that personality is mysterious and
irreducible has no scientific warrant, and is accepted chiefly
because it is flattering to our human self-esteem." If our Being
participates in something as mysterious and irreducible as
quantum physics—and how could it not?—the presumption
ought to be on the side of extraordinary human complexity.
If this elevates us in our own regard, well, sometimes the truth
must be accepted, whatever its consequences. I hasten to add
that we must assume we share this complexity with all Being—
quantum doesn't play favorites. This might lead to a revival
of that fine awe at the wonders of creation so characteristic of
theology.

•

To what extent is reputation a factor in our beliefs, opinions,
and controversies, even the weightiest of them? I am interested
in Edwards as a philosopher-theologian consciously working
within the intellectual tradition of New England Puritanism.
He is regularly described as the best philosophic mind this
continent has produced, and no one knows anything about
him except that he wrote a sermon about a spider. These two
facts sit oddly together. Surely his status as a philosopher and
man of letters should not be overwhelmed by a single sermon

of a hortatory kind common in eighteenth-century preaching. But it is. I am interested in American institutions and reforms that began in the Puritan Northeast. But, oddly enough, the states that banned and opposed slavery after the Revolution, as they could not do while they were colonies under British law, the states that advanced women's rights and achieved levels of literacy never before seen in the world, the states that practiced the purest form of democracy yet seen in the world, are thought of as peculiarly harsh and intolerant. This stigma, based solidly and immovably on ignorance of New England culture and of the world that was its context, ought not to overwhelm its crucial contributions to what is best in American culture. But it does. Somehow we are taught to sneer, and the sneer is a final and sufficient judgment on people and things of the highest interest and importance. It has been my eccentric fate to be attracted to subjects that have been excluded from the historical conversation by an aversion of which no account can be made— so deeply has the aversion itself obscured any knowledge of the matter in question. John Calvin is an instance, of course. Why not read the most influential theologian of the Protestant Reformation, who was also the most widely read writer in England during the English Renaissance and a profound influence on American civilization, as they still say, providing no particulars, though the fact is taken to be regrettable on balance and to make our culture an object of aversion. Why not look at the Geneva Bible, Shakespeare's Bible, and Sidney's, Milton's, Spenser's, Bunyan's—which was out of print for hundreds of years, treated as a crude production, the so-called Breeches Bible of the Puritans, though the King James Version was a virtual reprint of it, minus the scholarly and interpretive notes and with changes of translation that muted certain political implications. The King James Version appeared in 1611, at the end of Shakespeare's career, too late to have been known or used by him. The chronology is straightforward, and still it is almost impossible to make the case that Shakespeare was not mightily influenced by a text that did not yet exist. This notion has done almost as much to sanctify the volume as anything between its covers. The English Civil Wars of the seventeenth century were the first modern revolution, precursors of the American and French Revolutions. The disorders that surrounded them set off a great migration to New England, a decisive influence on our national beginnings. Most educated Americans are unaware that there ever was a civil war in England, or a commonwealth government there. The words *Calvinist* or *Puritan* are associated with each of the things I have named, and a strong negative energy attaches to those words. So with Edwards also, who tends to be treated as if damnation were his idea. The American Puritans were the most progressive population on earth through the nineteenth century at least. They deserve notice.

All this is to prepare two points having to do with prejudices and their power, with fixed assumptions that distort our thinking gravely. First, in the old quarrel inexactly described as the conflict between science and religion, the side that associates itself with science is generally assumed to be the side of intellect and reason, as I have said. Second, the side of religion is therefore by implication a defense against both intellect and reason, a conservative nostalgia threatened by indubitable truths science has revealed to us. And these things can indeed be true of those who have undertaken religion's defense, sadly enough. In accepting this posture, they grant the major premise of their opposition and greatly strengthen its case.

Russell, a looming figure in the early twentieth century, was an influential advocate for what is called the scientific side. He writes about the "conflict" between religion and science, beginning in the Middle Ages, writing as if scientists and theologians were easy to distinguish in those days. After all, the system that put the earth at the center of the universe was no

Romish invention, no projection of religious dogma, though he writes as if it were. It was the work of Ptolemy, a second-century pagan, and was the predominant scientific view of the heavens, defended by scientists as well as by churchmen, not only because theology had grown up around it but also because with adjustments made over time it worked uncannily well. One moral to be drawn from the episode is that religion should not involve itself too deeply even with the most prestigious scientific thought, no matter how great the consensus that supports it. Russell makes much of certain remarkable theological doctrines of the time. Early sciences—alchemy, astrology, and medicine—were bizarre as well, though I am aware of no mention of the motivations of stones and paper. In any case, I just read an article about a hypothesis that would account for the empty center of our solar system, anomalous compared with the many planetary systems that have now been observed: Jupiter and Saturn drifted inward toward the sun, ground up super-earths and planetoids that would have made the system typical, then drifted back into remote space. I simplify, but elaboration would only make the tale more remarkable. If some farsighted fifteenth-century Dominican had ventured this hypothesis, it would certainly have seemed preposterous to a man writing in 1935. However wrong the Middle Ages were in the particulars, they were right in not excluding the fantastical from their notions of the true.

Russell used his learning in the science of his time opportunistically, as we can see now, when the appropriateness of analogies between human behavior and the ways of stones and paper is presumably rejected on all sides. While on the one hand the errors of science are generally honorable things, detours on the way to better understanding, on the other hand these notions of Russell's never had the slightest grounding in reality. The prestige of science derives from the assumption that it deals in truth, fact. This is its purpose and tendency, but at no point is the purpose assumed to be fully and finally achieved. Science is, after all, a strategy, a method, not a doctrine. This is the secret of its brilliance, its rigor, its general reliability. But reason is not strictly reason when it is leveraged against a faulty inference—that is, a bad guess. The list I made earlier of the various schools of thought, considered scientific in their time, that undertook to empty the heavens and enlighten human-kind by, oddly enough, demonstrating to them that they had neither self nor soul, were a series of bad guesses, not one of them the foundation upon which truly rational or scientific thinking could be based. Some of them, notably racial science and eugenics, played out in atrocities. The question of the ex-istence of God and all the rest is not affected in any way by the ineptitude of the case made against it. The prestige of science should not be affected by the fact that it is vulnerable to mis-use. But certainly historical perspective permits us to say that neither science nor reason, properly so called, was implicated in these earlier campaigns against religion. And again, a largely consistent position was maintained through all these shifts in rationalization—no God, no self. Religion could make the hu-manist case if its defenders were humanists. It could also make a rational and scientific case against scientism, if it were not daunted by the old habit of deference, prejudice turned against itself. The selfish gene should have been laughed off the stage years ago, and it isn't gone yet.

I personally don't believe that God would submit himself to proof. The very thought seems irreverent to me. I do enjoy the liberation of amazement that comes with seeing the world as the work of God, but that is another thing. On the same grounds I have no interest in claims of disproof. As character-istic as the debunking of human inwardness is the smallness of the reality posited in this scientistic worldview. If physics and cosmology are truly sciences, then there exists a body of excellent evidence that the scale and the varieties of Being vastly exceed anything an earlier generation could have imagined. This persuades me that reasoning about ultimate things cannot be based on the anomalous fragment of reality accessible to our awareness. The school of thought I speak of never leaves the little sphere of common sense, and indeed often adopts the rather condescending tone one takes in arguing from the stronghold of the merely obvious. I did mention Russell's allowing for the possibility of freedom on the basis of quantum indeterminacy— an appropriately tentative conclusion based on actual, empirically demonstrated science.

Here is one of those prejudices I mentioned, the assumption that fact and reason lie always on one side of this old argument, even though over time the terms on which it has proceeded seem quaint at best, even bizarre. This prejudice seems to be held universally and to have shaped the conversation decisively. For the sake of reason and science it would be an excellent thing to examine the degree to which either of them has actually figured in this controversy. Both of them are so central in this civilization that it is crucial to try to maintain some discipline in the understanding and use of them. In the meantime, I think the whole substance of the supposed controversy could be summarized as follows: Some people believe in God and some people don't.

Finally, that second prejudice, against humankind itself. It is striking and surely significant that denial of the reality of God is so consistently associated with a denial of attributes that historically are thought to be synonymous with human nature. The logic of this is not clear to me. Certainly the argument is made easier by the exclusion from consideration of things the species have done culturally, including, strangely enough, mathematics and science. Russell offers as fact the very familiar notion that humankind suffered a steep ontological demotion when the sun rather than the earth was accepted as the center of the solar system. If this argument was made by some reli-

gious authorities cautioning against the influence of Coperni-
cus and Galileo, there is no evidence I know of that this was in
fact its effect. We are talking about the period called the Renaissance, after all, which launched the long experiment in
expanding and celebrating human capacities that has been important, even definitive, in the history of the West. In any case,
it is simply strange to imagine that the status of the human
race, by its own reckoning, could depend on a map of the
heavens. Putting aside ancient cosmologies, skill, beauty, brilliance, wisdom, as well as accretions of power and wealth,
were always seen and valued in and by human beings. Russell
and others who repeat this canard seem to think that the religious authorities whom they otherwise disparage were right on
this crucial point. They embrace this supposed consequence,
the devaluing of humanity to the level their understanding of
reality sees as appropriate.

One might suppose that a writer who considers himself an
advocate for science would see a triumph of human reason in
the new cosmology that would support the rising humanism of
the age. Instead, as is conventional, he sees the supposedly
diminished human self-esteem that he takes to be consequent
upon it as another newly revealed truth—that our self-esteem
had been based on an error, a failure of understanding. This is
an arbitrary decision, by no means inevitable or even logical,
and therefore another indication of the importance to this
school of thought of belief in a diminished humankind. Then,
again conventionally, Russell says that the theory of evolution,
by demonstrating that we are related to the animals, lowered
human self-esteem. But this is a commonplace long before
Charles Darwin. When Hamlet called man the paragon of
animals, when Edwards says we are distinguished from the
animals by our being endowed with understanding and moral
sense, they are not saying anything new. The contention that
has arisen about the particulars of the creation of Adam is not

relevant to the question of our being, morphologically and biologically, animals. Edwards says, "Herein does very much consist that image of God wherein he made man . . . by which God distinguished man from the beasts, *viz.* in those faculties and principles of nature, whereby He is capable of moral Agency." Ordinary experience does suggest the legitimacy of this kind of distinction between humankind and the generality of creatures, putting aside every theory about how we came to be what we are. There are always self-professed Christians who can be roused to panic at anything remotely like an opportunity, who act as if the eternal body of Christ were under mortal threat because of some notion they find unlikable. They do much to affirm and encourage such notions. But the claim our kind make on our deep respect ought to be self-evident, together with our obligation to honor and value them. Why do religious people so often act as if respect for humankind were contingent on the interpretation of a few verses of Scripture? This tends very much to support the view that in fact human beings are not especially precious or remarkable. Does the phrase "the image of God" not imply a reality that should be manifest to our experience as Christians? For that matter, can anyone at all who has lived in a family, a community, a civilization doubt that they are, indeed, precious and remarkable?

Yes. There are sociopaths.

Exponents of the theories I have criticized are for the most part academics, who can and do, with every justification, point out that they are probably nicer than I am. But they can point to nothing in their anthropology that defines goodness or that obliges us to act on any notion of it except, tacitly, one that is conventional in society at large. Now, a given of these theories is that the norms of society and religion are artificial and oppressive, contrary to our deepest impulses and our truest nature. Their essential value is at best relativized. This is one consequence of the jettisoning of metaphysics. Edwards's thought is loyal to a tradition that does not believe our works in this life can merit any reward in heaven. Instead, he sees whatever is good or gracious or beautiful in any human act or thought as an emanation of the divine beauty, sacredness itself. A vision like his would make any other person potentially or, in any moment, actually a revelation of the nature of God, as the brilliance of creation is also. I find this a wonderful understanding of the highest human capacities, for generosity and love, equally with intelligence and aesthetic sense—the last of these, in Edwards's scheme, the means of our individual participation in a revelation that saturates experience, since Being itself is an emanation of God.

Other traditions articulate the felt value, even the holiness, of the highest human traits, in other terms but always with reference to eternity. These virtues endure beyond mortal life and are honored here and hereafter as a faithful anticipation of an ultimate reality. In the infinitely smaller conceptual world allowed to human existence when metaphysics is disallowed, there is no language to describe human conduct in moral terms. There is one account to be made—for generosity as for theft, for honor equally with shamelessness. Every act is at root simply a strategy of self-interest. If this is not an inevitable consequence of the exclusion of metaphysics, if it is not true necessarily that this should be arrived at as an unchangeable tenet, it is true in fact, a consistent assumption of these theories, phrenology again excluded. Exponents of these theories consider themselves to be loyal to truth and reason, at whatever cost to traditional beliefs and preferences. Truth and reason are estimable values, certainly. But is it true or rational to adhere to any one of the previous avatars of this theory? If not, then a burden falls on any subsequent version of it to prove that it amounts to more than a posture, an acculturated role or habit. Who can show me a shred of empirical evidence for the existence of anything resembling a selfish gene? The prejudice that allows these theories to claim the authority of reason and science is, among many other things, a slander on reason and science.

What will replace them? It never hurts to take a new look at things. I would be happy to recover respect for the aesthetic sense that allows human beings to act graciously and beautifully, and to be honored for their capacity to enact fine behaviors under the demands of, or in light of, the opportunities of endlessly new occasions. Let us face the truth, that human beings are astonishing creatures, each life so singular in its composition and so deeply akin to others that they are inexhaustibly the subject of every art. A tremendous freedom always lies behind prejudice and begins to be released the moment the errors that are the substance of prejudice are acknowledged as error. Our present world does not need to be offered cynicism as ultimate truth. It does not need new grounds for indifference to human life or contempt for the norms that discourage exploitation and violence.

The Divine

The William Belden Noble Lecture at
Harvard Memorial Church: April 4, 2016

When words drop out of use, meanings go with them, perhaps. When the sense of the significant changes, language changes, or so it seems. It has been characteristic of the modern West for generations to try to move away from a vocabulary that is charged with its own intellectual and cultural history, the shift being understood as advancing thought from the pre-scientific to the scientific or from the religious to the secular, these two motives being more or less interchangeable. There is nothing especially novel in this. Quakers noticed that the days and months were named for pagan gods and dignitaries and so they numbered them instead: First Day, Second Day. The French Revolution reset the calendar to Year One and renamed the months—Germinal, Floréal—but the pretty new names could not be made to adhere, or the Quaker numbers, either. So Janus still stands at the opening of the year, Mars still brings his tempests, the emperors Julius and Augustus still lord it through our high summer. Sun and moon, Woden, Thor, and Saturn still name our days.

Language changes, and language conserves itself. We human beings are the language makers, of course, but efforts like these to change it respond to an awareness that in very important ways language creates us. At best we try to suppress demeaning words because they are powerful—they effect the ways in which people are perceived and also their perceptions of themselves. We are seeing now that there are those who react to the use of such words as an assertion of power, something to be admired, something to be reclaimed. In other words, while a slur has no intrinsic meaning—think of the thousands of slurs coined for and by the hundreds of ethnic groups that make up this country—its power lies in the fact that where it is used an individual will not be considered in his or her own right, that the traits attributed to a disfavored group will be applied to her, dismissing out of hand her claims to respect, her circumstances, her achievements, which are in any case seen to be compromised by race or gender. It seems that we have, in this country at this time, an experience of disempowerment in a significant part of the population, and that the old despotisms of disparagement and abuse are reasserting their claims because they have retained the power of old injustices, no matter how far society may have moved in a better direction. The schoolyard wisdom is wrong. Words can be very like sticks and stones—crude weapons that are always ready to hand. The use of them requires no skill at all.

I mention this to make the point that, as present experience illustrates with painful clarity, we are profoundly enmeshed in language. Slurs have their power because we all acknowledge the kind of meaning they have, in the very fact of our recoiling from their use. So they live on.

What has crude, assaultive language to do with the odd assortment of pagans and pagan deities whose names, after millennia, haunt our calendar? What have either of these to do with the fact that there are words and concepts that do indeed fade out of use, despite the fact that we might sometimes feel the lack of them? Language is a universe. Its elements are truly various—given, to use a favorite word of mine. They act eccentrically in time. They elude generalization.

•

I have been thinking about the phrase "the divine." I cannot remember the last time I heard it in the context of religion. It is not synonymous with "the sacred," or "the holy," certainly not with "the spiritual." It is different from all these in that it refers directly to God, or, in the Latin of pagan antiquity, to a god. If we suppose that it has become rare because our vision of ultimate reality no longer centers on a divine being, this is an epochal change, certainly. We in the West tend to imagine that changes in our thinking are advances of some kind, or are at least made inevitable in consequence of cultural or material evolution. In the most horrifying period of recent Western history, when Europe might well have been entering a new dark age, Dietrich Bonhoeffer wrote that his was "a world come of age," which must be offered a "religionless Christianity." I take him to have meant, or at least to have been exploring the idea, that for Christianity to survive in modern culture, it must be relieved of its burden of ritual and myth. Bonhoeffer was a brilliant writer and an exemplary man. But it is difficult to understand how he could have seen collective maturity in a civilization then giving itself over to the myths and cults of an imagined primitivity and to the active rehabilitation of Norse barbarism.

In any case, this interpretation of modern culture as qualitatively changed by a new maturity outlasted the bizarre mutations that might seem to have challenged it, and will outlast them again, no doubt, since we have no reason at all to assume that they will not reemerge in one form or another, or are not reemerging now. If the West has an enduring faith in any one idea, it is that the West advances, that is to say, that it matures in the direction of enlightenment, with all this entails in terms of the loss of illusion and the rejection of error. We stigmatize what we feel we must reject, and this discourages a reappraisal.

As we do this, we build the thinking of an earlier period into our understanding of the world, when by the logic of our assumptions we should be as scrupulously aware of the potential for error in conclusions drawn fifty or a hundred years ago as of those drawn a thousand years ago. The errors of the long modern period might seem subtler to our eye than those of earlier centuries, but there is no reason to assume that they are less consequential.

What is myth, after all? It is narrative that conveys a kind of truth by nonliteral means. This is a definition meant to exclude the influence of a common second sense of the word, that a myth is unreal, untrue. Setting this aside for the moment, I will suggest that the primary meaning of the word *myth* as it has been applied to Christianity would be: those elements of the religion that it has in common with other religions. The ascendant West was ill at ease with the resemblance of its religion to non-Western religions. In its likeness to them Christianity must be primitive. Therefore these elements were to be eliminated to conform Christianity to the worldview of a mature civilization. If myth, or mythos, were really thought of as a higher, more complex articulation of truth that is in principle available to being restated in other terms, then there is nothing about it to embarrass or offend the rational mind. If it is the "truth" it proposes that is rejected, this is another issue entirely, in which myth as such is not implicated. Rather, the religion itself is tacitly called into question.

"The divine," *divinitas*, is a concept for which pagan Rome had a word Christianity could adopt without modification. To speak of the divinity of Christ has always meant not that he was a sacred or holy or spiritual man, though these things were true of him, but that he, uniquely, participated in the nature of

God altogether, that he was God. And that he is God, since this is not the kind of statement that admits of a true past tense. The Incarnation, the Trinity—these are names for things in which divinity as Christianity has long understood it is expressed and very tentatively described. It should not scandalize us people of the third millennium when language that reaches toward the essentially true departs from the standards of comprehensibility we would apply to experience—acknowledging, of course, that our experience is a brilliant translation of the infinite and volatile complexities of Being itself into a world and universe that, remarkably or providentially, seem to lie within our grasp. Science before the twentieth century supported the assumption that reason was, as the physicists say, flat, that like the laws of nature its rules were the same everywhere and in all circumstances, and that whatever they could not countenance was an error, a primitive survival, a mystification. Then along came quantum physics, relativity, a theory of cosmic origins, and science ever since has been continuously at work at a new poetry, trying to capture something of the startling elegance, novel to our eyes, that eventuates in everything that is. Crucially assisted by dark matter, of course, which seems to hold the heavens together and about which little else can at present be said. Only grant that a great, creating holiness is at the center of it all, and one must arrive at something like the extraordinary language in which the ancients invested their perceptions. For the ancients the great, creative holiness was the intuition, the conception, that forced their language so far beyond the limits of the commonplace. Science departed from its origins in religion not so very long ago. If these two great thought systems are not now once again reaching a place of convergence, the fault lies with religion, which, in a fit of defensive panic, has abandoned its profoundest insights and has never reclaimed them.

In the book of Acts, Paul, speaking to the Athenians, quotes one of their own poets, perhaps Epimenides, in invoking the God "in Whom we live and move and have our being." He recognized that behind all the idolatry there was a metaphysics. Christianity, as it spread into the world, seems to have assumed this. It adopts the generic word for God in the pagan languages, *Deus* in Latin, *God* or *Gott* in Germanic northern Europe. Whatever error might be liable to come with the use of a word associated for many centuries with Venus or Neptune, Thor or Woden, this did not weigh against a consensus about the reality of the divine across these very different cultures.

There is a precedent for this in the Bible itself. The first verse of Genesis reads "In the beginning God created the heavens and the earth." The word *god* translates very precisely the Hebrew *Elohim*, a plural form of a generic word for God or gods, angels or powers, in the Semitic languages of the ancient Near East. The name given to Moses at the burning bush, the Tetragrammaton, modifies *Elohim* in the second creation narrative, but in the first, the word appears without a modifier. A respectful reading might see this as reflecting an understanding of the emergence of Being as the act of a divine power whose reality is a human intuition as broadly shared as the affinity of languages will allow the text to express. El is the name of the god at the head of the Canaanite pantheon. The God of the Bible is called El in some poetic contexts. Many scholars see this as evidence of syncretism, or of a polytheism lurking behind the declared monotheism of the Hebrew Bible.

But the analogy to our own use of the word *god* should suggest otherwise. The controversy between science and religion comes down to a familiar question: Is there a god? That is, is there an intentional power expressed in the existence of things? If the character of this power were to be modified by the name and the traditions surrounding any particular deity, this would not change either the question or the answer, nor would the metaphysical implications of the answer be fundamentally different either way. If Babylonian Marduk is at the center of Being, heavens and earth are to be thought of as made from the corpse of a great serpent and humankind is an afterthought, tolerated for its usefulness in building temples and offering sacrifices. If the god the scholars call Yahweh is at the center, his creation is good, humankind bears his image and is the object of his deep attention and his care. These are great differences with profound implications, yet secondary in significance to that more basic question, whether there is a god, whether reality in itself is or is not of a kind to require an affirmative answer. I do not mean to imply that any sufficient proof can ever be adduced on one side or the other of the question, only that one or the other must be true and must always have been true.

Many of the religious among us have abandoned the divine as a concept, attempting to find a compromise position, which, in the nature of the case, doesn't exist. Anthropologists can speak as fluently as theologians of the sacred or the holy or the spiritual, taking them to be an artifact of culture if nothing else. For these scholars, patterns of behavior are sufficient proof that the terms are appropriate. The divine, by comparison, is a phrase that asserts the existence of a god or gods—that is, of a mode of Being not conjured from human fear or hope but prior to and independent of humankind, and profoundly efficacious, to be understood by tentative analogy to human consciousness, which it utterly transcends. The divine is understood to confer sanctity. It is acknowledged in the authority of the sacred but cannot be, so to speak, captured by it. All the temples to Zeus and all the statues of him were not to be taken for Zeus himself.

Say that this understanding of the divine was very broadly shared in the ancient world. Are these grounds for treating it as myth in any invidious sense? The modern West passed through its period of triumphalism, which has not ended yet, relegating all that was not modern or Western to the status of error, however pretty or interesting it might be in particular instances.

Through most of this period, till well into the twentieth century, science rejected what much of antiquity knew, which is that the universe had a beginning. The Egyptians, the Babylonians, the Greeks in Hesiod's *Theogony,* and the ancient Hebrews each tell the tale very differently, which suggests that it arose not from mutual influence but from the independent intuition of an original act or moment somehow still palpable after the billions of years that had already passed before the ancients began their speculations. These ancestors are not at all remote from us in cosmic time, of course, and the physical world we see, if we wander a little distance from its pavements and enclosures, is for all purposes the same world. We reasoned ourselves away from the perception of it as emergent at the same time that we began to think of our own ancient text as mythic in a pejorative sense. Our best minds knew less about reality than Moses would have told them.

This tendency toward dismissiveness persists. It seized the rhetorical high ground perhaps two hundred years ago and has never relinquished it. The anxiety it inspires in some quarters has yielded a literalism that is brutally disrespectful of the text. Among nonliteralists it has produced an evasiveness that shies away from the text, and from theological tradition as well. In many cases what is intended as resistance to literalism tacitly concedes the legitimacy of literalism because sophisticated assumptions about the ancient and the mythic make reductionist readings seem inevitable. The new atheists, claiming the authority of science, go on about the old man with a white beard seated on a cloud, or they chuckle and scold at the thought of an imaginary friend. The response among the pious has been in some cases to put Adam on a dinosaur, proposing a science of their own. There is little to choose between the two. In both cases there is a radical rejection of the language of the sublime, that is, of the divine. In neither case is there any conception of the beautiful. Say what one will about religion through the millennia, it has yielded a great bounty of art in every kind. When King Solomon set about building the great Temple in Jerusalem where the Lord would put his name, he brought in foreign craftsmen who built something very like the temples of their own gods. Presumably, to the eye of Solomon and all Israel, in its sacred architecture pagan culture could and did evoke holiness and sublimity of a kind appropriate to the Temple of the God of Israel. This is the kind of thing that is regularly seen as evidence of syncretism and interpreted as evidence that the whole of the religion of Israel came together piecemeal from surrounding influences. There is an impulse to debunk in academic writing that is so long established as to be unconscious in many instances. The impulse is only more persistent because it is now taken to be the tone and substance of disinterested scholarship, a correction against the biases of traditional piety that need not concern itself with biases of its own. And the fact is that Israel lived in a swarming world surrounded by cultural kindred absorbed in their own rituals and myths. They lived in history, like any other people.

But every argument for syncretism can also be taken as evidence that Israel saw a true sense of the sacred in the surrounding cultures—not in the particulars of their beliefs and practices but in the more primary fact that they had an intuition of the divine that did indeed bear some analogy to Israel's. In his Letter to the Romans, Paul says this about pagans and their religions:

> What can be known about God is plain to them, because God has shown it to them. Ever since the creation of the world his invisible nature, namely his eternal power and deity, has been clearly perceived in the things that have been made. So they are without excuse; for although they knew God they did not honor him as God or give thanks to him, but they became futile in their thinking and

their senseless minds were darkened. Claiming to be wise, they became fools, and exchanged the glory of the immortal God for images resembling mortal man or birds or animals or reptiles. (I:19–23)

God has shown himself to mankind plainly in his creation. The pagans know God, but their knowledge of him is warped and distracted by idolatry, worship of the creature rather than the creator. So the main point is established clearly here that behind all the passionate differences and all the polemics there is, in however fragmentary a form, a shared and true perception of the divine. Time forbids the citing of numerous texts to the same effect to be found in the Hebrew Bible, a natural consequence of its monotheism. The Athenians ask Paul to tell them something new and he responds by telling them something timeless. He says, God himself "gives to all men life and breath and everything." And he quotes from another Greek poet, Aratus, who says of God: "For we are indeed his offspring." Seen in this light, the similarities between Israelite and other religions should seem unembarrassed, a recognition and acknowledgment, not proof of cultural or textual pilfering. Above all, there should be no disparagement of implied claims of the religion of Abraham and Moses to immediate and original knowledge of God when all knowledge of God, insofar as it retains some character of truth, must be immediate and original—God has shown it to humankind in the things that have been made.

Let us say that there are grounds for speaking of the divine as mythic. It structures and characterizes reality, in the way of myth. It asserts the existence of a Being or beings aloof from time who bear some likeness to humankind. It implants concepts like virtue and transgression so deeply in reality that reality responds to them as part of its own fabric. It is like myth in that it has scale. It refers to duration no human will ever experience. It refers to eternity, thinking past the extreme finitude of birth and death.

And it considers the heavens. God only knows what night looked like when the last lamp went out in Babylon or Jerusalem or in Calvin's mountainous Geneva, and the great host of stars, innumerable as the sands of the sea, claimed its place in the firmament. On the one hand, since Galileo people have worked with passionate diligence to understand and observe the heavens, and what a sight they are. We have looked into Melvillean nurseries, and glimpsed the births of stars that came into being many millions of years ago, an odd privilege of our relation to space and time. We do these things that are the unimaginable realizations of antiquity's old longing, and there is scarcely a poem or a prayer by way of celebration. "It moves us not—great God, I'd rather be a pagan." That is Wordsworth, of course, who need not have wished for more than to be a Christian or a Jew in a place and time where the revelatory character of creation was acknowledged. But he is right, all in all. It is the absence of divinity that dehumanizes nature. There is nothing paradoxical in this thought.

Myth brings scale to the narratives that stir the human imagination. Old Marduk, whose loss to the pantheon is not particularly to be lamented, did make one pleasing proof of his standing among the gods of Babylon, who did not at first accept his claims to supremacy. He flung a constellation into being, then made it vanish, then restored it. He did other things less beautiful, which nevertheless yielded the Tigris and the Euphrates, heaven and earth. The heavens for most of us now are a kind of wearying ethereal sea that accommodates travel from one coast or continent to another, its vastness and even its turbulence largely forgettable with good earphones and a movie. Or it is the dumping ground, so to speak, of far more detritus than even its great volume can dilute. We keep an eye on it now to gauge its health, speculating nothing, concluding nothing, about humankind from our epic power to de-create. Properly speaking, we are the stuff of myth. And yet we have no language to address the scale of the experience we have, not only as dwellers in a cosmos but also as creatures whose thoughts naturally inhabit the vastnesses of myth, creation to doomsday, who see our galaxy as a path across the heavens, who spin new tales of the impossible even while we sleep. A splendid dignity is spread out over all this, whether recognized or not, by the divine, the good and glorious creator and center and substance of it all.

The American Scholar Now

Presidential Lecture at Stanford University:
October 29, 2015 (published in Harper's Magazine
as "Save Our Public Universities," March 2016)

Emerson's lecture "The American Scholar," which he delivered in 1837, implicitly raises radical questions about the nature of education, culture, and consciousness, and about their interactions. He is urging his hearers to make the New World as new as it ought to be, urging his audience to outlive the constraints colonial experience imposed on them and to create the culture that would arise from the full and honest use of their own intellects, minds, and senses. Any speaker might say the same to any audience. Every generation is in effect colonized by its assumptions and also by the things it reveres. The future, in the American experience, has always implied an inevitable departure from the familiar together with the possibility of shaping inevitable change. The historical circumstance of the country at the time Emerson spoke made vivid what is always true, that there is a frontier, temporal rather than geographical, which can and surely will be the new theater of old crimes and errors, but which can and will be an enlargement of experience, a region of indeterminacy, of possibility. The difference between any decade and the next makes this point.

In his introduction to *Democracy in America*, Alexis de Tocqueville says a very striking thing about the world then unfolding.

> From the moment when the exercise of intelligence had become a source of strength and wealth, each step in the development of science, each new area of knowledge, each fresh idea had to be viewed as a seed of power placed within people's grasp. Poetry, eloquence, memory, the beauty of wit, the fires of imagination, the depth of thought, all these gifts which heaven shares out by chance turned to the advantage of democracy and, even when they belonged to the enemies of democracy, they still promoted its cause by highlighting the natural grandeur of man. Its victories spread, therefore, alongside those of civilization and education.

Tocqueville, like Emerson, stood at a cusp of history where literacy and democracy were both assuming an unprecedented importance in the civilization of the West. Not unambivalent in his feelings about democracy, Tocqueville did see it as based on "the natural grandeur of man," brought to light by education. "Poetry, eloquence, memory, the beauty of wit, the fires of imagination, the depth of thought." These things are mentioned as rarely now as the object or effect of education as "the natural grandeur of man" is mentioned as an assumption of our culture or a basis of our politics.

Emerson delivered his address to the Phi Beta Kappa society after the publication of Tocqueville's first volume and before the publication of the second. He was speaking at a time when colleges were being founded all across America—my own university, Iowa, in 1847. The great Frederick Law Olmsted was at that time putting his aesthetic blessing on our public spaces, notably on college campuses, including finally Stanford.

The *Oxford English Dictionary* defines *campus* as an Americanism. The conventions established in the early nineteenth century have persisted in meadows and gardens and ponds that celebrate, if only out of habit, these cities of the young, these local capitals of learning and promise. Olmsted, like Emerson, would have seen something like the emergence of brilliant individuality in unexpected places that Tocqueville describes, strongly potential in American life though as yet suppressed, according to Emerson, by a preoccupation with the practical, with trade and enterprise, and suppressed as well by a colonial deference toward the culture of Europe. Like Tocqueville, Emerson is proposing an anthropology, proposing that there is a splendor inherent in human beings that is thwarted and hidden by deprivation of the means to express it, even to realize it in oneself. The celebration of learning made visible in its spread into the territories and the new-made states must have taken some part of its character from the revelation of human gifts it brought with it. It is interesting to see what persists over time, and interesting to see what is lost.

For those to whom Emerson is speaking, who have made a good account of themselves as students at Harvard, deprivation is the effect of an unconscious surrender, a failure to aspire, to find in oneself the grandeur that could make the world new. We know these people. In fact we are these people, proudly sufficient to expectations, our own and others, and not much inclined to wonder whether these expectations are not in fact rather low. We have, of course, accustomed ourselves to a new anthropology that is far too sere to accommodate anything like grandeur, and which barely acknowledges wit, in the nineteenth century or the modern sense. Eloquence might be obfuscation, since the main project of the self is now taken by many specialists in the field to be the concealment of selfish motives. How do we define imagination these days, and do we still associate it with fires? Unless it is escape or delusion, it seems to have little relevance to the needs of the organism for good or ill. So, like character, like the self, it is no doubt by now defined out of existence. We leave it to a cadre of specialists to describe human nature—a phrase that by their account no doubt names yet another nonexistent thing. It must be said that, at best, these specialists would show no fondness for it if they did concede its existence, nor do they allow to it any of the traits it long found ingratiating in itself. This is so true that the elimination of the pleasing, the poignant, the tragic from our self-conception—I will not mention brilliance or grandeur—would seem to be the object of the exercise. Plume-plucked humankind. Tocqueville and Emerson might be surprised to find us in such a state after generations of great freedom, by the standards of history, and after the vast elaboration of resources for learning in every field.

In fact it is this vast elaboration, epitomized in the American university, that proves we have had a loftier view of ourselves historically, and it is a demonstration of the change in our self-conception that our universities as they exist no longer make sense to legislatures and to people of influence, a phrase that, in our moment, really does mean moneyed interests. Traditional centers of influence—churches, unions, relevant professionals—have lost their place in public life, or they have merged their influence with the moneyed interests, speaking here of those churches that do maintain a public presence. From this perspective, the great public universities—and many of them are very great—are like beached vessels of unknown origin and intention, decked out preposterously with relics and treasures, ripe for looting insofar as what they hold would find a market, condemned to neglect and decay insofar as the cash value of what they hold is not obvious to the most astringent calculation.

There has been a fundamental shift in American consciousness. The Citizen has become the Taxpayer. In consequence of this shift, public assets are now public burdens. These personae, Citizen and Taxpayer, are both the creations of political rhetoric—it now requires an unusual degree of historical awareness to know that both "politics" and "rhetoric" were once honorable things. An important aspect of human circumstance is that we can create effective reality simply by consenting to the reality of the phantasms of the moment, or the decade. While the Citizen can entertain aspirations for the society as a whole and take pride in its achievements, the Taxpayer, as presently imagined, simply does not want to pay taxes. The societal consequences of this aversion—failing infrastructure, for example—are to be preferred to any inroad on his or her monetary fiefdom, large or small. This is as touchy a point as are limits on so-called Second Amendment rights. Both sensitivities, which are treated as if they were protections against centralization and collectivism, are having profound consequences for society as a whole, and this without meaningful public debate, without referendum. Citizenship, which once implied obligation, is now deflated—that is, given an artificial value by use that treats it as primarily a limited good that ought to be limited further. The degree to which Citizen and Taxpayer ever existed, exist now, or can be set apart as distinct types is a question complicated by the fact that they are imposed on public consciousness by politicians playing to constituencies, by interest groups, by journalism that repeats unreflectingly whatever gimmicky notion is in the air and reinforces it. It can be said, however, that whenever the Taxpayer is invoked as the protagonist in the public drama, stalwart defender of his own, past and potential martyr to a culture of dependency and governmental overreach, we need not look for generosity, imagination, wit, poetry, or eloquence. We certainly need not look for the humanism Tocqueville saw as the moving force behind democracy.

I will put aside a fact that should be too obvious to need

stating, that America has done well economically, despite passing through difficult periods from time to time, as countries
do. It would be very hard indeed to make the case that the Land-
Grant College Act has done us any harm, or that the centrality
of the liberal arts in our education in general has impeded the
development of wealth. True, a meteor strike or some equivalent could put an end to this tomorrow. But if we were obliged
to rebuild ourselves, we could not find a better model for the
creation of wealth than our own history. I do not mean to suggest that wealth is to be thought of as our defining achievement,
or that it is the first thing we should protect or recover. But
since money is the measure of all things these days, it is worth
pointing out that there are no grounds for regarding our educational culture as in need of "rationalization"—it must be
clear that I take exception to this use of the word—to align it
with current economic doctrine.

•

All this sidesteps the old Kantian distinction—whether people
are to be dealt with as means or as ends. The argument against
our way of educating is that it does not produce workers who
are equipped to compete in the globalized economy, the economy of the future. This has to be as blunt a statement as could be
made about the urgency, currently felt in some regions and
credulously received and echoed everywhere, that we should
put our young to this use, to promote competitive adequacy
at a national level, to whose profit or benefit we are never told.
There is no suggestion that the gifts they might bring to the
world as individuals stimulated by broad access to knowledge
have place or value in this future world, only that we should
provide in place of education what would better be called
training.

If all institutions feel this pressure in some degree, public
institutions feel it most continuously and profoundly. A univer-

sity like mine, founded almost one hundred seventy years ago, before Iowa would even have had much in the way of corn-fields, gives unambiguous evidence of the kinds of hopes that lay behind its founding and sustained it through many generations. From an early point it emphasized the arts. It was founded while Emerson was active and at about the time Tocqueville was published, and can fairly be assumed to have shared their worldview. So with many or most public universities in America. Accepting creative work toward a graduate degree, the MFA as we know it now, was an innovation of the University of Iowa. My own program, the Writers' Workshop, is the oldest thing of its kind on the planet. People do ask me from time to time why Iowa is in Iowa. For the same reason Bloomington is in Indiana, no doubt. If we were better pragmatists we would look at the fact that people given a relatively blank slate, the prairie, and a pool of public resources, however modest, are at least as desirous of the wonderful as of the profitable or necessary.

Atavism is a potent force in human history. There is the pull of the retrograde, an almost physical recoil, much more potent than mere backsliding, much more consequential than partial progress or flawed reform. The collective mind can find itself reinhabited by old ideas almost unconsciously, almost unwillingly. A word around which retrograde thinking is often constellated is *elitist*. Liberal education was for a very long time reserved to an elite, whence the word *liberal*, befitting free men, who were a small minority in Western societies. Gradually, except by the standards of the world at large, Americans began democratizing privilege. As Tocqueville remarks, heaven shares out by chance those high gifts of intellect and culture, which had previously been associated arbitrarily with status and advantage, and were now manifest as a vastly more generous endowment. We need only allow the spread of learning to see the brilliance potential in humankind.

But the memory persists that the arts were once social attainments and that the humanities suited one to a position of authority. What use could they be to ordinary people? What claim should anything of such doubtful utility have on the public purse? Or, to look at the matter from another side, why should an English class at the University of Wisconsin be as excellent as an English class at Stanford University, for a mere fraction of the cost? The talk we hear so often now about "top-tier universities," about supposed "rankings," creates an economics of scarcity in the midst of an astonishing abundance. And it helps to justify assaults on great public resources of the kind we have seen recently in Wisconsin and elsewhere. Public universities are stigmatized as elitist because they continue in the work of democratizing privilege, of opening the best thought and the highest art to anyone who wishes to have access to them. They are attacked as elitist because their tuition goes up as the supports they receive from government go down. The Citizen had a country, a community, children and grandchildren, even—a word we no longer hear—posterity. The Taxpayer has a 401(k). It is no mystery that *one* could be glad to endow monumental libraries, excellent laboratories, concert halls, arboretums, baseball fields, and the *other* simply can't see the profit in it for himself.

•

There is pressure to transform the public university so that less cost goes into it and more benefit comes out—as such things are reckoned in terms of contemporary economic thinking. That this economics could be so overbearingly sure of itself ought to be remarkable given recent history, but its voice is magnified in the void left by the default of other traditional centers of authority. In any case, whether and how we educate people is still a direct reflection of the degree of freedom we expect them to have, or want them to have. Since printing became well established in the West and the great usefulness of literacy began to be recognized, it has been as characteristic of cultures to withhold learning as to promote it. They have done both, selectively, and the effect of this kind of discrimination has been profound, persisting in the present, as it will certainly persist into the future. In most Western cultures the emergence of literacy in women lagged far behind literacy in men, and in many parts of the world it is still forbidden or discouraged, despite, or perhaps because of, the fact that this disability in women radically slows economic development, among other things.

Western "progress" is arguably an uncertain road to happiness, I know. But insofar as Western civilization has made a value of freeing the mind by giving it ability and resources, it has been a wondrous phenomenon. Wherever its strong, skilled attention has fallen on the world, it has made some very interesting errors, without doubt, and it has also revealed true splendors. In either case it has given us good reason to ponder the mind itself, the character of the human mind being so richly inscribed on the cultural experience of all of us, in the ways and degrees that we, as individual minds, are prepared to read its inscriptions.

"Insofar as." American civilization assumes literacy, it saturates our lives with print. It also fails to make an important minority of its people competent in this skill most of us could not imagine living without. Old exclusions come down the generations—we all know that parents are the first teachers. Old injustices come down the generations—why bother to educate people who have no use for education, the hewers of wood and drawers of water? The argument was made that peasants, women, slaves, industrial workers would be happier knowing nothing about a world that would be closed to them in any case. Therefore for a very long time it *was* closed to them, since they could be assumed to be ignorant of it. In the degree that all this has changed, social equality and mobility have followed. Many traditional barriers are lower, if they have not yet fallen.

What exactly is the impetus behind the progressive change that has been simultaneous with the emergence of modern society? Our era could well be said to have had its origins in a dark age. The emergence of the factory system and mass production brought a degree of exploitation of human beings for which even feudalism had no equivalent. The severest possible cheapening of labor in early industry was supported by the same theories that drove colonialism and chattel slavery. The system yielded spectacular wealth, of course, islands of wealth based on extreme poverty and on the profounder impoverishments of slavery. Comparisons are made between slavery and so-called "free labor," which seem always to imply that the second was more efficient than the first, therefore destined on economic grounds to become the dominant system, and to bring with it a general melioration of conditions. It is a very imprecise use of language to describe as "free" a labor force largely composed of children, who, on the testimony of Benjamin Disraeli among many others, could not and did not expect to live far beyond childhood. It is an imprecise use of language to call "free" the great class of laborers who had no rights even to shelter outside the parishes where they were born. The fact of social progress has been treated as demonstrating that laissez-faire works for us all, that the markets are not only wise but also benign, indeed humane. This argument is based on history that is effectively invented to serve it, and on a quasi-theology of economic determinism, a monotheism in that it cannot entertain the possibility or the suggestion that social circumstance can have any other origin than economics. Clever as we think we are, we are enacting again the strange—and epochal—tendency of Western civilization to impoverish.

We have come to a place where these assumptions are being

tested, in reality, at least, if not in our universities and think tanks. Reality is that turbulent region our thoughts visit seldom and briefly, like Baedeker tourists eager to glimpse the sights that will confirm our expectations and put us on shared conversational ground with decades of fellow tourists. We leave trash on Mount Everest, we drop trash in the sea, and reality goes on with its life, reacting to our depredations as it must while ages pass, continents clash, and infernos boil over. It is true that our carelessness affects the world adversely, and it is also true that the world can fetch autochthonous surprises up out of its fiery belly. The metaphor is meant to suggest that we are poor observers, rarely seeing more than we intend to see. Our expectations are received, therefore static, which makes it certain that they will be like nothing in reality. Still, we bring our expectations with us, and we take them home with us again, reinforced.

Historical time also has a fiery belly and a capacity for devastating eruptions. It has equivalents for drought and desert, for glaciation. Its atmosphere can dim and sicken. Any reader of history knows this. If the changes that occur in it are very substantially the result of human activity, they seem rarely to reflect human intention, at least when they are viewed in retrospect. They seem always to elude human notice until they are irreversible, overwhelming. Western civilization had had a significant place among world cultures in articulating the sense of vastnesses and richnesses in its painting, poetry, music, architecture, and philosophy. Then rather suddenly this great, ancient project was discountenanced altogether. The sacred has since been declared to have been a meaningless category, a name for something in fact compounded of fear, hope, and ignorance, and configured around certain ancient tales and ceremonies, a forgivable error in an earlier age. That it yielded works of extraordinary beauty and profundity was acknowledged fulsomely in modernist nostalgia, whose exponents saw

themselves as the victims of the transformations they announced
and, in a considerable degree, created. Grand-scale change was
in fact imminent and inevitable, of course. Empires were falling, technology was rising. Whether the new age need have
brought with it this mawkish gloom is another question. I propose that the thought we call modern was by no means robust
and coherent enough intellectually to discredit metaphysics
and theology, among many other things, though it did discredit them. To account for this I would suggest that its appeal
to the upper strata of culture was in the fact that it closed questions rather than opening them. Its nostalgias made it resistant
to reform and excused it from giving a rational defense of its
resistance. It created the narrative of a breach with the European past by ignoring European history. Granting the horrors
of the First World War, Europe seems to have comforted itself
by arming for the Second World War. That is to say, humankind has always given itself occasions for grief and despair, and
has seldom made better use of them than to store up grudges
and provocations to prepare the next occasion.

•

Human cultural achievements may be thought of as somewhat
apart from these periodic rampages. There are no grounds for
thinking of high civilizations as less violent than any others—
no grounds, that is, except in the histories and anthropologies
that are written by them. So long as warfare and other enormities are treated as paradoxical, anomalous, aberrant, we lack a
sufficiently complex conception of humankind. History can tell
us that neither side of our nature precludes the other. The worst
we do does not diminish the goodness of the best we do. That
our best is so often artistic more than utilitarian, in the usual
senses of both words, is a fact with which we should learn to be
at peace.

The arts have been under attack since Plato at least, on the grounds that they had no useful role in society. They are under attack at present. We have persuaded ourselves that the role of the middle ranks of our population is to be of use to the economy—more precisely, to the future economy, of which we know nothing for certain but which we can fairly imagine to be as unlike the present one as *it* is unlike the order that prevailed a few decades ago. If the present is any guide, we can anticipate further profound disruption. So such coherence as the economy has created in the culture to this point cannot at all be assumed. The reverence paid to economic forces, which, with the accelerating accumulation of wealth in very few hands, increasingly amounts to little more than faceless people with no certain qualifications playing with money, enforces the belief that our hopes must be surrendered to these forces. The coherence society might take from politics—that is, from consciousness that it is a polity, a human community with a history and with a habit of aspiration toward democracy requiring a capacity in its public for meaningful decisions about its life and direction— exists apart from these forces and is at odds with them. So far as they are determinist, and so long as they succeed in defining utility—that is, value and legitimacy—for the rest of us, we have surrendered even the thought of creating a society that can sustain engagement and purpose, beyond that endless openness and submissiveness to other people's calculations and objectives that we call "competitiveness."

At the moment, two things are taken to be true: one, that our society must be disciplined and trained to compete in a global market, and two, that these competitive skills have no definable character. Who might not be displaced by a computer or a robot? Who might not be displaced by an offshore worker, an adjunct? Economics from its brutal beginnings has told us that cheapened labor will give its employers a competitive advantage, and that costlier labor will drive industries into extinction or into foreign labor markets. Oddly, even monstrously costly executives seem never to have this effect. Economics has told us that labor both creates value and is the greatest cost in the production of value. When Marx wrote about these things he was using a long-established vocabulary, still descriptive now, therefore useful. There is nationalism involved in all this, historically. The colonial system, which was entirely bound up in trade and industry, enjoyed the power and the sense of grandeur of the old European empires. The global reach of the early industrial system made mass poverty a national asset, as it is now. According to the theory that rationalized it, the worker's wage could not exceed the level necessary to his subsistence— that is, the level necessary to leave him, more probably her, physically able to work. I believe this "brazen law," as they called it, is still in force in many of those societies with which we are told we are competing.

The most obvious evidence that the United States proceeded for a long time on other assumptions is our educational system, which is by now seen by very many people as an obstacle to our recruiting ourselves to the great project of competing in the world economy. If it is no longer clear what these singular institutions should be doing, it is pretty clear what they should not be doing, which is disseminating knowledge and culture, opening minds. The dominant view now is that their legitimate function is not to prepare people for citizenship in a democracy but to prepare them to be members of a docile though skilled working class. It has been characteristic of American education that it has offered students a great variety of fields of study and a great freedom to choose among them. It has served as a mighty paradigm for the kind of self-discovery Americans have historically valued. Now this idea has gone into eclipse. The freedom of the individual seems to have been reduced to a right to belligerent ignorance coupled with devotion to a particular reading of the Second Amendment. Other than this they are offered a future in which their particular interests, gifts, and values will have very minimal likelihood of expression, since they are very likely not to suit the uses of whatever employment is on offer. They must give up the thought of shaping their own lives, of having even the moral or political right to try to stabilize them against the rigors and uncertainties of the markets, those great gods. All this assumes, of course, something that has never been true in this country, that the society and economy will be dominated by great industries that make more or less uniform demands of their workers, as those primordial cotton mills did. We are encouraged to accept the inevitability of a dystopia, the brightest hope being that we or our children will do better than most people.

An early step in making all this inevitable is the attack on higher education, a resurgence of that old impulse to force society into the form that is considered natural and necessary, an impulse that only grows stronger when society as it exists seems recalcitrant. The fact is that, in general, our system of higher education could hardly be less suited to serve the unspecific but urgent purposes of the economy of the future presently imagined for us, which really bears more resemblance to that forgotten past, that dark age, which taught the benefits to the few of cheapening the labor, that is to say, depressing the living standards, of the very many. This is an object mightily assisted by high levels of unemployment and by access to labor markets where large-scale poverty is endemic. A rationale for all this is that Western prosperity sprang from the dark age of early industrialism. Post hoc, ergo propter hoc. This is a tendentious reading of a very complex history. Henry Ford's realization that workers should be paid enough to be a market for the things they made, an inversion of the old model, might be said to have come from his experiencing the limits of what Marx quite accurately called the expropriation of the worker. The so-called consumer society followed on Ford's innovation. This was novel, an object of derision at home and abroad, and it is what we are losing now as unemployment and the exploitation of cheap labor in other countries exerts a continuous downward pressure here. A consumer society is one in which people in general can engage in discretionary spending. It is characteristic of Americans that whatever they are or do is what they also ridicule and lament. But in fact the margin above that grim old standard, subsistence, is the margin of personal freedom. And, granting fads and excesses, interesting uses have been made of it.

And as one important instance, for a long time, by world and historical standards, we have educated a great many people at great cost. Our discretionary spending has also been expressed as a willingness to be taxed for the common benefit. Without question the institutions we have created have added tremendous wealth to society over time. But we have been talked out of the kind of pragmatism that would allow us to say: This works. No comparably wealthy society has proceeded on the utilitarian principles that would ration access to varieties of learning in the name of improving a workforce. One might reply that there has never been a country to compare with this one in terms of wealth. True enough. One conclusion we might draw from this fact is that what we do works. At the very least, it does not impede the great cause of wealth accumulation that, come to think of it, never is the stated object of competitiveness, any more than is liberty or the pursuit of happiness, the general welfare, or, indeed, the examined life. By its atavistic lights we should be prepared to navigate uncharted seas, assuming always that nothing else is offered or owed to us but work, which is itself highly conditional, allowed to us so long as no cheaper arrangement can be found. With all the urgency of this argument, holding up to us this dismal, threatening future, no mention is made of the fact that great wealth will indeed accumulate. It will not be distributed, however. The most efficient system ever devised for the distribution of wealth is a meaningful wage. The most effective means of depressing wages ever found is the mobility of capital, that same accumulated wealth, which can move overnight to a more agreeable climate. Our workers—that is, all of us, more or less—are already prepared to understand that in abandoning America it is only obeying that brazen law. There will be a hint of rebuke, as there is now, in the fact that we failed to be competitive, which might have something to do with currency fluctuations or with the misfortune of living in a place that is a little too fastidious in the matter of breathable air and drinkable water. This rebuke will echo through society, demonstrating to many the absolute need to jettison these standards, their immediate cost precluding any thought of their long-term benefit. Attending to public health is distributive, since it entails particular costs to achieve a general benefit associated with a general ability to prosper. I avoid the more familiar term *redistributive*, since it implies a real, prior ownership of wealth from which a general wealth is subtracted. This notion is not supportable, philosophically or economically, though at the moment it is very powerful indeed.

I mentioned before that all this is somehow entangled with patriotism, with nationalism. There is a great scrum going on, now and also forever, since this model of economy has taken over so much of the world. China seems to be slowing, so India will emerge as the great competitor, presumably. We will marvel at the vast percentage increase in one measure or another of their well-being, as we always do, which any country in the world with a big enough population will demonstrate, since there are smart people everywhere and since infusions of money and industrial technology will have these effects anywhere. Their middle class will expand, as ours would too, given capital and new infrastructure and manufacturing, though it would grow less dramatically percentage-wise since it has been very large historically. Still, at some point these measures of the prosperity of, say, India would begin to be presented to us as alarming trends. They would be taken to mean that we were about to be vanquished, left in the dust of mediocrity and decline. Our cult of competition does not seem able to entertain the idea that two or more countries could flourish simultaneously, unless, of course, they are European. It does not permit the thought that our response to the economic rise of India or China or Brazil might properly be to say: Good for them. This is the use that is made of the old habits of nationalism. We are always ready to be persuaded that we are under threat. While care for our terrain and people and future can be tarnished as socialism, to be swept up in a general alarm that impoverishes them all is somehow American. What nonsense.

Let us call the stripping down of our society for the purposes of our supposed economic struggle with the world the expropriation of our workers. Academics have made absurd uses of Marx's categories so often that there are risks involved in even alluding to them. But Marx was critiquing political economy, and so am I. And nothing was more powerful in that brutal old system, now resurgent, than downward pressure on wages. Americans think Marx was criticizing America, an error of epochal consequence, propagated in the university as diligently as in any right-wing think tank. They think that political economy, that is, capitalism, was our invention and is the genius of our civilization—the greatest ever, by grace of capitalism, so they say. Indeed, unread books may govern the world, not well, since they so often are taken to justify our worst impulses and prejudices. The Holy Bible is a case in point. Then again, there is the history of academic so-called Marxism to misinform us. It is certainly true that as colonies created as extensions of the British industrial system, notoriously involving the Atlantic slave trade, our earliest beginnings have always haunted us and harmed us, too. Still, access to land, scarcity of labor and its mobility, and the communitarian ethos of the northern colonies changed the economy in fact, then in theory. The iron law of wages lacked the conditions that enforced it in the old country. If Jefferson's "happiness" is given its frequent eighteenth-century meaning, prosperity or thriving, then the pursuit of happiness—a level of life above subsistence—would become possible as it had not been for any but the most exceptional members of the British working class. If political economy is capitalism, then the American colonies began to vary away from capitalism long before the Revolution. In this new environment only chattel slavery could preserve certain of its essential features, notably the immobilization of a workforce maintained at the level of subsistence and a radical polarization of wealth. Again, these were the plantations of the British industrial system, producing cotton for the cotton mills of Manchester. It is remarkable how often they are treated as if they were preindustrial, precapitalist, as if cotton and indigo were comestibles and sugar was a dietary staple, and as if the whole arrangement did not run on credit and speculation.

Well, obviously I am very critical of the universities, too. They give prestige to just the kind of thinking that undermines their own existence as humanist institutions, especially in economics but in many fields influenced by economics, for example, psychologies that subject all actions and interactions to cost-benefit analysis, to—the phrase should make us laugh—rational choice. And this bleeds out to the humanities, of course, which are utterly, hopelessly anomalous by these lights, and have run for cover to critical theory, which is tortuous and dreary enough to look like a lot of work and impenetrable enough to evade scrutiny. In every case the conception of what a human being is, and with it the thought of what she might be, is made tedious and small. The assumption current now, that the test of a university is its success in vaulting graduates into upper tiers of wealth and status, obscures the fact that this is an enormous country, and that many of its best and brightest prefer a modest life in Maine or South Dakota. Or in Iowa, as I find myself obliged to say from time to time. It obscures the fact that there is a vast educational culture in this country, unlike anything else in the world. It emerged from a glorious sense of the possible and explored and enhanced the possible through the spread of learning. If it seems to be failing now, this is true because we have forgotten what it is for, why the libraries like cathedrals, why the meadows and the flowers. They are all a tribute and an invitation to the young, who can and should make the world new, out of the unmapped and unbounded resource of their minds.

Grace and Beauty

The Comparative Literature Lecture Series at
Princeton University: April 7, 2016

I have read enough about the fundamental complexity of all things, down to the very protons and neutrons, to feel at ease saying this: Beauty disciplines. I know my two-word sentence is not intelligible by conventional standards. I hope by means of it to move a little beyond these standards and to begin to justify my doubts about their usefulness.

The fact is that I have begun to feel both intrigued and comforted by the thought of everything we do not know, which is almost everything. The 95 percent of the mass of the universe that is dark matter holds the galaxies together, so they say. It is like a parable, this aloof and unknowable power sustaining us, the patron, so to speak, of the spangled heavens, which are so grand to our sight, and baubles when the universe is thought of whole. Whatever it is, it is utterly unlike the matter that is familiar to us, so I have read. How excellent it is that anything could be so unforeseen. And just as excellent, and fully as remarkable, that humankind has managed to catch a glimpse of it. Increasingly I think of the mind and the universe as one great system, and the unknown and uncomprehended in their infinite variety as sutures, fontanels, that accommodate the growth of human awareness. I'm thinking of the sutures in the skull, of course, that foresee and permit the great expansion of the brain unique to our species. This is a faulty metaphor for a number of reasons. At some point the fontanels do close, while nothing we have learned implies that the unknown is by any means reducible, let alone exhaustible. Wallace Stevens says, "The squirming fact exceeds the squamous mind." *Squamous* means "bony." Flawed as it is, I find my metaphor more serviceable, better suited to my purposes, though there is no poet I return to as often as I do to Stevens, and among his poems, few more gratifying to me than "Connoisseur of Chaos." Brilliant consciousness pondering the imponderable. Stevens is the great realist. "How high that highest candle lights the dark." Yes and amen.

By implication, Being is addressed to the mind as the mind is addressed to Being. Both should be thought of as emergent, Being infused with its roaring history and on its way to somewhere or something, but, given the difference between its time and ours, as if paused to tolerate our contemplation of it. And then the mind reaching after it. To call it Deus absconditus would not be wholly wrong, since it is both hidden and manifest, elusive and radically sustaining. I suppose I always find myself writing theologically because only theology supports an ultimate coherency that can embrace equally the true, the tentative, and the flawed, as reality itself embraces them—which is only to say that we, our erring kind, are as intrinsic a part of reality as mice and moonlight.

•

There is tremendous play in reality, or, to put the matter another way, there are far too many layers and orders of complexity in all of Being to abide the simple accounts we try to make of things. This complexity is dynamic because from moment to moment every layer of complexity introduces any number of variables. I am aware that play and variability might not be exactly the terms I need. If they do not describe the workings of things intrinsically, but only as they are experienced, they do well enough for my purposes, since my interest here is in reauthorizing experience, felt reality, as one important testimony to the nature of reality itself. The tendency of the behavioral sciences, in their accounts of the evolutions of intelligence and language ability and also their stark models of human motivation, are parsimonious in ways and degrees experience cannot justify. And since we all do live with our motives, even struggle with them, and since we all spend a great part of our time putting thoughts into language, mere proximity to the phenomena should give us some credibility as witnesses. We choose an utterance, a gesture. By these means we identify ourselves and, in the same moment, discover and create ourselves. If it does not seem quite true to say one acts freely, the problem may lie at least in part with the common understanding of that abstract entity "one," the individual self, and with our habit of subordinating important but unacknowledged sources of manifest behavior to the behavior we think of as willed, even when it is not enacted. In other words, there are no grounds for saying that our tedious, impolitic selves, our conventional selves, however much they give us to dread or regret, are less free than any other behavior. If we understand our lesser selves as a product of social conditioning, as much can be said of our best selves. True, since Freud the commonplace has been that our darker motives, being more primitive, are therefore more authentic, therefore freer, insofar as the word can be said to apply to this model of the human psyche. Neither statement is true or sufficient, of course.

I know that my years at the work of writing fiction have conditioned my thinking about many things. The problem of finding and sustaining a credible character, a creature made of words on a page, which, or who, can seem to a reader to be worth attending to, perhaps caring about, brings all sorts of questions with it. Character implies consistency of a kind. A word, even a punctuation mark, can be out of character. There is an inaudible equivalent of a clang or a clunk where this kind of mistake is made. To ignore it is an option the writer really does not have. It is fair to call this an aesthetic response, and also a test of the phenomenon of credibility, that Ariadne's thread. What fiction is not experimental? What fiction does not work in delicate signals, flickers of sensation evoked by language that simulate the ways in which we know what we know?

But consistency cannot mean predictability, which yields didacticism or melodrama. The old Kantian moral imperative, that a human being should be treated as an end rather than a means, can be restated as an aesthetic imperative radically limiting the degree to which character can be put to the writer's use, whether to represent a type or to make a point. These rules of mine are ignored all the time, of course, by the authors of valuable books. I do not want to imply that literature is or should be limited or judged by one set of standards. I am speaking only of my own sense that to have the feeling of human presence about him or her a character has to seem free and constrained simultaneously, and that when this ceases to be true, credibility is lost. From this I have concluded that a better understanding would create a synthesis of these states, though so far I can only think of them as being in opposition to each other.

Practically speaking, when I am writing I tend to think of a character as having a palette or a music. An aesthetic, in other words. While this is in some ways constraining, it establishes the limits within which substantive invention is possible and, more to the point, within which variation is meaningful. These limits liberate the character, a fact that would be accounted a paradox if it were not so familiar. There are analogies in every art, which permit me the use of these metaphors.

Now, if I were to give a character a childhood trauma, say,

or if I were to make her materialistic or pietistic or paranoid, then she would most likely be acting out the behaviors we are conditioned to expect of people of whom such things are true. Then characterization preexists the character, and to the extent that it does, she is deprived of autonomy. If, on the other hand, she has a kind of coherency of tone and manner, which might be called a repertory of behavior if this could be understood as something emergent, self-renewing, self-elaborating, then these same things could be true of her without any loss of autonomy.

This is beginning to sound a little like Edgar Allan Poe's "Philosophy of Composition."

I absolutely never think out characterization in terms like these before I write, or as I write. But I do work from a sense of the experience of human presence, which forbids that diagnosis or moral judgment should have a central place in my attempts to conjure it. I reflect on my own exclusions, and when I do this in retrospect it can seem as though I have proceeded on the basis of a theory rather than by following the grain of the credible as it presents itself to my mind. The standard I use is strictly experiential. What is the specific absence I feel when I miss someone? The most estimable person on earth could not fill the place left empty by a dear friend, even if it is never clear at all why that friend should matter so much. What is the abstract, the ghost, that persists in the mind, meaning him or her and no one else? What makes the atmosphere of a house change when some particular person walks in the door? Or to put the matter another way, how does our brain compose the ominous strangers who come to us in dreams, with their greasy hair and sidelong looks, full of insinuation and much too believable? Why just that coat? That crudely bandaged hand? Every detail is perfectly evocative of someone we don't want to be so uncannily aware of us. I tell my students to ponder the difference between knowing about someone and knowing him. There was a time when they were inclined to provide a curriculum vitae by way of characterization, and it was necessary to remind them of the powerful distinctiveness of actual or dreamed or remembered human presence.

What all this has to do with grace or beauty is not obvious at this point, I know. And to compound every difficulty, I will add another word to the discussion, an old and philosophical word, *entelechy*, which means "the active principle of wholeness or completion in an individual thing." I have been thinking about this word for years, since I found it in the introduction to an edition of Leibniz's *Theodicy*, a book I seem to have begun at some point, to judge by underlinings and coffee stains, and then to have put aside, taking away no impression except of this one word and its definition. I love to look at old books for some of the same reasons botanists like to study old vegetable strains. They have not been through the often highly dubious processes of refinement that have weeded out vigor and complexity, and flavor, too, from the contemporary language of ideas. *Entelechy* means "soul" in some contexts, which discourages its use. And it is teleological by clear implication. So I had this word in mind for years without having any use for it.

Then, because teaching and writing made me reflect on how fiction emerges and, within fiction and perhaps every other art, how good choices are made, I came back to the idea of "the active principle of wholeness or completion." As a fiction develops, a writer has the exhilarating experience of losing options, of saying "Of course!" to things that emerge on the page with an aura of necessity about them. A great part of the pleasure of reading Dickens comes from the strange compound of utter originality and perfect inevitability invested in his best characters. After one or two brilliant details, every subsequent choice is disciplined by them. The characters, as writers so often report, have taken life and will go their own way, and their creator is obliged to respect and be grateful for their autonomy. Grace and beauty are, in the same way and in the very fact, intrusions upon authorial intent because the fiction has found its way to its wholeness and completion. They also emerge on the page, asserting an authority the writer should be grateful to acknowledge.

I am very much in the habit of going to contemporary science for analogies when I want to lift my thinking out of a course that seems conventional, which in my internal vocabulary is a synonym for deeply suspect. It seems to me, now that I grant myself the term, that there is entelechy everywhere, from the seed to the flower to the seed again. But the concept does not flourish in an environment where Darwinist assumptions prevail, with their anti-teleological answer to every question—the organisms who lack a given trait or have it in a relatively deficient form are less likely to survive and reproduce. Change is accidental variation winnowed and shaped by selection. A cuttlefish can camouflage itself instantly by becoming like the stone behind it, because the ones who couldn't do this did not survive. The most complex phenomena are ultimately that simple in the Darwinist view.

New research in genetics describes the heritability of acquired traits, especially, it seems, if they are the consequence of trauma. And the fluent changes that occur within the genome, for example, make the simplicities of the Mendelian style of explanation seem very quaint. But simplicity is tenacious, and the arguments for and against are plagued by circularity. Teleology of whatever kind has been groomed out of the language in which we talk about reality, meaning that other relevant questions, about the nature of time first of all, have no place in the conversation.

Before the modern period the natural world was assumed to reflect design and intention. This way of stating things did indeed tend to close down inquiry. In order to advance, science had to proceed on other assumptions. But brute reductionism also closes down inquiry. And this can only be particularly true when language is meant to exclude the possibility of interpretation that might be encouraged by tradition and by a kind of common sense. The odds are very good that our understanding of many things is faulty, and that it is premature to attempt to weed out what might appear to be imprecisions but are as likely to be a sort of aura of lingering possibility, intuitive play.

It has been found recently that there are two immune systems in the human body: the intricate one science has long been aware of, and another, simpler one consisting of cells distributed throughout the body, which in the tongue sense bitterness. These cells identify and react to bacteria and toxins immediately, while the more elaborated system takes hours or days. A shorthand explanation for the redundancy would be that the first system is a kind of holding action to compensate for the slower response of the second system. Then again, since nature is elegant, the first system might also prepare for the onset of the second one, signal it as to the nature of the threat to the organism, or tend to aspects of the threat that by their nature need to be dealt with as quickly as possible. These deployed taste buds were originally discovered in the lining of the lungs. There is teleology in this kind of language, in the suggestion that such things happen in order to protect the organism, rather than that they happen and persist in offspring because they do, fortuitously, protect the organism.

In this instance, as in a million others, it is impossible not to feel admiration for the resourcefulness and ingenuity of the body. There can be no doubt that this redundancy of immune responses in fact confers a great survival benefit on an organism. My own theology forbids me to interpose theological interpretation between whatever is to be known and any understanding that might be appropriate to it. To do so is, I believe, a presumption, however pious, that often tends to obscure whatever new marvels lie behind any present one. I'm impressed by great early scientists like Isaac Newton, deeply religious men who were scrupulously attentive to the given world. Still, granting that in cases like this one Divine Providence explains too much, it is true that natural selection also explains too much.

I am absolutely not making the case for any kind of nostalgia when I say this. It is not nostalgic to express a doubt about the adequacy of a concept, even without reference to the fact that this one emerged, granting precursors, in the middle of the nineteenth century. I have said that I wish to reauthorize the testimony of experience, assuming that the brain and the senses are a part of nature. Who would dispute that they are? Scientists are as much inclined to dualistic thinking as the rest of us, and some of them are very inclined to alienate the mind from the world by dwelling on its long history of illusion—which might otherwise be called its long progress to our present state of knowledge, since there is no reason to assume that a higher primate should be capable of high-order intellectual clarity or interested in achieving it. It is easy to forget what an anomaly we are. Allowance being made, of course, for the propensity toward error we have always demonstrated, and which becomes evident only in retrospect, allowing any present time— our own, for example—to believe it has matured beyond this propensity.

The fact remains that there is no other origin for the human mind which is not dependent on theistic assumptions we have agreed, in my case for theistic reasons, not to make. I propose two things: first, that if the mind is to be thought of as a product of the world, or of the processes of which the world is itself a product in its substance and in its history, then the mind ought to be of great interest as evidence about the nature of Being. It is the ultimate known instance of complexity organizing itself, not only to be efficacious in innumerable ways but also to be free—to use a word it is difficult to use with precision. That said, it is only because we are so profoundly anomalous that we have any use for it at all. Therefore it is a subject that is even more interesting than it is difficult.

We say the mind is creative, a phrase that certainly implies a meaningful freedom. I have said a little about this kind of creation as I experience it when I write. It is free in this sense— the world would certainly never have felt the lack of an imaginary minister dying in Iowa in 1956 had anything intervened to stop me from writing a book. I would have felt no need to give an old man imagined life, and death, if I had not realized one afternoon that there was a highly particular voice in my head. For me the impetus behind the book was simply that it was in my mind. I have never written a novel for any other reason. Teaching has provided me with an interesting life and a good income; nonfiction and the reading and research it requires are very satisfying to me. But from time to time I realize I have a novel in mind, and then it is a matter of consuming interest to me to see what it is.

I overstate, of course. I am at risk of another kind of dualist thinking, representing my mind as a rather autonomous being in its own right, which now and then asserts its notions and preoccupations, obliging me to collaborate in realizing them. My mind and I. Since I have set about the project of reauthorizing experience, I can only report that the dichotomy sometimes feels this absolute. In the deeper sense of the word, what does a mind know, and how does it know?

Once I solved a word puzzle in a daily newspaper. It was a quote from Robert Schumann. It said that to compose music one need only remember a song no one has ever heard before. This is another kind of liberating constraint, the sense of answering to what is unconsciously and intimately known, perhaps known more deeply because it is still very widely potential, the song we could not know we yearned to hear. The impact of this sentence of Schumann's was certainly greater because it emerged out of bleary gibberish, just below the comic strips and beside the crossword. I would never have expected to find a thought there that was so perfect an instance of its own truth, something I would not have thought to say but was more than ready to affirm.

Am I implying teleology here? Does art call up a response that is essentially the recognition of a new thing? This sounds like a paradox, and to call something a paradox too often ends discussion. Earlier I introduced my favored word, *entelechy*, and then I left it behind. But it is precisely useful here. The active principle of wholeness or completion in an individual thing. I would say it is true of art generally that it occurs along a continuum between expectation fulfilled, however surprisingly, and expectation disrupted, however profoundly. Is it ever possible to expect Lear to enter carrying the dead Cordelia? Expectation might be called the emotional investment of the audience (meaning those who experience an art, as distinct from those who make it, and who must also participate in this same expectation in a way that makes either fulfillment or disruption a meaningful choice). Certain critics have been so struck by the social or communal aspect of participation in an art that they have reduced fiction to a species of automatic writing—and, by extension, I suppose, painting to automatic painting and so on. The writer is thought of as entrapped, incapable of saying or meaning anything other than whatever her culture induces in her, strive and struggle as she might. This makes interpretation easy, which it really ought never to be. It also accounts rather brusquely for genre and for cultural and national aesthetic traditions. To mention that memory of a song no one has heard, to invoke Stevens's phrase "the voice that is great within us," seems like mystification, except to people like Schumann and Stevens, who might be assumed to speak with some authority. Experience demands a richer vocabulary than theory can give it, for all its neologisms.

"It can never be satisfied, the mind, never." That is Stevens again. The mind is always in process, moving in time through the currents of possibility, realizing formally meaningful things in and from the flux of consciousness, paragraphs and poems that have an overplus of meaning even the writer would not have recognized if certain words had not come together in a certain order. The ways in which they are satisfying—to the ear, to the senses, to cultural memory—fill them with meaning. So, beauty disciplines. It recommends a best word in a best place and makes the difference palpable between aesthetic right and wrong. And it does this freely, within the limits it finds—cultural, material, generic. Another paradox, perhaps, a discipline that is itself free, and free to make variations on such limits as it does choose to embrace. Beauty is like language in this. It can push at the borders of intelligibility and create new eloquence as it does so.

•

I am treating beauty here as an active principle. I use elegance as a virtual synonym for it, pleased that elegance has status by association with good thought, though I try not to exploit this. I do not mean to say that one thing or another rises to the standard of beauty, rather I propose that beauty manifests itself in one thing or another, even asserts itself when accident permits. In saying this I intend to suggest a kind of force active in reality, perhaps very pervasively, that we have no instruments to measure or record except our minds and senses. Consider the ancient, perhaps universal association of beauty with power. The greater the god, the more splendid the temple, as if like were meant to conjure like.

My impulse is always to reach for metaphors, and the comparisons that present themselves to me here are to stones or ice

ong many things, a sense of or participation in the fullness
an act or gesture so that the beauty of it is seen whole, the
ap and the landing. Ethically it means an understanding of
he wholeness of a situation, so that everyone is understood in
her humanity, the perceiver extending no more respect to herself than to others, understanding any moment as a thing that
can bless time to come or poison it. As an aesthetic, for the
novel, at least, both the first and second definitions are in play.
Theologically, grace must include the fact that we have untried
capacities to live richly in a universe of unfathomable interest,
and that we can and do, amazingly, enhance its interest with the
things we make. Isn't it true that we actually add things to the
universe, the great plenum? And this is true, I would say, by
the grace of God.

or sandbars in a river, all of which are in th.
very shapely. The lovely forms they take c
obstruction of the river water. At the same tin.
modation of the currents slows their own erosic
say they collaborate in persisting as themselves. The
more satisfying because both of these things are tr.
Elegance upon elegance. When I write I make it a rule
do anything—choose a name or a detail of any consequ.
for only one reason, or two reasons. Or three, ideally. T.
for me, an important scruple, on the principle that things
simultaneous and reciprocal in their nature, the river and t.
stone. When at any point this is not acknowledged, there is a
fraying of the fabric of the imagined world. This sounds very
intentional. It would be truer to say that on such grounds my
mind warns me away from ideas I might myself have considered pretty good.

Through the whole length of this essay I have been trying
to earn the occasion to say that our intuitions having to do
with the way things are and become are real enough to participate in the elegance of meaningful complexity, which may
be one definition of beauty, a necessary if not a sufficient one.
These intuitions include a compounding of time, so that we can
see how things tend, and how they might complete themselves
out of the constrained variables of the reality we posit for them.
I can see I am assuming that these things occurring in time
encounter a kind of contrary wind, what time itself might be if
it were symmetrical, or if it is, for that matter. The completion
of a character or a fiction, a play or a poem, must have the look
of teleology, a denouement that seems prepared and inevitable,
that seems to have approached, not simply to have eventuated,
to have arisen within the arbitrary limits imposed by every
good choice made in the course of its invention, not as a fore-
shadowing but as a reality still imminent. Entelechy.

I suspect I have not mentioned grace at all. To me it means,

A Proof, a Test, an Instruction

The Nation, *December 5, 2016*

Let us say, as a thought experiment, that History and Providence conspired to create a president suited to twenty-first-century America. He might unite in his own person the two races that are shorthand for difference and division within the society, and have deep personal bonds with both black and white. Race has only the meaning culture gives it—and we learn every day that culture is a heavy-handed enforcer of the distinctions it has made. An ideal president would be one suited to his circumstance, to dealing with the potent aftershocks of an unjust and violent history. If it were clear that he loved and honored, and identified with, both streams of his heritage, he would bring as much humanity to this grievous old affliction as any one person could bring to it.

Only imagine how the unacknowledged empire our country has become would be made more knowing and refined if this president had the memory of passing his childhood among the children of societies that seem remote to most of us, chasing a tattered kite down a muddy road, hearing the call to prayer, learning new forms of courtesy, seeing the effects of lawless government on the lives of good people. Again, if this president had family who were part of the emergence of Africa from centuries of colonialism, a continent at the threshold of the world's future, a complex and fragile phenomenon capable of igniting and also extinguishing extraordinary individual gifts, he would have a vantage point uniquely suited to his responsibilities toward this volatile planet. In both cases he would have ten thousand times the understanding that is supposed to be acquired in congressional junkets and sophomore years abroad.

This is a kind of understanding individual Americans are happy to claim on the slightest grounds. Oddly, at the same time the public seems to be flattered by the notion that a "real" America would be more provincial than it ever was, isolated from the effects of foreign influences as colonies in a mercantile empire, then as an immigrant country, never could be. Those who speak of the United States as great, formerly if not at present, must acknowledge that immigration has been concomitant with our greatest moments, wherever they wish to locate them. It is perverse, though clearly effective, to treat deep experience of other cultures as compromising. The candidate John Kerry spoke French—so much for him. So did Jefferson and Franklin and Adams, and they read it, too, as educated Americans did during that seminal period, to our benefit, no doubt.

The United States is a very great power. It created its modern posture against an adversary it took to be equivalent to itself, perhaps even more powerful. The opponent has fallen away, more or less, and America is left with an overhanging capability to do harm, which is an important definition of power. This capability may no longer be suitable for deterring threats to us, but it is real and undiminished. As we learned in the course of this instructive election season, there are those who think that since we have it, we might as well use it. Not against Russia, of course, that important region in the new nation of Oligarchia, but against ragtag radicals who torment regions that do not need the further catastrophes our power would visit on them. No war will end war, short of Armageddon. So we had better consider other options. A president for whom other societies are not abstractions, who knows that the children of our enemies are as silly and lovely as our own children, would be well suited to helping us live more consistently with our values, granting all the obstacles history has put in his or her path.

•

The success with which Barack Obama has been estranged in the minds of many Americans, made to seem foreign on precisely the grounds that made him singularly qualified for his office, reflects a refusal to accept what America is—not only a multiethnic and multiracial nation but a pervasive cultural and economic presence in the world, with responsibilities equal to our influence, a daunting thought. We are mighty and the world is, in every way, fragile. Tact and restraint, where possible, are indicated. But we—politicians, journalists, cultural figures—do little to encourage a temperament suited to our role.

The growing din of our politics, and of the media fantasists who create terrifying worlds of threat and deceit and who increasingly shout down our politics, is not likely to yield a mature consensus about our role and our obligations. It is true historically that Americans in meaningful numbers have mocked and bedeviled our great presidents. They, being great, have tended to do good things for good reasons, and therefore to be able to answer reasonable criticism. This fact has led their detractors to resort to scurrility potent in its time—Abraham Lincoln was mixed-race, Franklin Roosevelt was Jewish. And now Barack Obama is Muslim. The notion, given force by the insistence of those who propagate it, is that Islam itself is evil and full of insidious intent, as Judaism was said to be in the 1930s by those who wished to discredit Roosevelt. The object in every case is to instill the belief that a great deception has been carried out, the true character and motives of the president are sinister, his government is illegitimate and must be opposed. I do not share the exceptionalist or providentialist faith that malicious behavior, outright slander, is somehow vindicated by the fact that we have survived it so far. I don't accept the view that playing on prejudices is just another part of political give-and-take. I think history has indulged us, allowing us to get away with abusing the democratic system in ways it will not sustain forever. Would anyone object to what I have said here? Well, in fact, Barack Obama would object.

•

It is a remarkable thing to have some meaningful conversation with a president of the United States, in this case a man young enough to be my son. Barack Obama is gracious, poised, and intense in the face of concerns and demands I cannot imagine. There is a sentence in a benediction common in mainline churches like his and mine—"Return no one evil for evil, but in all things seek the good." It seems to me always that his remarkable dignity and resilience must have its source in a transvaluation of this kind. He is extraordinarily alert. His attention runs a little ahead of the moment, to the next question, to the courtesy or reassurance he thinks the moment might be about to demand of him. It must be clear to anyone who has read his books that he is eager to learn from any encounter that might yield insight into a kind of query he brings to experience, which is, I think, an openness to an extremely inductive understanding of value, one that he is always ready to expand and refine. Though he would not apply such words to himself, the president is a philosopher, perhaps a theologian.

In the land of the blind the one-eyed man might seem delusional. There are risks in having an interesting mind in this odd climate we have made for ourselves. There are risks also in being in fact faithful to the faith so many of us claim. The president is taken in some quarters to be non-Christian because he is disinclined to hate his enemies. This can only mean that an uninstructed and unreflective "Christianity" has indeed taken hold in the population. The wrath of man worketh not the righteousness of God, according to the Epistle of James. But we have lived for years with the raucous influence of self-declared Christians who are clearly convinced that their wrath and God's righteousness are one and the same. Then when the president, though he is insulted, balked, and provoked, refuses to yield to anger, his self-possession is apparently unreadable. A considerable part of the population must have ceased to recognize and respect piety, not to mention simple dignity.

President Obama would say that my thinking is far too harsh, distracted by the nonsense of the moment, and that the essential thing, the thing that always wins out finally, is the goodness and wisdom of the American people. Only confidence in the ultimate wisdom of the people makes democracy sustainable through crises. The dynamic of the system assumes dispute and contentiousness, but respect for this dynamic and for those who sustain it, however heated the argument, is vital to democracy. In the long term, on the whole, respect will prove to have been justified, and to have kept contention from flying out of control. I hope he is absolutely right, and that his capacious optimism can embrace my indignation, as, by his lights, a necessary energy, together with all the contending passions that drive the country forward.

•

President Obama is fascinated by the cohesion of communities and societies, by the numberless people who day after day do the numberless things that sustain the life of a city. He has seen what happens where cohesion fails, in America and elsewhere, and this no doubt makes him more aware than most of us are of its value, its beauty, its enormous fruitfulness. This awareness of the value of community also gives context to his equal and deep respect for all lives lived honorably and responsibly, and to his desire to help the marginalized enrich and enjoy the good life of community.

This is a consistent element in his thinking. He often quotes the phrase "a more perfect Union," which is first in the list of purposes for which, according to its preamble, the Constitution was ordained and established. The language assumes union, and acknowledges at the same time that this union is flawed and difficult. The comparative "more" implies that it will be improved rather than perfected by the new Constitution—realism on the part of the Founders, no doubt, who were already dealing with contending regions and interests. But that "more" also implies relative perfecting yet to be done, a continuous adjusting of law and custom to more nearly align them with the ideals expressed in the Declaration of Independence and the First Amendment. It is because there is the fact and the strength of union, whatever its failings, that these failings can be alleviated or overcome.

I was in college when Margaret Mead was in her glory and anthropologists could still claim to find societies untouched by the modern world. The idea was that in such places human nature would have been preserved in a purer form than in the rationalist and technological societies of the West. By observing these societies we could learn what we are essentially and how we ought to live. These societies were gentle, violent, uninhibited, and so on, depending, it came to seem, on the preferences of the anthropologist. People who have no historical memory in the Western sense and who are engrossed in their lives may not think to wonder what drove their ancestors to the depths of a forest and deprived them of the benefits of better resources and wider contact. In any case, the "primitivity" of these populations could in general be called poverty. Globally and historically, it would seem to be natural in human societies to create wealth, however badly they distribute it. So the isolation of such groups was probably more defensive than Edenic.

In retrospect this thinking seems akin to some of the less savory rages of decades just preceding it, having to do with purity and authenticity, the radical undermining of self and identity supposed to result from foreign influence and racial or ethnic mingling, the same kind of nostalgia that had mocked up Norse cults and Druidic rituals and that is stirring among us now. Cities in those days were called inhuman. These days they are called war zones. It all seems credible at any given time, perhaps in part because the ideal of the organic society, philosophically respectable since 1800, has predisposed us to accept it. In course of time it exhausted its field of research, since the researchers themselves were a corrupting Western contact. An anthropologist told me that he and his colleagues now do polling.

The question at the center of it all was and is how societies cohere, and what in them promotes human flourishing. The United States, by the theoretical lights of the old anthropology, was impossible. It was the great instance of a society that was not organic, not rooted in ancestral soil and ancestral blood but instead a quasi-nation fabricated from materialism and from certain discredited Enlightenment ideas. When I was in school it was a commonplace among foreign observers and certain American savants that we did not and could not have a national character or culture. We could not even know what it was we lacked, that being profundity, which, to the deracinated, is only a word. We were theoretically impossible, like so many of the planets that circle other suns. But there they are, and here we are, endlessly circling a few old texts and an idea or two, stable through continuous change while other countries falter. Our culture has inordinate reach and very substantial prestige. Our national character is as distinctive as any.

Nostalgia falsifies. It encourages the notion that we must once have had the authenticity and fellow feeling supposedly to be derived from a common stock. Colonial New England was as near as America has ever come to ethnic and religious homogeneity, and here is how the theologian Jonathan Edwards, in 1746, described religious culture among his contemporaries: "The daughter of Zion (the church) in this land now lies on the ground, in such piteous circumstances, as we now behold her; with her garments rent, her face disfigured, her nakedness exposed, her limbs broken, and weltering in the blood of her own wounds, and in no wise able to arise." Religious life went on, of course, in New England as elsewhere. Edwards says, "God's people in general have their minds unhinged and un-settled, in things of religion . . . and many are brought into doubts, whether there be anything at all in religion; and her-esy, and infidelity, and atheism greatly prevail." These would be the Nones. Our laws and customs allow for our being a contentious people, yet wherever disputes arise panic ensues. We really should take whatever comfort we can, and draw what-ever conclusions we must, from the fact that we are prone to alarm, a little inclined to frighten ourselves on slight pretexts.

Marx laments that the solidarity of the English working class was drained away by the California gold rush. In the early twentieth century the German language competed seriously with English to become the national language until the World Wars suppressed it. We speak of our history in ways that imply continuities where there were in fact continuous intrusions of external events, wars, famines, and persecutions abroad, as well as the effects of internal developments, for example, the cotton trade and the forced immigration of Africans as slaves, the recruitment of foreign labor to build the railroads or work in the steel mills and coal mines. All this is subsumed under American history, as it should be. But the word *American* encourages selective memory, and the Africans, Chinese, Polish, and Welsh are lost to the notion of a population always English-speaking, always western European. The Midwest is seen as homogeneous—German Catholics, German Lutherans, German Mennonites. The lions have lain down with the lambs.

The miracle of this country is that, by world standards, it is a union, stable and coherent, even as its heterogeneity increases in every generation. To call this a miracle is only to say it is a fact that at this point lacks explanation. The idea of the organic society, united by blood, faith, language, and culture, attractive as it may sound, actually tears societies apart, since some intolerable difference can always be found, some old wrong remembered. These have been the grounds for separatist movements in Britain and Europe, for conflicts in India and the Arab states. Those who invoke the idea of a "real America" would like to import a problem history has so far spared us. Take just the assertion that America is a Christian country. There is a history of appalling conflict among the churches and sects called Christian, which, by the grace of God, they left on the battlefields and scaffolds of Europe when they came here. The moment Christianity is established we will begin to notice that it is extremely various, and we will begin to think about who the real Christians are, a group more than liable to exclude me, of course, since my coreligionist the president is excluded already.

Those ideas that have so far held us together are very beautiful. That is their power. That they could have had the authority for us they have had is a thing worth noting, even while the crudest passages of our history make it clear that we can resist them fiercely and distort their meaning utterly, and that at best we are slow in understanding how very much they imply. Surely they offer more basis for a generalization about human nature than any number of cave paintings or kinship systems precisely because they are not local and they are not relics or survivals. They enlist the loyalty and fire the aspirations of a vast and various and continuously changing population through generations and centuries. Insofar as we feel the difference between what our country is and what these ideals proclaim—human equality realized in sacred and inalienable rights—they are always in advance of us. It is in this sense that the genius of our past is the promise of our future. It is in this sense that we can always speak of hope.

•

My respect for Barack Obama is vast and unshadowed. Given the information, advice, and reflection his decisions have proceeded from, I might have made other choices from time to time. But this by no means casts doubt on his wisdom or motives, any more than it endorses mine. A modern president is alone with endless decisions, many very grave. It is an accident of history that the weight of the world should fall on his or her shoulders, a consequence of our relative stability in a disorderly world and of the basic effectiveness of our political system, which have been indispensable to our "greatness," if one is inclined to use the word. To have been unfailingly dignified, gracious, competent, and humane under such pressures is a very moving achievement, an endurance that is more than heroic. That this president had no help from his opposition, that they did what they could do to shake and discredit him, to weaken him in this country and therefore in the world, and that he kept his poise through it all and met the demands of his office with deliberate, gentlemanly calm is a gift to our history, an example every one of us can learn from. It is true that he righted the economy, reformed health care, and protected our domestic tranquility as effectively as the availability of homicidal weapons will permit—all great achievements. He has had little help from certain of his friends, who think it is becoming in them to express disillusionment, to condemn drone warfare or the encroachments of national security, never proposing better options than these painful choices, which, by comparison with others on offer, clearly spare lives. The president has done nothing more important than to stand against, above, the vulgar, mean-spirited noise that disheartens the public and alienates good people from politics, which is the one true, essential, and indispensable life of democracy.

I have had a singular relationship with President Obama. I cannot imagine a greater honor than his having called me his friend, but if I call our relationship more than meaningful acquaintance I might suggest a degree of personal familiarity that I cannot claim. We have had conversations. His expressed interest in my work has had a marked effect on my career, very marked in Europe because he is held in such high regard there. The association of his name with mine abroad has let me see him as he is seen where the miasmas of polemic do not obscure him, as a gracious, good, and brilliant man. There he is a vindication of American democracy, while here every means has been tried to deny the public the consequences of having chosen him.

Having spoken with the president, having had some direct experience of his humor, his intelligence and courtesy, and his goodness, I consider it probable that those who have opposed him so intractably did so because they knew how remarkable a leader he could be. They were threatened with the possibility of a great president, one who could lead the country in a direction they did not favor and give prestige to a vision they did not share. At the incalculable cost to the country of exciting racial animosities in response to his historic election, they have damaged him as they could. So this other greatness, his accepting the discipline that comes with a reverence for the people and the country, has been thrown into prominence.

There is a beauty at the center of American culture which, when it is understood, is expressed in a characteristic eloquence. Every new articulation renews the present life of the country and enriches historic memory to the benefit of future generations. Barack Obama speaks this language, a rare gift. He is ours, in the deep sense that Lincoln is ours, a proof, a test, and an instruction. We see ourselves in him, and in him we embrace or reject what we are.

The Beautiful Changes

The Veritas Forum at Northwestern University:
April 15, 2015

One wading a Fall meadow finds on all sides
The Queen Anne's Lace lying like lilies
On water . . .
—Richard Wilbur, "The Beautiful Changes"

I have come to the conclusion that reality in its nature precludes nothing, that its operations might be taken to reflect God's freedom on the one hand and his courtesy on the other—freedom to act outside the notion of possibility we abstract from the lawfulness of the world he gives us to inhabit, and courtesy that makes the world in fact lawful, allowing us to be capable within the limits of given reality to build and plan, to see our intentions through to their effects, to pass through the strange, rich stages of mortal life. God's freedom is expressed in what is usually called miracle. But I think the world of human experience itself should be thought of as miraculous as well, root and branch, more miraculous in nothing than in the lawfulness that differentiates it so sharply from the seeming antinomianism of deeper reality. The dazzlements of the subatomic notwithstanding, nor the torrential expansion of space-time, the world of our experience feels knowable, stable, and predictable, and it usually is. In saying this I wish to establish first of all that divine freedom preexists and infinitely exceeds the reality we know, and that our reality is an act of divine restraint, a covenant made with earthly life that puts self-imposed limits on a power that would otherwise overwhelm us, would effectively annihilate us.

This little garden, earth, implies an act of creation which was radically, for us incomprehensibly, free. It implies an act and an intention that are expressed in the world of our experience designedly or arbitrarily—it would be given certain features and qualities, to the exclusion of an infinity of others that, if they had been chosen, would have had a part in it. Its given qualities are therefore no basis for reconstructing the creative act itself, however expressive they might be of the intent behind it. In other words, what seems to us possible and reasonable on the basis of our experience cannot be understood as conditioning or limiting reality *beyond* the structures of our experience. This fact is as true and important for a physicist as it ought to be for a theologian. The physicist would, of course, put aside any thought of intent, any teleology, but the theist need not, must not. And as much as I respect science and its methods, here the theologian can claim a great advantage, conceptually speaking. She need not struggle to breathe life into a purely materialist cosmos. She need not attempt a grand unifying theory out of the heterogeneous parts of known reality. She need not leave unaddressed the fact of the extraordinary role of human consciousness in the cosmos, of which physics is one great instance. On the other hand, she is free to absorb into her account of reality elements that are anomalous, not to be arrived at by positivist reasoning. So imperious is the materialist approach to reality that it considers whatever it cannot capture by its methods as effectively nonexistent, for example, the human self, the human mind. It marginalizes to the point of disappearance things we generally consider abstractions, for example, justice, wisdom, and beauty. The theologian may and must grant these even an especial reality.

Some part of a definition of beauty ought to be that it is an aspect of experience that can, and possibly should, compel attention and also reward it. To say this is to grant it an objective existence of some kind, a place in the economy of needs and rewards that bonds humankind to the world, that engrosses the mind in experience. Yet the idea of beauty varies from one perceiver to the next, one decade to the next, and from culture to culture. At the same time, it is so important in the shaping of human life that the sense of it may do more than any other influence to make a culture distinctive. The Parthenon, St. Basil's Cathedral, the Taj Mahal variously and authoritatively epitomize the aesthetics of a singular place and period. Sometimes with a little instruction we can recognize varieties of beauty we could never otherwise approximate or even imagine. If existence were designed to engraft us into the world, to charm and engage us, what could be better suited to accomplishing this than beauty, with its inexhaustible openness to variation, with its frangible and circumstantial rules and limits, which enable invention and tantalize perception? The theologian can say that beauty eludes definition because it expresses the grace of God, like other elusive things, say, time and light. It takes its nature from its purpose, its intended effect. Photons famously elude definition—I am not transgressing against reason when I say that essential aspects of reality confound our categories or that they are mutable in relation to their perceivers. I am simply allowing my account of reality some of the breadth appropriate to its subject.

Much thinking about human things has been captive for a very long time to the methods and biases of anthropology. And anthropology has been governed by the assumption of an original simplicity in all things human, complicated over time, at least among the majority of the species, until we arrive at modernity. A misunderstanding of non-Western languages was based on, and has encouraged, the idea of an original simplicity. It appeared to justify the notion that their speakers were themselves primitive. But no matter how serious the problems with this schema, no matter how much complexity is always discovered in supposed simplicity, this model has never really been replaced.

Both language and beauty have mutability and accommodation as qualities that are essential to them. Both shape and are shaped continuously as they are realized in our reflections, choices, and creations. Like the genome, both are uncannily well suited to exist, to flourish, in time. Futurity is implied in them in the fact of their constrained mutability. If the starting point for language was not an original simplicity, a business of threats and warnings, perhaps, how else is language to be accounted for? What magic or miracle could have intervened to yield the very great complexity that characterizes human utterance as we know it? This is a real question. The theologian might say that language is essential to human nature, and that it bears relation to the expressed intent manifest in all creation. In·the beginning was the Word. This is a statement of faith, granted. Still, it is fully consistent with the great potency of language. If our interest is in the given world, the world of experience, then unserviceable theories of origins ought to be put aside in favor of attention to the things themselves, leaving accounts of beginnings to the sacred unknowable—or to the empirically unknown and perhaps unknowable. Surely no theory should persist simply for want of a better one, when the theory clearly distorts its purported subject.

Beauty is equally inaccessible to positivist accounts. It has no consistent usefulness, is the product of no fixed colors or proportions, is not reliably associated with well-being. It is indeed in the eye of the beholder, an eye that can be helped by instruction and experience, is in any case much influenced by them, and may, by its decisions, refine and extend the consensus surrounding the beautiful, at least within the limits of a culture and period.

·

I may seem to be comparing unlike things. While forms and manifestations of language are very real and constantly present to us, beauty is ordinarily treated as an abstraction, this despite its unquestionable power in our experience. I do not say "a conception of beauty" because there is an urge or a tropism that lies behind all conceptions of beauty, wildly as they differ, and it is this that interests me.

I have come to doubt the usefulness of abstraction as a category, not only because of its suggestions of static unworldliness but also because it distracts attention from the active and vital properties of these entities that so variously weave our lives into them as they preserve and transform history, culture, speculation, and belief, as well as the interior narratives of all our individual lives. Justice, another great abstraction, is defined differently in every age and culture, and is felt as a reality billions of times a day as it is approximated or satisfied or offended, or as it is modified in light of circumstance. It has a very great practical power in any moment, though it too is subject to change, whether through increases in refinement or lapses into malice or revenge. A creation that was arbitrary in the way I suggest might include the fiat "let there be justice" or "let there be beauty," each having the properties I describe intrinsically, not as proceeding from circumstance, or as having somehow evolved from material conditions with which they have no kinship.

Science tells us that any number of universes are possible in theory, and that life is so adaptable it could occur in forms unimagined by us. So science and theology can agree on one great point: Our reality has properties that could have been radically unlike those we know and experience. If Being is a cascade of accident, each moment determining the particulars of the next and therefore excluding other possibilities, we are still left with the fact of the very remarkable substances and energies that are and have been so beautifully configured at every scale. Be that as it may. Theology on the other hand asserts intention rather than accident, and in doing so it captures an essential characteristic of reality, that is, its coherency and mutability, its temporal being as both—and simultaneously—self-identical and subject to and capable of varieties of change too numerous to reckon. The biblical creation narrative allows us to say that the world was made to have the qualities of life, that is, to exist in time, to change and be changed freely, within real but rarely absolute limits. Be fruitful and multiply and fill the earth. Nations and languages arose out of the growth and dispersing of population. Profound differences did not impinge upon essential identity, as science can tell us, though historically and at present the differences seem to matter most to us. There is a mighty paradox in identity. The infant and the old man are one self. The life-changing event can only modify a particular life, which came before it and will continue after it. Yet the change is real, even profound. And beauty, intrinsic and perceived, attends on every change, transforming itself, refining itself to engage the altered mind again. This renewed encounter with beauty is often experienced as a manifestation of grace. Beauty awaits our notice, while, as experience, it is eloquently modified by our histories and temperaments, speaking to us one by one, soul by soul.

Beauty is grandly present in the architecture of the cosmos, minutely present in the structure of the atom, and yet we humans can seem capable of utter indifference to it. But I have begun to feel that our ability to do wrong is the basis of our moral nature, that our bias toward error gives meaning and urgency to our seeking after truth, that our blindnesses make the beautiful, pervasive as it is, always an object of discovery, a thing to be yearned for. Just as the norms of our experience of existence are radically untypical of the universe of Being we can reasonably infer, with its entanglements and indeterminacies, its dark matter and antigravity, so we are singular among creatures precisely in our capacity to refine and elaborate our understanding in the awareness of its shortfall. It is this in us that has made tiny blue earth a singular, seraphic presence in the great cosmos, watching and pondering, rapt with wonder. We can feel deficiency in what we know or do, we can hear inadequacy in our most painfully considered phrases. And gracious and chimerical beauty will bless us with the certainty that there is more to be hoped for, more to be tried. The theologian can say all this implies divine intention and also continuous, loving engagement. Because God has created the universe, humankind is at the center of it all.

Our Public Conversation: How America Talks About Itself

The Page-Barbour Lectures at the University of Virginia:
February 22–26, 2016

Recently I read a brief overview of myself and my work, an article on the Internet. It said that if someone were bioengineered to personify unhipness, the result would be Marilynne Robinson. The writer listed the qualities that have earned me this distinction—I am in my seventies, I was born in Idaho, I live in Iowa, I teach in a public university, and I am a self-professed Calvinist. Ah, well. I will only grow older, I am happy in Iowa, my religion is my religion. That I was born in Idaho will be true forever. So I can put aside any slightest, unacknowledged thought of satisfying the standards of hipness. The review was cautiously positive despite all this, warning and alluring and also flattering its readers with the assurance that in me they will find thinking that is very unlike their own. Fair enough. The article did make me think, though, how inclined Americans are to find their way to some sheltering consensus that will tell them what to wear, what to eat, what to read, how to vote, what to think. There is nothing new in this observation of mine, though perhaps I am unusual in considering these aggregations in terms of the mass of things they leave unconsidered, neglected, and unknown.

Looking back I realize that I have spent a great part of my

adult life working to rescue wounded or discounted reputations. I've always known that there are risks. To say that Jonathan Edwards is not hip is to test the limits of understatement. As much might be said of Shakespeare's Henry VI plays, John Calvin, Puritanism. At this point in my life there can be no doubt about the tropisms of my mind and soul, even though for a long time I thought I was just tidying up a few misunderstandings for my own sake, before I went on to other work. I somehow thought I was devoting the time to people and things that lacked poetry, were utterly unpoetical—believing what was always told me, implicitly and explicitly. These stereotypes are hard to eradicate, however unwelcome they might be. Distinguished names associated with Puritanism in England include Edmund Spenser, Mary and Philip Sidney, Arthur Golding, Thomas Middleton, Fulke Greville, Andrew Marvell, John Milton, John Bunyan. In Britain, social and legal disabilities as well as outright persecution discouraged nonconformist loyalties, especially before and after the parliamentary revolution and the Commonwealth. So the style of thought, the worldview, associated with Puritanism naturalized itself to the environment of the dominant culture. But about these figures I have named there is no ambiguity. It is true that their writing does not satisfy the polemical sense of the word *Puritan*, which is so overwhelmingly its modern sense that the most careful efforts at historical precision in the use of the word are always compromised by its associations with priggishness, acquisitiveness, hypocrisy, narrow-mindedness, and fanaticism. Still, for years I accepted, or did not know how to reject, the bleak stereotype, when it is precisely the poetry of Puritanism, and more generally the use and celebration of the English language always associated with it, that has enlisted my devoted attention.

I am fascinated by history, and I don't know what it is. I believe that, whatever it is, it is profoundly important, and I don't know why. I am especially fascinated by erasures and omissions, which seem to me to be strongly present in their apparent absence, like black holes, pulling the fabric of collective narrative out of shape. Europeans often say our culture is Puritan—Lollard, according to Freud—and we don't know enough history to understand what they might mean by this. We have made a project of freeing ourselves of even minimal standards of taste or discretion, and still the word clings. Ethical rigor, aversion to display, the ideal of vocation are all diminished things among us, and still we are Puritan. Most recently I heard us denounced in these terms at a dinner table in London. How horrifying our rules against sexual harassment! It is the most natural thing in the world for students to fall in love with their professors, subordinates with their superiors! And so on. My suggestion that this might all seem very different from the perspective of the student or the subordinate, and my thoughts about fairness, merit, and so on, were not of interest. They were merely one more Puritanical pretext for denying the pleasures of life. I think in many cases *Puritanical* may simply mean "reformist," tending to assume that even very settled cultural patterns and practices can be called into question, that they are not presumptively endorsed by culture, that what is traditional cannot claim therefore to be rooted in human nature. We tend to forget that our revolution was one in a series— Geneva expelled its Savoyard rulers and was governed by elected councils. The Dutch expelled the Hapsburg emperor and in the process trained sympathetic British volunteers who took the experience home with them. Then with the Puritan Revolution England tried and executed its king and attempted a decade of parliamentary government. More than a century later the American colonies rejected monarchy as a system on the basis of the abuses of the king then in power. This is not logical, strictly speaking, but it affiliated the Americans with the great precedent of the English revolution, the revolution of Milton and Marvell. The most revolutionary idea contained in all this is that society as a whole can be and should be reformed. This Puritan energy does indeed continue to animate American life.

•

Sometimes on the strength of a reformist movement history is recovered—there are innumerable instances of this in the last half century, in this country often as a consequence of the civil rights movement. In Europe, perhaps as a secondary consequence of this movement, Britain, the Netherlands, and other countries have begun to acknowledge the enormous extent of their roles in the Atlantic slave trade. It says a great deal about human consciousness, collective and individual, that a phenomenon of such scale, duration, and consequence could be obscured so thoroughly. One of the many advantages of my long life is that I remember how things were before that old oblivion began to break up a little. The past really is a foreign country, even the near past, the one you have lived through. You have to have been there to have anything like a true sense of it. This does not make the past understandable, any more than living now makes the present understandable, but it does allow you to call to mind the cohesion of its elements, from which the whole strange mind-set derived its authority, as dreams and eras and cultures do, always including our own. We continue to learn how important slavery and racism have been to the construction of Western civilization, literally as well as figuratively. Without question we have vastly more to learn. Through all this it is important to remember that history that is grossly incomplete can feel coherent, sufficient, and true. The reality of history, whatever it is, is perhaps best demonstrated by the power it has when the tale it tells is false.

Coherence means something like "stickiness, adhesion." An assumption, if it is firmly held, and especially if it is unconscious, will attract information that preserves or renews its stability, testing its credibility as information by its stickiness, rejecting anything that will not be assimilated to it—unless, and then only in certain cases, some external shock or some shift of consensus causes it to decohere, to lose the logic of its structure. If you are deep in a dream and someone knocks at the door, that giant, elusive spider you are now trying to kill with a hammer will vanish at the next knock, and the coherency that made the creature real and threatening will disintegrate. And in half a minute that logic will be wholly irrecoverable. Any model of reality tends to perpetuate itself if it can, on a principle of coherence peculiar to itself, and this is true of the narratives of history. It is somehow also true of history itself— true, that is, of whatever has actually happened, the unacknowledged history that haunts us, and perhaps also invests our societies with their distinctiveness, like that Puritanism of ours. I have read that the interaction of dark matter with itself is based not on gravity but on friction. I have no idea what this might mean, except that, dark matter being by far the preponderant form of matter in the universe, good old gravity could be only one relatively minor structuring principle of it all. In their absence from our awareness essential things are not missed, though still they are present and essential.

I have been reading things Shakespeare and his audience might have read in order to understand both of them better. Literacy was high then, driven by tracts and pamphlets that were addressed precisely to those who, in other generations, would have had very limited access to printed or written material and little or no ability to read it. There were widely circulated newspapers that covered the wars on the Continent. There were chronicle histories, which implicitly addressed the great questions of royal succession and legitimacy. Most popular of all these during Shakespeare's lifetime was a great tome, larger in each of its editions—*The Actes and Monuments of the Martyrs*, by John Foxe. The book is famous for its illustrations depicting

martyrdoms, and for the care and the remarkable sophistication of its printing. But I had never seen it. I went to the Folger
Library in Washington, D.C., and asked to look at it, assuming
that an eminent Shakespeare library would have copies of a
book he and his audience would have been very likely to have
had some acquaintance with. In fact they had, they told me,
only one copy that was in good enough condition to be looked
at, and that one only because a scholar using the library had
arranged to have it bound at his own expense. Foxe's book of
martyrs was a central text of English and American Puritanism. It is a polemic, certainly, a prerevolutionary work. But it is
also an extraordinary work of historical documentation in
English, Latin, and, where needed, Greek. The chronicle histories bear no comparison to it. Its importance as an extraordinary
specimen of Renaissance publishing should be sufficient by itself to protect it from being left to molder away from neglect in
an archive devoted to Renaissance culture. I feel I am probably
fair in taking the marginalizing of Foxe's book to be an effect of
its association with Puritanism, a sort of editing of history, which
I must assume is important in very many contexts but which I
notice in this one instance because of my particular interests.
That said, Shakespeare is hardly an interest I can claim to
have to myself. There is a Toryism in Elizabethan studies that
yields a model of culture that must exclude, for example, this
important book, because its very importance throws many
things into question about Shakespeare and the public he addressed. A comparable and related phenomenon is the history
of the Bible of Shakespeare, Milton, and Marvell—that is, the
Geneva Bible, which was out of print from 1644 to 2007.
There is a great deal of reverence accorded the King James or
Authorized Version on the theory that it was the watershed for
all that wonderful language, and this despite the fact that it was
published in 1611, when Shakespeare's career was at an end.
The Geneva Bible was the Bible of the Puritans. It is the King

James Version, just not yet shorn of the marginal commentary that instructed its readers in the Reformed understanding of the text, and not yet purged of language that might seem politically dangerous. What did Scripture look like to the generations who saw it in a form not "authorized," that telling word? How many thousands of scholars have *not* wondered how Shakespeare's work could have been influenced by a book published in 1611? Very many American scholars are royalists of the imagination, wistful onlookers, too in love with their Elizabethan world picture even to acknowledge how badly it accords with the actual brilliance and spirit, and repressiveness and violence, of the age.

•

I have arrived at the conclusion that American history is substantially false, though not exceptionally so, and that many of these falsifications go back to a source that is older than the country, earlier than the colonies. I dwell on American history because it is mine, and because it is the screen on which the national psyche is projected. I would like to think America might go on for a very long time, always recognizable in its best qualities, however it may transform itself otherwise. I assume most Americans would agree that the essence of the project did find classic expression in 1776 and 1789. It seems to me that for the survival of our experiment to be even imaginable the country must know itself much better.

A thousand problems arise immediately, of course. I was talking to people in a library in Iowa City about the abolitionist movement and the Civil War. A woman came up to me afterward in a state of scarcely controlled irritation and asked me why any of this should interest her, when no one in her family was even here at the time of the Civil War. She had a point. The true history of the United States is rewritten day by day. Yet the fact is that we were a string of British colonies for almost as long as we have been an independent country. And during that long time the trade and industrial policies of British and other European governments established slave labor in the Americas. So far as we can know, nothing of greater consequence ever happened on this continent, except for colonization itself. The Civil War is only the most spectacular instance of its impact on our civilization, which is ongoing, as we all know. It is true and always to be remembered that the great influx of Africans was a gift to the culture that has given it a brilliance and rich distinctiveness the whole world enjoys. That they came as captives and lived as slaves is an inexpressible grief and transgression.

In other words, it is not ethnocentricity that makes early America of such interest to me. On the contrary, ethnocentricity is what makes our history avert its gaze from our Anglo-European origins. We prefer to speak as if our society had neither source, context, nor analog, insofar as its doings are or have been in any way regrettable. We were somehow spontaneously generated, like toads from the mud of the Nile, and were instantly up to our special version of no good. To want to keep discredit to itself, to insist on the utter uniqueness of its sins and errors, might seem generous or rigorous in a country, but it is neither of these because it has nothing to do with the truth. In Adam's Fall we sinned all, the English in Ireland, Australia, the Caribbean and here, the Belgians in Congo, the Spanish in Argentina, the Russians in Ukraine. The list is infinitely far from complete, as we all know. Its beginnings are undiscoverable. Phenomena of the kind it names are infinitely far from being ended. If we could let ourselves have anything like a real sense of history, we would not be so continuously surprised and bewildered by its latest permutations.

It seems conventional among historians to say that the American Revolution wasn't about much, that the liberalizations brought on by the evolution of the British parliamentary system would have yielded the same freedoms without all the uproar. This view of things is deeply uninformed, because we avert our gaze. And it has the effect of making the generations who began and sustained the Revolution of little historic interest. In the South were the plantation owners, with all the problems this involves. In the North were the Northerners, generally described as Puritans or Calvinists, with all the problems this involves. We have left ourselves nowhere to place our sympathies. Our solution is to project on England and Britain an imagined aloofness from our sins and errors despite the fact that problems that perplex and disgrace us descend from our long colonial period and its aftermath, during which time Britain emerged as a great industrial power on the back of all that uncompensated toil in American cotton fields.

What does it matter? Everything always matters. Years ago, during the thaw in relations between the United States and Russia, I went to an exhibition of the Romanov jewels. Off to the side, out of the way, there was a display of photos and newspaper articles about the Russian intervention in the Civil War on the side of the Union. Tsar Nicholas II sent his fleets to the harbors of New York and San Francisco, where they remained through much of the war. He did this to prevent intervention on the side of the South by England and France, which along with Russia were the great powers of the time. The British had begun a gradual emancipation in the West Indies in 1837. But they came very near attempting to enforce a "peace," that is, a permanent division of this country that would have left American slavery intact and ensured the flow of American cotton to those nightmarish factories in Manchester and Lyon. There was much gratitude and celebration here over the arrival of these formidable Russians, to whom we might in fact be said to owe our national existence. How did we manage to forget this? The 1860s are a much-studied period in our history, needless to say, and by world standards not a very distant one.

Might this intervention not have been a good thing to remember, during all those years when Russia was made to seem so intractably alien to us? But the tale does not reflect well on England or France. It does not cohere with our image of northern Europe as our always better self. I propose this as an instance of that tendency of fact, of truth to be excluded when it is not assimilable to some settled and preferred vision of things, a vision it would complicate. Truth would be a leaven in the lump, so to speak, giving the whole narrative an element of truth in the form of complexity.

Complexity is powerfully stripped away by half-informed or uninformed aversion. Why should people so often feel what amounts to contempt for figures, even entire populations, about whom they know nothing and will learn nothing on the grounds of this same aversion? The word *Orwellian* has been worked nearly to death because it is so very useful. Consensus really ought not to trump reason or preclude it, though it does, routinely. And reason always tells us that human beings and their societies and histories are mingled—that is, never only to be condemned, sometimes ingratiating or admirable. Decent mutual respect depends on an awareness of this fact, that is, on good history.

A conscious strategy currently favored for excluding complication, usually on the pretext of acknowledging complexity, is cynicism. The tsar had his own motives. True enough. People do. No doubt he had a number of them. This really does not neutralize the fact that the British and French had their motives, too. By the blunt measure of their potential impact on human lives, these were, at best, far inferior. We have brought home from our wars, cold and hot, this habit of impervious antagonism, antagonism as loyalty, which dovetails neatly with our version of cynicism, better called intellectual lassitude. We have allowed ourselves to become bitterly factionalized, and truth has lost its power to resolve or to persuade.

There is a mystery in the fact that by means of these truth-excluding encapsulations, besides making our society foolish and vulnerable, and in some ways ineducable, we do preserve, very effectively, negative beliefs about ourselves. My earliest memories take up after World War II, when movie theaters still ran ads about the need to relieve hunger and poverty in war-torn Europe. The camera dwelt on a little boy in short pants and bare legs alone in a dark, narrow street. I remember a German immigrant neighbor, an older woman who scolded my mother as if from a moral height for the inadequacies of her knitting, for her buying soap when she ought to have been making it. Her houseplants, she said, were a disgrace. My mother was impressed, even deferential, though not to the point of making soap. The neighbor was a product of her moment, a priestess in the cult of *Heimat*, but we would not have known. There were a number of freshly arrived Europeans then. I remember an old man who practically lived at the mayor's office, and who scolded whomever was polite and could spare a minute with the fact that democracy was wasted on Americans. More generally, I was educated to the belief that this country was an awkward attempt at a civilization, a crude imitation of something profound and elegant and intrinsically elsewhere. Objectively speaking, this is remarkable, considering what was then the very recent history of Europe. Be that as it may, the admiration for things European, whether in any instance it was justified or not, came paired with the implication that nothing so excellent or so profound would be possible here. I've read a good deal of Fascist literature over the years, and I know it was believed and taught and spun into philosophy and philology all over the Continent that mingled and rootless people who spoke an adopted language could never even know how utterly they fell short—of profundity, of authenticity, both important terms of the time. By these lights such people were a corruption, a threat to the organic integrity of any true culture. A splinter in the flesh, Hitler said. In our deference to European thought we applied this thinking to our hapless selves and kind, never reflecting on the uses that had been made of it in Europe or the biases it legitimized here.

I have never admired deference. I was dosed with Sartre and Artaud, as any college girl then would have been. I felt their nausea. It made an Americanist of me.

But for those whose tolerances were different from mine, figures like these defined the future. It was not a very interesting or habitable future, but in the short term it opened the way to study abroad. Juniors returned knowing better how to hold a fork or a cigarette. They had heightened social confidence—they had checked an important box. None of this ends with adolescence. Or this adolescence never ends. It seems to be true now that there is no Europe of the kind to potentially unleash new literary trends or to make us line up around the block for a new French or Italian movie. Without any particular object of emulation to measure our deficiencies by, the sense of deficiency is at least as strong as ever.

It is absurd that the products of a civilization as old and solid as this one should forever be such colonials, feeling sophisticated in the fact that they have and confess such deeply internalized prejudices against themselves. A few years ago I was seated near an American couple at one of those dinners they have at Oxford before a lecture. The Americans were doing something I see very often. They were saying that in the States there were no such events as these, that intellectualism was held in contempt there, and so on. They were earnest and insistent, even a little bit loud. I said, That might be an overstatement. They reacted, again predictably, as if the fact were plain and must be faced. When they were told that I was the lecturer, they were irritated. Not only had they been interrupted mid-kowtow. They had come out for an evening of stimulation among their betters and they had found me instead. Why

do so many otherwise presentable people think they can in-
gratiate themselves with foreigners by talking this way? I take
ingratiation to be part of the motive behind it, or the hope. A
small thing in the great scheme, granted. But it enacts as
much as it expresses that internalized prejudice. Put aside the
notion of country and imagine 320 million souls who happen
to be passing their mortal time on this continent. Why should
we discourage them from major aspiration? Say 15 percent are
black, 51 percent are women. Is it at all consistent with their
aspirations to be told that whatever their gifts, an ultimate mediocrity awaits them? I don't know how damaging this really
is. I certainly felt the weight of it when I was young. I see
students who seem to think they are excused from the kind of
effort they might make by the belief that there is no audience
in this country for serious literary work, for ideas. Some first-
rate writing is being done here now, and finding a readership.
Still, I hear again and again that Americans hate books and ideas,
that demanding novels don't find publishers. This gloom,
which is mutual condescension, is unshakably in love with its
certitudes.

Then there is the matter of our press, our public discourse,
which looks more and more like self-parody. The purport of all
the jeering and slurring and scaring seems to be that democracy is indeed wasted on Americans.

Well, democracy is my aesthetics and my ethics and more
or less my religion. I am very grateful that my life has passed in
a society where the influence of a democratic ideal is sometimes great, sometimes decisive. A thing I have long regretted,
though, is that I have been significantly distracted from this
privilege, and from the experience of my life and the lives
around me, by generalizations about us all that are meager and
belittling at best. When I was still vulnerable to those unan-
chored comparisons that are always made of us and that we
seem always to welcome as truth, I thought we as a culture

might *be* especially materialistic, especially intolerant, especially violence-prone, especially indifferent to the finer things. Now as I watch this supposed populism that invites some part of the public to identify with all these things as indeed American, as the voice that *really* is great within us, a sort of utterly corrupted Whitmanism, I fall to wondering how the grand experiment has been brought to such a pass. And this brings me back to history.

·

I am always writing about that broad area that lies between expert opinion and public assumption. It is broad in the sense that it reflects the state of knowledge in far the greater number of people, not at all in the sense that the difference between expert views and public assumptions is typically great.

The film *Amistad* is based on an important event in American history and is intended as a serious treatment of it. In 1840 a Spanish ship carrying African captives in the Caribbean was seized by the captives. The navigators, who were spared so that they could take them back to Africa, misled them and sailed north. They were found off the coast of the United States, arrested, and brought to New Haven, which was an important abolitionist center. This came to the attention of Lewis Tappan, who organized a very distinguished legal defense to clear them of charges, including murder, and to free them. The case went all the way to the Supreme Court. When they won, Tappan arranged for them to return home to Africa.

In the film nineteenth-century New Haven looks like a set for the Salem witch trials. There are randomly assorted details to suggest a pervasive religiosity—a troop of nuns pass through the street, a close-up shows crosses on chains dangling from Bibles. Simpering, black-clad women poke crosses at the Africans through the slats in a picket fence. Puritans, as these people are clearly meant to be and would have been, more or less, did not dress in black and did not use crosses, which they regarded as icons. The Africans, watching black-clad people kneeling in the street outside their jail window in some clumsy and unspecific show of sympathy and evangelism, remark, with subtitles, that they look unhappy. This moment hardly seems necessary, since the cliché is so commonplace that even George H. W. Bush was aware of it. When they fell to thinking about it, a great many New Englanders were indeed unhappy about slavery, and about the Fugitive Slave Law, which was germane to this case and which was meant to implicate Northerners in the enforcement of slavery. This is the kind of unhappiness that should be associated with intelligent humanity, not with gloomy fanaticism. But they were Puritans, and therefore, as cliché would have it, cankered souls who simply hated life. I will not pause over the fact that this region at this time was producing a body of literature of great beauty and depth, which is generally considered a sign of cultural health.

So, given the conventions that shape the film, what is to be done with the figure of Lewis Tappan, a great early emancipationist who devoted himself and his fortune to the cause? Among many other things he was one of the founders of Oberlin College, an institution of singular importance in advancing abolition and in asserting the equality of all races and both genders. In New York City, Tappan's business was burned, his house was ransacked with him in it. He went right on, rather jovially and very constructively, supporting abolition.

In the film he remarks to his black colleague that it would be better for the cause if the Africans were to die. There it is, the stereotypical fanaticism, the inevitable underlying pathology that contaminates what would otherwise be generosity and idealism. There is no truth in this, of course, but it satisfies the expectations of convention and also of cynicism. Movies love the underdog, here a rumpled young lawyer invented to fill this role. But a movie with any claim to historical significance would find the underdog in Tappan and the figures he recruited to the freeing of the Africans. That they were men of standing in their society did not make them powerful against a hostile president or the slave interests in Congress, as the length of this struggle and the larger struggle for emancipation makes clear. The controversy surrounding the *Amistad* and the determination of the case are very important, so why not give a true account of them? Reality is interesting.

Well, for one thing, to do so would disrupt some deeply entrenched notions. Lewis Tappan, that Puritan, used moral and religious language to make his case against slavery. This may mean he was, as they say, holier than thou. I freely concede that he was holier than me, if we are to be judged by our works. Better, or easier, to reinforce those stereotypes, available as they are, undisputed as they are. Popular culture has its own systems of self-perpetuation.

One last thing. There is an idealized Englishman, in the movie a naval officer who destroys a slave castle he has discovered on the coast of Sierra Leone, a place whose existence until then might supposedly have been only rumored. Since Sierra Leone was the center of the British slave trade from the sixteenth century, when it was sanctioned by Queen Elizabeth, to the early nineteenth century, this is clearly implausible. But the movie gives us someone to admire—not a taciturn, stoical New Englander but a taciturn, stoical Briton. We are very accustomed to the idea that qualities that are handsome on one side of the Atlantic are unhealthy, soulless, reprehensible on the other. Puritanical, in fact. The convention is that Puritan culture was stunted intellectually, emotionally, and morally by the religious tradition that also founded Harvard and, of course, Yale, to name only local examples of their remarkable institution-building and their devotion to learning.

•

Lately I have been reading, and reading about, another Puritan, Oliver Cromwell. In his case the expert view is typically quite different from his popular reputation, to the extent that he can be said to have a popular reputation. So far as he does have a place in the general public's mind he looms as a giant monolith on the darkest terrain of unhipness, towering over even Edwards and Calvin on that Ultima Thule where the sanctifying words *comme il faut* are never spoken. Scholarly opinion reflects an awareness of Cromwell's importance to early modern history, and a fascination with his essential opacity despite his relatively long and well-documented public career.

Cromwell, at age forty, having had no experience to prepare him, joined the army of Parliament in its war with Charles I. Over time it became apparent that he had a genius for warfare, especially for the use of cavalry. He rose through the ranks on the basis of great personal courage and an unbroken history of success in combat, attracting and retaining an army that came to be regarded as the preeminent military power in Europe. Through all this he remained dutifully subordinate to his commander, Lord Fairfax, and after the death of Fairfax, to Parliament. Over time his New Model Army became an interest and a political force in its own right. Finally Cromwell emerged, in a country profoundly disrupted by years of civil war, as head of state. For about ten years England experimented with forms of Republican or Commonwealth government. After Cromwell died, his son and successor proved unable to govern, and the monarchy was restored.

All this is of interest because it might be called the beginning of American history. Those abolitionists in New Haven were the cultural and, in many cases, literal descendants of the supporters of Cromwell, who came here in search of religious freedom—as we often say, without elaboration. The English Civil Wars tend to be known, if they are known at all, for the trial and execution of the reigning king, Charles I. Granting

that the trial can hardly be said to have made the legally difficult case that the king was, or could be, guilty of treason as the
law then stood, and granting that decapitation is an ugly fate,
neither of these was crude or cruel by the appalling standards
of the time. Nor, for that matter, by comparison with the French
Revolution, which came more than a century later, and which,
though it was closely modeled on the English example, utterly
exceeded it in vindictiveness and bloodshed. In any case,
among the king's judges, called regicides, three were sheltered
in New Haven and one was buried there. Others who did not
escape England suffered the "superfluous death," too ghastly to
describe, which was the usual fate of condemned traitors and
which the king had been spared. Connecticut was a natural
refuge for those fleeing the suppression of the Commonwealth
side after the Restoration. A colony had been founded there in
1635, before the outbreak of war in England. According to the
eleventh edition of the *Encyclopaedia Britannica*, Saybrook "was
planned as a settlement to which for a time it was thought Lord
Saye and Sele, Lord Brooke . . . Oliver Cromwell and other
independents would immigrate." Independents are more commonly called Puritans. So the seeds of radicalism and revolution were planted on our soil almost a century and a half before
independence.

Then again, American history may have had an earlier beginning yet. There was a period of reform and unrest during
the brief reign of the boy king Edward VI, who ascended the
throne at the age of nine and died when he was fifteen. As the
successor to his father, Henry VIII, he came to the throne in a
time of turbulence. The Church of England had rather newly
been severed from Rome. With the radical exception of the
king's having put himself in the place of the pope, Henry VIII
intended a minimum of change in theology and practice when
he broke with the Catholic Church. But the Reformation was
at its height on the Continent, and Edward VI, who passed

seamlessly from tutelage to precocity and who was fluent in many languages and a devoted student of Scripture and theology, attempted to model his church and society on European examples. This meant a great destruction of art, prayer books, and ritual objects. It meant also a great relaxation of censorship laws with a consequent explosion of publishing, much of it of religious literature, though early vernacular works such as *Piers Plowman* also enjoyed great popularity. It meant that the laws dating back to Richard II that punished heresy with death were repealed, and, with two exceptions, the burning of people as heretics ended while Edward lived. This was a radical departure from the practice of his father. While the stripping of the churches is often treated as harsh and philistine, the disuse of the stake and gallows is never discussed in aesthetic terms, though surely it should be. Edward repealed as well most laws concerning treason. He was succeeded by his half sister Mary, who reversed these reforms.

This child king, beloved as he seems to have been by the people, was given no tomb. According to the historian Diarmaid MacCulloch, his grave is marked only with "a simple modern slab." My 1911 *Britannica* has little to say about him, none of it kind. Rumors that he was alive persisted for years after his death, and it is good they were false, the article says, "for Edward showed signs of all the Tudor obstinacy, and he was a fanatic into the bargain, as no other Tudor was except Mary." Attacks on the child began early. In the words of a contemporary, "If ye knew the towardness of that young prince, your hearts would melt to hear him named, and your stomach abhor the malice of them that would him ill. The beautifulest creature that liveth under the sun: the wittiest, the most amiable, and the gentlest thing of all the world." Edward was ten when this was written, and there were already "them that would him ill." The convention of blaming the king's advisers for grievances would certainly be plausible here, since his

collaborator in these reforms, and surely in part his instigator
as well, was his uncle and Lord Protector, Edward Seymour,
1st Duke of Somerset. According to the *Encyclopaedia Britannica*,
Somerset's ideas "were in striking contrast with those of most
Tudor statesmen, and he used his authority to divest the government of that apparatus of absolutism that Thomas Cromwell
had perfected. He had generous popular sympathies and was
by nature averse to coercion." Somerset's downfall, which
led to his execution, is generally considered to have resulted in
part from his conciliatory response to Kett's rebellion, an armed
popular rising protesting the impoverishment that came with
the privatization—that is, the enclosure by landlords—of the
common lands that were historically a resource of the poor.
Kept apart from all this, apparently, is the issue of religious reform, which is laid to the child king's precocious and intense
piety, his fanaticism—though it was marked by that reluctance,
entirely untypical of the times and his forbears and his successor, to burn heretics. In *The Winter's Tale*, Paulina says, "It is
an heretic that makes the fire, / Not she which burns in't."
The same critique could be applied to the word *fanatic*. Surely
it is bizarre to harbor historical animosities toward a doomed
child.

The problem seems to be that, as head of the church,
Edward was a Puritan before the word. MacCulloch is careful
to insist that he and his circle were not Calvinists, offering no
grounds for this assertion. Calvin in fact corresponded with
Edward and Somerset. In one letter he responds to a request for
his advice on completing the reform of English church and
society. He dedicated both editions of his *Commentary on Isaiah*
to Edward, and sent him a brief commentary on a psalm he
thought might interest him. Many particulars of the Edwar-
dian church are consistent with Calvinism. For example, Edward
ended the requirement of clerical celibacy and introduced
English into the Eucharist. And, tellingly, Thomas Norton, a

poet and politician who made the first English translation of Calvin's *Institutes of the Christian Religion*, was a member of Somerset's household, his secretary, and the son-in-law of Edward's councillor and archbishop, Thomas Cranmer, who also corresponded with Calvin. About Norton my doughty old *Britannica* has this to say: "Norton's Calvinism grew with years, and towards the end of his career he became a rabid fanatic." After three hundred fifty years the embers were still hot.

I am suggesting that a polemic with its origins in American prehistory has more or less expunged, has at least alienated, an important part of our colonial and national history, the part that is appropriately called Puritan. This could not have happened if we had not collaborated in it decisively, of course. Why would we have done this? And why am I perfectly confident that we will persist in it? It can't be the whole problem that when people feel they know who to blame or to snicker at, they seldom feel the need to know more.

The alienation of New England from our sympathies has, oddly enough, at the same time made it more or less the epitome of our origins, an enclave of the provincial and fanatical in a world that was, by implication, reasonable and relatively humane. How many witches had been burned in Britain and Europe before a Puritan set foot on American soil? How many had been burned before the word *Puritan* was coined? Were there never witch trials in the colonial South? Did only Puritans devote themselves to rigorous piety? It is bizarre that they are isolated by association with attitudes and practices that were, if anything, less characteristic of them than of British and European culture as a whole. The implication that they were exceptional in these things implies that we can simply assume contemporaneous cultures—the American South, for example—may be understood with unspecific reference to a standard of reasonableness that is never to be assumed anywhere. And this erases history that would give context and meaning to a great deal that has been thought and done here, some of it, the Puritan impulse toward reform, their passion for education, and their genius for institution-building, a heritage of great value.

A true genealogy of American Puritanism leads back through the English Revolution, through the brief reign of a tombless and disparaged child, and back farther yet to the masters of the old vernacular style, the Lollards and Wycliffites who discovered the beauty of the language of common life, and of common life itself, and were the originators of the great dream rehearsed in that language through so many generations. In this light we can understand John Winthrop, and Lewis Tappan as well.

•

The period between the fall and death of Charles I and the restoration of the monarchy in the person of Charles II, the so-called Interregnum when England was governed by Parliament and Cromwell, took place at a time when colonies were established in America, firmly enough to have some sense of themselves as societies and recently enough to feel very intimately involved in English affairs. They were governed under charters granted by the Crown that forbade the establishment of laws inconsistent with what was then, before the parliamentary revolution, British law. During the civil wars that engrossed the mother country, and during the Protectorate of the Puritan Cromwell, the colonies could only have had an interregnum of their own. England had more urgent demands on its attention, for one thing, and for another, Massachusetts and Connecticut would have been as unanimous in their support of the Puritan side, perhaps, as Cromwell's army itself. Early American history is not my field, but I have read enough, unsystematically, to attach some significance to the fact that I have seen scant mention of the effects of either the wars or the Protectorate in New

England, immediately important as they were to the American settlement. The severing of British and American history at this point is completely artificial. Men left New England to fight on the side of Parliament and Cromwell. Cromwell's own chaplain was formerly a minister in Massachusetts.

Puritanism was a political as well as a religious movement— indeed, the two were simultaneous. The colonists were moved by beliefs about religion and society that were closely related to those held by Cromwell and his army, and by the dissidents in Parliament. There is every reason to note differences of opinion among Cromwell, army, and Parliament, and there is no reason to assume unanimity among any group of colonists. But the English factions hung together well enough to sustain and win two major wars against the royal army and the Scots. It is clearly important to acknowledge a high degree of consensus among them, as well as their strong association with New England colonization. As I have said, Cromwell was personally involved in the founding of Saybrook, Connecticut.

When that good Englishman John Winthrop spoke in 1630 about the city on a hill, he was appealing to his hearers as people creating a model society whose success or failure would be known to the world. Describing elsewhere the decision to admonish a tradesman for taking an excessive profit on his goods, Winthrop says it was decided that the first of the "false principles" that had misled the tradesman was "That a man might sell as dear as he can, and buy as cheap as he can." This admonition was necessary since the man was, says Winthrop, "a member of a church and commonwealth now in their infancy, and under the curious observation of all churches and civil states in the world." Such minuteness of attention is only imaginable given the actual frequency of travel to and from New England and the continuous communication of England with the colonies. It is interesting to consider by what standards the great world was assumed to be judging this new commonwealth—clearly it is not one that we bother with now, or regard as having any tendency to diminish the brightness of that same city on a hill.

In any case, New England, so far from being the isolated refuge of an austere religious minority, was a laboratory for a kind of social order being tried in parts of Europe and soon to be tried in England itself. Winthrop's speech aboard the *Arabella* anticipates the Interregnum by more than a decade. It is only its inexplicable isolation from British and European history that allows it to be read as a very early celebration of an American nation. It is in fact a utopian vision of a society whose relations are based on charity, using the word in the biblical sense, meaning love. The religious critique of existing social order from the Puritan side was that it was unbiblical, un-Christian, in the fact of its being based on status, wealth, and power, all of which preclude the thoroughgoing mutual liberality Winthrop calls for, using just this word. He was the governor of the colony, and might have been expected to mention the usual texts about how authority is to be honored as an instance of God's providence. Instead, he sees the bonds of society in mutual care and service. This particular vision has a long and deep history in English culture, going back to *Piers Plowman* and forward to William Blake. It was the vision of the Quakers and the Levelers. Shakespeare pondered it as the regime of his forests and wild places. This is not to say that anarchy in any sense of the word lies behind Winthrop's vision, only that the essential, primary order for his commonwealth would be a matter of maintaining these bonds of mutual affection. Strictures against profiteering should be thought of in this light, then and now, at least insofar as the health and cohesion of society are valued.

Colonies actually governed by British law as it stood before the Civil Wars were necessarily limited in their options. That

they were frustrated in their attempts to legislate for themselves is among the grievances listed in the Declaration of Independence. But in the seventeenth century, while the monarchy
was in crisis, then dissolved, they began to create laws of their
own. In practice these codes did not survive the Restoration,
but insofar as they are discoverable they are evidence of the
social theories of the colonists. Given their kinship with the English dissidents, it seems reasonable to suppose that they are
also an indication of the thought that lay behind what would
be called the Commonwealth, that is, the revolutionary government of Parliament and Cromwell.

I have come across references to a code drawn up by the
colony of New Haven. I happened to learn about the Massachusetts Body of Liberties of 1641 many years ago from a
mention in a letter to the editor in *The New York Times*. I can't
really be sure to what extent the gap in history I sense here is
really an artifact of my own lack of thoroughness in looking
into the field. But my decades of browsing predispose me to
thinking that a subject I have never seen raised or alluded to
has probably dropped out of American history. This period,
from the point of view of the general public, is a complete
blank, except for the few caricatures sketched into it of witches
and somber men with buckles on their hats. How much for-
mulating and publishing of laws happened in New England in
the Cromwell period I don't know. After the Restoration, del-
egates from New England went to London to reestablish their
charters. I am glad to have happened upon the Body of Liberties, which is a very interesting document, brief and clear,
anticipating the American Bill of Rights in defining liberty in
largely negative terms. For example, item 46 says: *"For bodily
punishments we allow among us none that are inhumane, barbarous or
cruel."* Anyone who has any acquaintance with contemporary
English or European history knows what a radical departure

this is. Cromwell as Lord Protector tried to reform what he called the "wicked and abominable" sentences of the criminal law, but failed to gain the approval of Parliament.

The Massachusetts Body of Liberties lists twelve capital crimes: idolatry, witchcraft, blasphemy, premeditated murder, murder in rage, murder by guile (they seem to have wanted to arrive at the number twelve), bestiality, sodomy, adultery, kidnapping, false witness against the accused in a capital case, and insurrection or subversion. All of these but the last have warrant of Scripture, which is cited. If this code seems severe by our lights, a bitter consequence of Puritan religious zeal, in fact it very much limits the list of capital crimes, and in particular it excludes from the death penalty what were overwhelmingly the crimes of the poor. Under English law theft and also idleness or vagrancy were punished by hanging. Early American law is always said to be based on English common law, without elaboration. Then either the use of the gibbet in such cases did not accord with common law but was prevalent all the same, or American practice and theory departed in important ways from this precedent.

I looked up common law in my *Britannica*. The article is brief, one column devoted to this important subject. Common law is, the article says, "probably best defined with reference to the various things to which it is opposed." These things are statute law, equity, civil law, canon or international law, and "local or customary law, as the general law for the whole realm." Quoting further: "Blackstone divides the civil law of England into *lex script* or statute law, and *lex non script* or common law." The latter, he says, "consists of (1) general customs prevailing in certain districts, which are the common law strictly so called, (2) particular customs prevailing in certain districts, and (3) laws used in particular courts." Inevitably the article concludes that common law "is the foundation of law in the United States." How anything so amorphous and indefinable could be the basis of anything is a question worth looking into. It is not even the basis of English law, surely, because it can be contravened by these other systems. "Occasionally," says the *Britannica*, the term *common law* "would appear to be used in a sense which would exclude the law developed by at all events the more modern decisions of the courts." The notion of common law, which suggests a kind of common decency brought to bear on disputes and transgressions that required public resolution, is hard to discover in practice. I am persuaded at this point that the notion that our legal system is based on it is simply a cliché. There is a kind of English "law" that serves much better as progenitor, the biblical/utopian codes proposed by dissident groups like the Lollards and the Kentish rebels in Kett's rebellion. It is this nucleus that is to be the basis of the new society whose character and viability will be of such interest to the world.

Into the twentieth century there was a body of law called Poor Law, which very narrowly governed the lives of the mass of the British people. Mention of it is omitted in this *Britannica* article, though a full six pages are devoted to it elsewhere. They deal in grueling detail with pauperism and workhouses, a system still very much up and running in 1910, still taking its ethos explicitly from a statute of Elizabeth I. There is no difficulty whatever in finding evidence of its reality and importance. If it is relevant to the development of American law, it is inversely relevant, in that our laws do not include an Ordinance of Labourers, a special legal system meant to govern the working poor. It is over against its strictures on movement and association that the First Amendment of the Constitution should be understood. That said, Poor Law does appear to be the basis for laws that protected the institution of slavery in America.

The idea of a *lex terrae*, a "law of the land" that constrained the king and limited other law, was important in the time of Edward VI, when George Ferrers, a member of his court, first

translated the Magna Carta into English. What this famous document ever meant in practice, whether in Latin or in English, is
an open question. Poor Law, which was national in scope and
as nearly uniform as it could be made, seems, however, to have
produced a sort of holocaust of the redundant, carried out by
legal means over generations. The common folk, who were, in
law, "the poor" if they lived by their labor, would be unlikely
to have endorsed this, they being potentially so vulnerable to
it, so helpless in the face of it. As Sir Thomas More pointed
out, Moses has no capital punishment for crimes involving
property, to which the English poor were often driven. In the
Body of Liberties, the laws of Massachusetts were brought into
line with Old Testament law and became relatively modern and
enlightened in their biblicism. In this at least, thank God, we
have followed Moses. I can't imagine that he any more than
the Puritans would find our recent zeal for endless incarcera-
tion admirable, though it is marginally less abusive of the poor.

New England Puritans are very often said to have aspired
to theocracy, even to think they had achieved it. In the first
place, it is difficult to imagine a more theocratic arrangement
than one that assumed the divine right of the king. Charles I
was persuaded that he had no one to answer to but God alone.
Then again, if the pope were granted final authority over every
regime in Christendom, this could certainly be described as
theocratic as well. Two "liberties" in the Massachusetts code
shed light on the question. First, "Civill Authoritie hath power
and libertie to deale with any Church member in a way of Civill
Justice, notwithstanding any Church relation, office or interest." In other words, membership or standing in the church
should not at all exempt anyone from the ordinary functioning
of the law, as clergy have been exempted traditionally. Second,
"No church censure shall degrade or depose any man from any
Civill dignitie, office or Authoritie he shall have in the Commonwealth." The decisions of a church will not interfere with

the workings of civil government or with the standing of anyone as a member of civil society. By the standards of the time
this is an extremely clean separation of church and state, depriving the church of powers to coerce that were still very
important elsewhere. These are not the laws of a theocracy, as
should be clear by comparison with virtually any other society
contemporary with it.

In any case, the tendency of historians to treat Puritans as if
they were interested in religion in only the narrowest sense—
altar or table, Communion in one kind or in two—overlooks
other scruples, also religious. For example, the Body of Liberties not only forbids horrible punishments, which often involved dismemberment, but also specifies that the body of the
executed should be buried within twelve hours. Under Elizabeth severed heads and limbs were hung on walls and in trees
in various places and left there, to widen the impact of royal
justice, presumably. The heads of Cromwell and two men close
to him were displayed for decades on pikes over the Palace of
Westminster. Cromwell died a natural death and so was exhumed and executed posthumously. Only a strong wind finally
brought his head down from the pike. It might seem a minor
courtesy that the head of Charles I had been surgically re-
attached to his body and that he had been allowed to remain
in his grave. Still.

A great deal is made of the repressiveness of the Puritan reformation of morals under Cromwell, his attempt to suppress
swearing and drunkenness. It is true that he had led a terrify-
ingly efficient army over the length and breadth of England,
and into Scotland and Ireland. Certainly he had blood on his
hands. But if the Puritan departure from the penal horrors enshrined in law were thought of as a part of the reformation of
morals—to me this seems appropriate, since they would spare
society as a whole much terror and degradation—the ban
on swearing would be comparatively minor, even pardonable.

Again, it should be noted emphatically that under Cromwell no one was executed for his religious beliefs. In his letters Cromwell advocates consistently for freedom of conscience. These would have been important enhancements of the quality of life. It should be noted that the Massachusetts code does not list heresy among capital crimes—or mention it at all, for that matter. We know the colonists did expel people from their settlements on these grounds. Total reformation never comes at one stroke. Still, on balance, what is often called Puritan intolerance might as fairly be seen as Puritan tolerance. Winthrop says this about the expulsion of Anne Hutchinson: "So the Court proceeded and banished her; but, because it was winter, they committed her to a private house, where she was well provided, and her own friends and the elders permitted to go to her, but none else."

•

So American culture sprang from English dissenters. What has this meant? The Carolinas were colonized after the fall of Cromwell and the Restoration, and named for Charles II, then king. The Fundamental Constitutions of Carolina was drawn up, commissioned by the king and written, it is said, by John Locke. No doubt the tendency of colonies to legislate for themselves was to be forestalled by this constitution, which would have established an authoritarian class system based on landownership. It created carefully delineated ranks and degrees and provided invented names for them. Somehow the colonial governor, William Sayle, who was a Puritan, never found the right time to put this constitution into effect. It would have created a kind of idealized England from the monarchical point of view, where landholding and authority were fixed and simultaneous. It would have precluded long-standing issues.

From the early Middle Ages the dream of the English poor was secure access to land, which they claimed as a right based in tradition. This access was threatened and progressively ended by enclosures, the seizing and hedging in, the appropriation for private use, of land that by custom had been available for the use of the community. Enormous flocks of sheep displaced villages, their inhabitants turned out to wander the roads and in the worst cases to starve or to be hanged for vagrancy. This endless, irresistible disaster was written about in the early sixteenth century by More and is the context for his *Utopia*. The First Fisherman in Shakespeare's late play *Pericles* speaks of "rich misers" like whales who "never leave gaping till they've swallowed the whole parish, church, steeple, bells, and all." Oliver Goldsmith, writing in the eighteenth century, describes a ruined village where "one only master grasps the whole domain," and a landscape where once "scattered hamlets rose," but now "unwieldy wealth and cumbrous pomp repose." Enclosure was a revolution from above that created abject dependency in the huge class of the poor by seizing commons and excluding the community from the use of this traditional resource. The visionary literature of England idealized the echoing green, the world as it was before this systematic creation of poverty and destruction of the poor—a world modest, joyful, familial, and as if unfallen. This vision remained powerful even as the society urbanized and the loss of the commons became more a symbol of profound discontent than a present grievance for those who involved themselves in protests and uprisings.

Englishmen in the New World found a harsh life, one that did not lend itself readily to the Arcadian aspects of this vision. But Puritan New England did have a particular ethos of community of the kind Winthrop urges and celebrates in his *Arabella* address, which is as indebted to English social history as to Scripture, insofar as the two can be distinguished. Its early exponents were Lollards, after all, in fact or by association.

The Earl of Somerset, Lord Protector of Edward VI, was one of a number of wealthy and powerful men who would take the side of those who resisted enclosure. Cromwell seems to have been another. His history before the age of forty is very little documented, but during that time he was a modestly substantial landowner, educated in Cambridge, who served in Parliament. His aristocratic connections by blood and marriage, though not direct, were not insignificant, either. It was in this earlier period that he was called "Lord of the Fens." This was an irony. It seems Cromwell tried to prevent the drainage, therefore the making suitable to conventional farming and enclosure, of land that had sustained a population of the very poor. Before Cromwell, the Protector Somerset had attempted to intervene on behalf of a rising against enclosures called Kett's rebellion, an attempt that began his fall from power. John Kett himself was a landowner who sympathized with, then led, and finally died in this insurrection. In other words, neither Somerset nor Cromwell was involved in class war as that phrase is normally understood. There were then two contending visions active, both of them believed by their adherents to be based on Scripture, one claiming a basis in antiquity, the other a basis in an ideal primitivity—when Adam delved and Eve span, when Christianity was still pure of accretions. This latter was Puritanism, the tradition of Cromwell's rearing and education, the tradition he helped to establish in Connecticut.

The emergence of Cromwell and the relative effectiveness of his government until his death would be difficult to account for if it were the novelty and departure history often suggests. But, first, it was a Calvinist revolution of a kind for which there were earlier precedents in Switzerland and the Low Countries. Second, its ethos and policies had precedents in the reign of Edward VI. While Catholic Mary ruled, many leading Protestants went as refugees to Geneva, including some who had been figures close to Edward. There they produced the Geneva Bible with its Reformist notes, the Bible of Shakespeare and of the American colonists, and there they felt very directly the influence of Calvin, whose contempt for monarchy in general seems to have eluded scholarly attention. Many Englishmen went to the Low Countries to fight on the Protestant side, including Sir Philip Sidney, who famously and graciously died there. In other words, there were important models of stable Protestant regimes that had overthrown their traditional rulers, and English people of great influence had the opportunity to study them at length and at close range. The severing of English from European history in this period is as unaccountable as its severing from American colonial history.

And, of course, the neglect of English history by those who write English history is equally arbitrary. Later writers give the reign of Edward VI short shrift. But during the Renaissance and Reformation Foxe's *Actes and Monuments* was the most popular history among contemporaries. Foxe says this:

> These meke and gentle times of king Edward, have thys one commendation proper unto them for that among the whole nomber of the popyshe sort, of whom some prively did steale out of the realme, many were crafty desemblers, some were open and manifest adversaries, yet of all that multitude, there was not one man that lost hys lyfe. In summe, during the whole time of the vi yeres of this king, much tranquility, and as it were a breathing time, was graunted to the whole churcuhe of England: So that the rage of persecution, seasing, & the sword taken out of the adversaries hande, there was now no danger to the godly . . . Briefly during al this time, neither in Smithfield, nor any other quarter of thiss realme, any was hard to suffer for anye matter of religion, either Papist or protestant, eyther for one opinion or other . . .

Since Foxe was a Protestant, as most of his readers were also, presumably, his celebration of an interval in which neither

Protestants nor Catholics were violently persecuted, as both
had been at various times under Henry VIII, suggests a devel-
oping consensus in favor of this degree of toleration, at least.
Jeanne d'Albret, who became the queen of Navarre shortly
after Edward's death, executed no one on religious grounds
during her seventeen-year reign. She was an ally of Calvin's
and corresponded with him as Edward and Somerset had done.
So in this regard Cromwell might be thought of as part of an
emerging movement, and also as engaged in the restoration of
welcome reforms that Mary had swept away.

There was an intellectual underground in England, a long
tradition of radical thought that went back to John Wycliffe
and William Langland and emerged in the speeches of the common soldiers in Cromwell's army when they held their remarkable debates about the nature of the society that should emerge
from the ruins of the old order. This tradition would have
given the moment the tentative familiarity of an expectation
fulfilled. Cromwell would certainly have been influenced by
it, through long familiarity with the "godly men," the "plain
russet-coated fellows" who made up the solid core of his army.
The English historian Christopher Hill argues that Milton was
influenced by the thinkers of this underground. It is entirely
probable that he was, not only because of its importance to
the revolution but also because it was a deeply rooted literary
tradition.

Early in her reign Queen Mary declared "an inhibition by
proclamation" meant to deter dangers to her realm "through
diversity of opinions in questions of religion." It forbade un-
authorized preaching and interpreting of Scripture, and also
"playing of interludes, and printing of false-found books, ballads,
rhymes, and other lewd treatises in the English tongue, concerning
doctrine, in matters now in question and controversy, touching
the high points and mysteries of Christian religion; which
books, ballads, rhymes, and treatises, are chiefly by the printers

and stationers set out to sale to her Grace's subjects, of an evil zeal, for lucre and covetousness of vile gain." This is quoted by Foxe, to whom these strictures would clearly apply, as they would also to John Day, the printer and publisher of many dissenting works, including the *Actes and Monuments*. Foxe had remarkable access to documents far older and rarer than this one would have been, and his reports of them are highly consistent with their use by later and modern historians. So either his faithfulness to them is confirmed by others or he is simply considered reliable, despite his being an apologist and polemicist for the faction whose zeal the queen would like to inhibit.

The kind of censorship called for by Mary was not unusual, though it was intermittent. Clearly nothing of comparable severity had been imposed by Cromwell, though we know from Milton's *Areopagitica* that Parliament did begin to require a licensing of books. Roger L'Estrange, proposing a regime of censorship to be imposed by the newly restored Charles II, after the fall of the Commonwealth, called for a reduction by two-thirds of the number of active printers; raids to seize prohibited books, whether new, republished, or concealed; rewards for informants who knew of the existence of forbidden books; and punishments for those informed upon, anyone involved in their making or distribution, including stitchers and carters. The "ordinary penalties" are proposed: "Death, Mutilation, Imprisonment, Banishment, Corporal Peyns, Disgrace, Pecuniary Mulcts." He says, "For the Authors, nothing can be too Severe, that stands with Humanity and Conscience. First, 'tis the way to cut off the Fountain of our Troubles. 2dly. There are not many of them in an Age, and so the less work to do." He quotes treasonous views that are in print, for example, this: "Princes Derive their Power and Prerogative from the People, and have their Investitures merely for the People's Benefit." And this: "Kings are Accountable to the People, I do not mean to the Diffused humours and fancyes of particular men in their single and natural Capacities; but to the People in their Politique Constitution, lawfully Assembled by their Representative." Certainly there are better grounds for finding the basis of our laws in this suppressed and defeated Commonwealth movement, which contributed so largely to our early population, than to an elusive "common law."

•

In his introduction to the first volume of *The Writings and Speeches of Oliver Cromwell*, published in 1937, the Harvard historian W. C. Abbott says, "If Calvin's *Institutes* provided a logical system of theology to set against that of Rome and his government of Geneva became a model state, his doctrines and practices combined to inspire an almost fanatical (that word again) devotion among his followers. It is one of the greatest mysteries of the human spirit that a faith founded on the assumption that man's fate depends not on his own free will and acts but was predestined from the beginning, should have moved its devotees not to supine inaction but to deeds of heroism and self-sacrifice as vain as they were exalted unless they were 'of peculiar grace elect among the rest.'" It is always fair to wonder if anyone, even a scholar as generally scrupulous as Abbott, has actually read the *Institutes*, and if he has, how he would define the words *logical* and *system*, very commonly invoked, or how, they being granted, they limn out a "mystery" that seems to him to make no sense at all. But this observation is nearly inevitable wherever any reference to Calvin and his influence is made. Perhaps by 1937 it was already mere reflex. It does not respond usefully to the fact, which he notes, that Calvin's influence is strongly, even uniquely, associated with potent activism. Here I will mention Lewis Tappan again, who was in fact fairly representative of his culture and his times. I could mention John Brown.

Some light is shed on Abbott's mystery by the life of

Cromwell himself. A man who, without training or experience, discovered at the age of forty that he had a genius for the use of cavalry in battle, and beyond that for warfare, including the organization and control of a highly effective army, might really wonder how these things befell him. He might think in terms of fate even if he were not theologically predisposed to. People in at all comparable circumstances often do. There are surprises in life that refuse to be understood in the simple terms of act and consequence. It seems reasonable to assume they come most frequently to those who throw themselves into the arms of fate, or Providence, rather than to those who proceed by calculation. Human estimates of the possible tend to be conservative. And our estimates of the effects of our actions and intentions are very far from reliable. It seems odd to me to think an act of heroism is "vain" if it does not count toward one's own everlasting benefit. Any reader of classical literature would know that heroism occurs among people who never think in terms like eternal salvation, and who really are fatalists. Again, however, this is just the little storm of perplexity that is always stirred up by the mention of Calvin, a figure of great importance in early modern history as his mention here should remind us, who ought to be looked at seriously on these grounds alone.

In any case, Abbott does quote, from the dedicatory letter that prefaces the *Institutes*, a passage that both justifies revolution and describes the form it should take. " 'Let us not think,' wrote Calvin, 'there is given no other commandment but to obey and suffer . . . I affirm that if they wink at kings willfully raging over and treading down the poor community, their dissembling is not without wicked breach of faith, because they dreadfully betray the people's liberty.' " It is odd in this context that Abbott does not say who "they" are who are to defend the people's liberty. "They" are parliaments, magistrates of the people. Cromwell took part in a war already begun between king and Parliament, was obedient to Parliament in his role as military commander, and attempted for years to establish what might be called parliamentary government, ironically at last dismissing Parliament and ruling alone, just as Charles I had done. In Geneva there were governing councils in place long before the Savoyards were driven out and before Calvin's arrival. They continued to govern. This kind of continuity must have seemed possible for some time in England as well. The worthies who signed the American Declaration of Independence and negotiated the Articles of Confederation and the Constitution were acting as representatives of the people and were generally accepted as such. After its revolution, France attempted parliamentary government and ended up with the emperor Napoleon. Though this model has not been consistently successful, its successes have been sufficient to make it important to the emergence of the modern West. In this context, the Cromwell period is again no anomaly, and the Calvinist basis of its activism is not far to seek. The idea that there is liberty that inheres in the people and that kings have no right to abuse is consistent with interpretations of the Magna Carta that emerged under Edward VI and Somerset. It is important to remember that both the Magna Carta and Calvin's *Institutes* were translated under their patronage. The second of these might well have influenced the reading of the first, since in the charter there is no comparably explicit assertion of what might be called the unalienable rights of the "poor community" over against the king. The claims of the Magna Carta are entirely of, by, and for the barons, whose appeal to custom had no positive implications for the people custom allowed them to despoil.

•

What is lost in the fact that our early history is distorted by suppressions and omissions? I was surprised by the importance of women in the literary culture of the Renaissance—specifically Calvinist women, who patronized and protected writers and who themselves wrote poetry and drama and made translations. Lucy Hutchinson, the wife of a regicide, wrote an epic based on Genesis and made the first complete translation into English of Lucretius's *On the Nature of Things*. Anne Vaughan Lok wrote the first sonnet cycle in English. Mary Sidney wrote tragedies as well as the greater part of the verse translation of Psalms begun by her brother, Philip. I have come across the names of many more than I have had time to look into. The rise of English as a literary language would have been an encouragement to women, who were not often educated in the use of Latin. In any case, this period was clearly a stimulus to literary expression as well as to theological and other learning in women.

•

When I write about the character and importance of Puritanism, it is not with the intention of suggesting that we could or should return to it. It was as much a long historical moment as it was a distinct tradition. Its struggles with orthodoxy, and the marked tendency of its own institutions to decry elements of orthodoxy, were a consequence of the fact that orthodoxy was inconsistent with its own tenets. It was meant to be reformed and continuously reforming. The hardest definitions it made of itself were an effect of its defenses against the pressures of an environment in which "nonconformity," as it was called, was subject to exclusion from civic life. The acts of uniformity imposed by Elizabeth and others, which were meant to enforce by fines weekly attendance at an Anglican church, together with exclusion from university, public office, property ownership, and so on, were the kind of thing that harden the perimeters of any minority. These strategies of self-defense tend to become identifying features of the group, from the point of view of members as well as outsiders, no matter how arbitrary they are in their origins. Protestant men from certain regions of Europe, especially clergy, still wear beards beneath their chins because the soldiers who once harassed them wore mustaches. To doff their hats or not, to stand or kneel or not, were choices that were meaningful in highly particular settings, and signs of their participation in particular controversies. Once in America, without the context that made them meaningful, these customs began to seem anomalous over time, and provincial. In the early nineteenth century Harvard became Unitarian while Yale adhered to its ancestral Congregationalism. Amherst and Andover were founded to shore up the old religion, which changed under their influence in ways that would seem unexpected, given the assumptions we would be likely to bring to the idea of a restored Puritanism. These two schools, with Yale, became the front line of the abolitionist movement. They helped found and staff other new colleges in the disputed territories of the Midwest, which in turn became outposts of abolitionism. Higher education—liberal education—became a very important medium for the advancement of radical social reforms. The movement that scattered these colleges over the landscape, a very distinctive feature of American civilization, has had immeasurable consequences, including its contributions to the ultimate elimination of slavery.

Since my interest here is in putting both American Puritanism and certain writers in context, I will consider for a moment the family of Emily Dickinson, citizens of Amherst. Dickinson's grandfather was among those who felt passionately that the loss of Harvard to Unitarianism had to be compensated by the creation of a new school to train Congregational clergy. He poured so many of his resources into the project that he went bankrupt and had to go west to recoup his losses. Where did he go? To Lane Theological Seminary in Cincinnati, Ohio, where he seems to have looked after the school's finances and invested in land. Lyman Beecher was the president of Lane, and Calvin Stowe taught there—the father and the husband, respectively, of Harriet Beecher Stowe, who lived in Cincinnati from the age of twenty-one to the age of thirty-five. Lane was at the time the largest Protestant seminary in the country, and the Beechers, and increasingly the students as well, were involved with abolition and the Underground Railroad. This provided the material for Stowe's famous novel. Old Dickinson came home and the college was opened. Amherst provided a low-cost education to aspiring clergy and opened its classes to auditors as well—townspeople and younger students like Dickinson herself. Congregational clergy were trained in the liberal arts before they began their theological training, so Amherst was a rich resource for its community. Dickinson briefly attended nearby Mount Holyoke College, a school meant to provide a low-cost education to young women from the poor hill towns around Amherst. The school was founded on what was called the manual labor system. Everyone at the school, student or faculty, contributed work to the running of the school. The president, Mary Lyon, baked the bread. This system was characteristic of colleges founded by the antislavery movement, for example, Knox College and Oberlin. It was meant to keep higher education affordable, to erase social inequality, and to create a more "useful" educated class. It was directed against slavery in that it encouraged the individualism of self-sufficiency as opposed to the habits of exploitation of others associated with slavery and social inequality.

Mount Holyoke was one of a number of colleges or seminaries established in New England during this period. Women's higher education was part of a movement toward gender equality associated more broadly with antislavery. We tend to think of these female seminaries as sequestering, perhaps, but they in fact provided young women with a privilege unique in the world at the time, a rigorous education comparable to the education enjoyed by young men, and on terms that were intended to make them accessible, to remove financial barriers. All these schools have evolved into institutions of a very different kind, with a very different impact on society, and the genius of their early years and first intentions is by now a lost memory. They are worth considering not only because they help to interpret the vast development of the educational culture so characteristic of this country but also, for my purposes, because they are the self-interpretation of the last population who identified, without irony or affectation, as Puritan. They were the most radical social reformers this country has ever seen, in part because they had an extraordinary opportunity to put the impress of their values on a civilization very much in a formative stage, in part because they felt, and they were right to feel, that the civilization was tending away from them. The Unitarianism of Harvard was seen even then as more sophisticated, if not more learned, than the old religion. I will observe, in earnest hopes of being corrected, that Harvard figures very little in this epic tale. I know of no college founded from Harvard in this period. Troops of young Yale Divinity School graduates went out into the wilderness to spread enlightenment in a true sense of the word among these new towns and populations. They left a heritage that, if it were known, might even give goodness a good name. The whole movement had a kind of heroic generosity in its design and intention that is rare in history, and it persisted through decades, planting colleges throughout the Midwest, and in Colorado, California, and Hawaii. Josiah Lovejoy, a famous antislavery martyr in Illinois, was a Princeton man. I await information that will correct me—it appears from my reading that sophisticated Harvard did not exactly throw itself into this great work.

So Emily Dickinson, in going to Mount Holyoke, was stepping into the stream of a reformist movement. We all know that she soon stepped out of it again. Why she chose to go home to her family we will never know. There is a tendency to present her as captive to a rigid society, but the female seminary actually offered intellectual liberation not available to women

My point is that everywhere Dickinson looked there was radicalism of some kind, reform of some kind. Her reactions to it all, so far as I can tell, are undiscoverable. Clearly, however, the cliché of her being an intellectual captive in a frozen world is simply wrong. Perhaps her brother's long and open affair with Mabel Loomis Todd and the stoicism with which it seems to have been accepted is another light on the radicalism of the time and place. The ideal of Puritan reform was not essentially nostalgic but was instead primitivist. It reexamined the most fundamental institutions, including social hierarchy—including, emphatically, marriage. It gave no presumptive positive significance to the fact that social relations of any kind were long-standing or seemingly universal, and this included gender relations. This is true at the same time that marriage as covenant was, according to Calvin, the bond most favored by God. This vision of it is an aspect of the rejection by him and other Reformers of priestly celibacy and of celibacy in general as a more sacred condition than marriage. The idealization of marriage changed the understanding of it in ways that might not have been foreseen. The first modern divorce was granted in Calvin's Geneva.

In any case, I have omitted one great factor in all this, which is the Second Great Awakening. A few preachers, Charles Grandison Finney notable among them, set off a lengthy and, again, radical religious revival that swept the Northeast, especially upstate New York, the motherland of American religions. Finney was a lawyer and church musician who underwent a profound religious experience, trained as a minister, and became a revivalist, which at that time was a highly respectable calling, aspired to by learned men, a credential that qualified one for a college presidency, for example. The conversion experiences that drove this awakening and their consequences are best described by William James in *The Varieties of Religious Experience*. He was writing after the heat of the moment had

in any other society of the period. Whatever her reas[on]
did well, giving the world a body of work it would b[e]
poorer without. In going home, it must be noted, she [did not]
seclude herself from the distinctive radicalism of her tir[me and]
community. She could hardly have done so, becau[se the]
Dickinsons were very much involved in it, at least by as[socia-]
tion. Her brother, Austin, was a close friend of Frederick[Law]
Olmsted, the great landscape designer and abolitionist. [They]
wandered around the local woods together finding native [veg-]
etation suitable for planting on the Amherst green and the [cam-]
pus of the agricultural school that would become the Unive[rsity]
of Massachusetts. And Dickinson wrote to Thomas Wentw[orth]
Higginson asking for his response to her poetry. Higginso[n, I]
hasten to note, was a graduate of Harvard Divinity School. [He]
was not only a great abolitionist, the commander of a bl[ack]
regiment in the Civil War, a friend and supporter of John Brow[n,]
but also a strong proponent of women's rights and worke[rs']
rights before and after the war. Clearly she knew to whom s[he]
was writing. Higginson is himself a wonderful essayist, bo[th]
brilliant and ingratiating. He traveled to Amherst to meet th[e]
poet who had written to him, and then wrote a singularly fin[e]
evocation of her. After Dickinson's death her sister brought th[e]
trove of her poetry to him, and he edited and published it[.]
This story is very often told in a way that makes a villain o[f]
Higginson. He is supposed to have made the wounding assess-
ment of her work that discouraged her from publishing more
than a scant few poems. Clearly, however, Higginson was a
gifted man, strongly predisposed to reading a woman poet
with great interest and respect. His report of his encounter with
her certainly reflects this. If he tried to nudge her toward slight
changes that would make her strange and difficult poetry a little
more accessible to the general reader, this is surely a forgivable
error in an editor responding to the work of someone so complex and elusive.

passed, more or less, but describing to his Scottish audience the demonstrable, transformative effects of these highly individual raptures that Americans were inclined to pass through. The conversion, as in Finney's case, was not a change of religious belief but an intensification of it. This was hoped for and encouraged as a sign of one's acceptance by God. It was the experience of all but two of the students at Mount Holyoke while Dickinson was there, one of the two being, of course, Dickinson. It is all rather hard to imagine now. But James's point, and a thing well worth noting, is that these most intense excitements, passing through whole populations, had consequences that were overwhelmingly benign. These excitements were too much for some to endure—hospitals in affected regions were prepared to treat what they called "religious hysteria." But there was no ramping up of old hostilities, no one was burned or hanged. Certain offshoots were trivial or absurd, of course. But a great part of these energies went into antislavery activity. Finney himself became a professor, then the president of the new Oberlin College, accepting the appointment on the condition that all races and both genders would be admitted on equal terms. The philanthropist behind the creation of Oberlin was no other than Lewis Tappan. He created it as a place where abolitionist students, expelled from Lane Theological Seminary for their radicalism, could complete their education and express their radicalism without inhibition, which they did.

So when these self-professed Puritans, who had effectively lost any place in England and knew they were losing ground in America, set out to renew their tradition, the effort was marked by intense piety, the founding of many schools intended to promote reform, and utopianism striking enough to earn a mention in Engels's essay on the viability of Communist societies for both Brook Farm and Florence, Massachusetts. There is a tendency among historians to treat the efflorescence of Puritanism as a departure from it, or a rejection of it, a pure consequence of the polemically negative characterization of Puritanism. In fact all those schools, the reforms in the status of women, the conscious inculcation of a work ethic as a rejection of the association of status with leisure based on exploitation were not changes that made us more like the rest of the world. In fact, they made us more like ourselves, and our better selves. All this brought on the Civil War. It could hardly do otherwise. Of course it would be truer to say that slavery itself brought on the Civil War.

•

Again, I am aware of exploring lost history. I mentioned how aware I am that I bear the stigma of living in Iowa and of teaching in a public university. This country grossly impoverishes itself with this condescending or contemptuous dismissal of vast reaches of its terrain and the multitudes who live and die there. I have been asked a hundred times why I teach at Iowa, by people sophisticated enough to know that in my field anywhere else on earth would be a step down. So perhaps I teach at a public school in the Midwest because I am an elitist. I have my own reasons for being glad that Iowa is in Iowa. I would never myself have discovered the region or its history, which is an epochal part of our national history and which settled into my literary imagination as satisfyingly as the prairie instructed me in a new aesthetics.

And I take comfort in the fact that the state has no death penalty, that there are earnest and ambitious efforts to educate people in prison. I am pleased that Iowa has one of the highest literacy rates in the country and the fourth-lowest rate per capita of gun ownership. If I were to use that profile to choose a better state to live in, I would be hard-pressed to find one. I am pleased that marriage equality was recognized early in Iowa, and that, since it was a territory, Iowa has had no laws forbidding interracial marriage and no laws permitting segregation in schools. If I were to add these to the profile, my choices would be narrower still, probably approaching zero. Every four years the national media come to Iowa to photograph cows. Since I am a connoisseur of forgotten places, I have a house in upstate New York. I could demonstrate for the press the existence of many cows, just a cab ride and a train ride from Trump Tower. Speaking of which, or of whom, I don't appreciate being blamed by *The New York Times* for that phenomenon, that most New York phenomenon, a sort of political Paris Hilton, famous for being famous by virtue of their own fascinated attention. There's no point mentioning that Donald Trump didn't win Iowa, since Ted Cruz did.

In any case, rumors persist that Cleveland has an orchestra and also a clinic. Chicago has some interesting architecture and a few decent universities. There's a museum in Kansas City whose Ancient Near Eastern collection is more or less inexhaustible, if you like that sort of thing. There are those for whom Ann Arbor is a synonym for paradise. I joke, of course. A region of sixty million people of every possible ethnicity, thickly strewn with colleges and universities and with a long history of relative wealth, is no simple "heartland," no backwater or cultural desert. If population density is productive of desirable traits, it has its great conurbations. I will mention, however, that Iowa City is larger than Periclean Athens.

I am weary of omissions, of failures to acknowledge. People can be convinced that they live in a small country, for all purposes, where there are few options, and markers of success or failure that will be recognized anywhere. My reformers had a glorious sense of space and freedom, very deeply impressed by obligation. They made it, by human and historical standards, a great theater of heroic generosity, which, despite all, is sometimes palpable still. At this time the country needs to regain equilibrium and direction. It needs to recover the memory of the best it has done, and then try to do it all better.

Mind, Conscience, Soul

Plenary Address at the Religious Affections in Colonial
North America Conference, Huntington Library,
San Marino, California: January 27, 2017

I am deeply indebted to Jonathan Edwards. Reading him in college—assigned portions of *The Great Christian Doctrine of Original Sin Defended*—made me aware of a much more plausible ontology than anything compatible with the ugly determinisms on offer then and now in courses on philosophy and psychology. I could put a name to my discontents because I had an older brother who shared them. But I got past them finally one particular afternoon, reading from a nineteenth-century edition of Edwards's *Works*. Everything about this assignment suggested drudgery. But that hour felt like an awakening, so to speak, as if a great burden had been lifted from my soul. I recognize the irony of my having been rescued by precisely this text. In it Edwards describes Being as emergent and the continuities we depend on not as intrinsic but as wholly sustained by God. So reality is indeterminate within a very broad and arbitrary frame of probabilities and possibilities, until it happens. In other words, Edwards dismisses the narrow causal channel of conventional deterministic thinking, which is also essential to Freudianism, Skinnerism, Marxism, or neo-Darwinism. His purpose is to defend the traditional doctrine that implicates all generations in the sin of Adam, without reference to individual transgression. He asserts another, higher-order determinism, which is the freedom of God, constrained only by his own nature. Very characteristic of recent theories about humankind is the assumption that we are the creatures of our race or genes or the traumas we have suffered or the shape of our brains. These theories have been put aside one after another as they are found to be based in errors of fact that yield errors of reasoning, or vice versa. Edwards taught me how to understand that something much richer and stranger is going on than any of these schemes can begin to suggest. I realize I am involving myself in complicated thoughts about a treatise that is not my subject. My purpose is simply to say that I have long seen Edwards very differently than as the black-clad cleric with spiders on his mind. His conception of Being as emergent opened Emerson, Dickinson, Melville, and Whitman to me, and William James as well. He helped me wonder constructively about what Puritanism actually was. He certainly made me wonder what I was looking at when I read his work and theirs.

It seems the universe is a kind of foam, huge voids with filaments of conventional matter, galaxies, constellations, and so on surrounding them like the skin on bubbles. These voids grow. They put enormous pressure on matter, pressure so great that the force of it is attributed in some part to dark energy, of which we know nothing. It, with these voids, may account for the accelerating expansion of the universe, with consequences so profound that a human observer, however well equipped, living one or two billion years from now (granting that there might be such a creature), would see nothing but void. I offer this as a metaphor for contemporary American intellectual life, which is also a thing of forceful and expanding voids, driven by a nameless energy that pushes reality out of shape and might ultimately push it out of sight altogether. I am not talking about popular culture or about the impact of new technolo-

gies. There is really nothing very new about the phenomenon
I describe. If there is anything essentially American about it,
this is probably true because we educate such a large part of
our population. We educate them or, more properly, we condition them in a way that makes them averse to knowing all
kinds of things. We teach them that they already know what
it is essential to know—that certain things are worthy of
unvarying and uninformed contempt. Many people are aware
that Edwards wrote a sermon about hell and damnation. Many
highly educated people are aware that Edwards is generally
considered the finest philosophic mind this continent has produced. They all have the same fixed ideas about him and his
America, learned from the same high school or college anthol-
ogy with the same excerpt from that sermon, which is offered
as an epitome of New England thought and culture, though it
is certainly not characteristic even of Edwards's writing, let
alone his theological tradition. The void Puritanism has merged
with the void Calvinism, swallowing Edwards along the way,
to constitute a vast ignorance of early American history, a negative
energy that obviates any awareness of contemporary British
and European history, with which early New England history
is so deeply intertwined. Specialists might think I overstate. But,
in my experience, specialists also are afflicted by the problems
that come with this strange attrition, this general emptying out
of whole fields of effective knowledge.

America always has the great, interesting problem of arriving at some understanding of itself. History is entirely germane
to this project. We have lived with norms and institutions we
value. How did they develop? What have they meant to earlier
generations? How have they been articulated and extended? The
word *conservative* seems to have some authority among us, but
how many of us know enough to be sure when our institutions
are being defended and when they are actually under assault?
We should have learned by now that the whole civilization

could drift off its moorings amid much waving of flags, much loud talk of former greatness.

Ideas about the nature of a good society were developed and applied in New England. They did not originate there. There were precursors on the Continent and in England. For my purposes, it is enough to say that the Puritans were intent on a reformist experiment in New England, which was as much political as religious. The Southern colonies, by contrast, were socially dominated by the Church of England, the capstone of Royalist conservatism. When the parliamentary revolution, also called the Puritan Revolution, took place in England, many New Englanders crossed over to fight for Oliver Cromwell. There were perhaps ten years when Puritans actually governed a commonwealth in England, a prosperous nation by its own recent standards and despite the turmoil that typically follows revolution. Cromwell died and his son quickly failed as his successor. The British call this period the Interregnum, a word that marks an absence almost as complete for them as it is for us.

The void that has swallowed early American history has swallowed this crucial passage in Anglo-American history. British historians typically say that Puritanism ended in 1689, at the time of the Bloodless, or Glorious, Revolution, which might as well be called the unresisted invasion of England by William of Orange and a sizable army. This must mean that Puritanism ceased to be a threat to the established order in Britain, therefore that it is understood as primarily a political movement. It continued to flourish in America well into the nineteenth century, depending on definitions, and is still dominant among us, according to foreign observers in those diminishing instances in which they think we are being overly fastidious about something. In any case, the writers Edwards cites and quotes at length in *A Treatise Concerning Religious Affections* are almost all Puritans of that old Cromwellian generation, active about a century before Edwards. All those I will quote are from this period, my point being that in this treatise Edwards is making a defense of a stable, elaborated tradition, not merely engaging in controversy. If there is a question in anyone's mind whether Edwards, writing in the mid-eighteenth century, is himself a Puritan, his choice of references makes his own identification with them very clear. He does not quote to argue from authority, rather from affinity. He uses them to identify a core Puritanism, over against religious excitements he and they denounced as hypocrisy.

The work of the many Puritan writers who flourished in the Cromwell period was, even at the time, recognized as a striking element in the life of the movement and the culture. The British Puritan William Greenhill, in a preface to *The Sincere Convert*, by Thomas Shepard, the Anglo-American founder of Harvard, says,

> Did ever any speak, since Christ and his Apostles, as men now speak? We may truly and safely say of our divines and writers, The voice of God, and not of man: such abundance of the Spirit hath God poured into some men, that it is not they, but the Spirit of the Father that speaks in them . . . What infinite cause hath this age to acknowledge the unspeakable mercy of God in affording us such plenty of spiritual tractates, full of divine, necessary, and conscience-searching truths, yea, precious, soul-comforting, and soul-improving truths! . . . In good books you have men's labor and God's truth.

At the time of the Restoration, Roger L'Estrange, the royal government licenser of the press, laid out his plan for suppressing insurrectionist writings by radically limiting the number of presses, destroying condemned books, and severely punishing anyone who owned them or had any part in distributing them. He recognized that many printers would go out of business

because the books he would be suppressing were the books people wanted to buy. It would be most efficient, he said, to eliminate writers, since there were few of them in any generation.
But John Milton and Andrew Marvell are noted Cromwellians,
better understood in the context of their remarkably prolific
generation. Shakespeare was the older contemporary of writers
such as Richard Sibbes and William Ames, and he is fascinated
by subjects that fascinated them, for example, the potency of
conscience. (The American historian Perry Miller has said the
Puritans "abhorred freedom of conscience," on grounds he does
not divulge. Glib as he is, thin as his scholarship is, I appreciate
him as a nameable misfortune.) In any case, it is remarkable
how cleanly the Reformation has been severed from the English
Renaissance, and how little attention is paid to the popular audience that writers and playwrights enjoyed in this period. It is
simply annoying to have studied the period off and on for decades without ever seeing a reference to these important figures.

The political character of Puritanism as part of an international movement is easily demonstrated. Many dissenters
had gone to centers of Reform learning in Geneva, Strasbourg,
Wittenberg, and elsewhere. Hugh Peter, born and educated in
England, served as a pastor in England, then in Rotterdam
among the English there, then from 1635 as a pastor in Salem,
Massachusetts. He returned to England seeking financial
support for the colony and became involved in the incipient
revolution as a chaplain, soldier, and close associate of Cromwell.
In 1651, during the Puritan ascent, he published in London a
little book titled *Good Work for a Good Magistrate; or, A Short
Cut to Great Quiet*. It is a small compendium of proposed reform, too interesting to be dealt with more than briefly here. It
states that "none can bee free of great injustice, who by persecution for Religion take away liberty of conscience . . ." It is to
be noted that under Cromwell no one was prosecuted for his
or her religion. The little book includes provisions liberal by

modern standards, that doctors and lawyers should be paid at a fixed rate from the public treasury, for example. On the subject of crime, it says, "Let no Malefactors against the light of Nature, and civil society, escape punishment, but be justly and speedily punished, not in prisons beforehand, by cold, heat, stink, famine or any other way, but out of humanity, let them be comfortably provided for, till sentence bee given, and then let Justice take place; That all Murderers, Thieves, Whoremongers, Adulterers, False witnesses, evil speakers, deceivers, Bankrupts, Drunkards, Traitors, Blasphemers, and all manner of evil doers may be duly punished, rather inclining to mercy than cruelty, and always with a merciful heart." I am sure we moderns do not meet this standard.

In one respect Peter is definitely harsher than we are. He proposes "that they, who under pretense of able men, under color of Merchandise, get other men's goods into their hands, and yet, when they need not, bankrupt themselves on purpose to deceive others, and enrich themselves, be sorely punished, as very great thieves." Further, "that no bankrupt may ever after come into any office, or bear any Rule in Church or State." He says, "One Bankrupt doth more hurt than twenty thieves that are put to death, or sorely punished for it." I have quite recently acquired a context that allows me to understand what is referred to here.

In any case, the only early legal system I have seen that is comparable to this one for gentleness and moderation is the code titled the Laws and Liberties of Massachusetts, promulgated three years earlier, in 1648. This code remained the basis of Massachusetts law until our Revolution. In form and content it anticipates the American Bill of Rights. In both cases, Cromwell and Parliament were dominant in England, and the social thought behind the laws was Puritan. Compare Dale's Laws, a body of laws imposed in Virginia in 1611, with its many death penalties for minor theft, for speaking ill of the

English governors of the place, for running off to the Indians, and, on the third offense, for skipping church. (This horrible code was to be read in church on every Sabbath.) Or compare the Fundamental Constitutions of Carolina, approved by the British governors of the territories of the South from Virginia to Florida. This design was promulgated in 1669, after the Cromwell era and outside the sphere of Puritanism. It was meant to establish a fixed, hierarchical, land-based aristocracy, a virtual feudalism. Whether these laws were practical or sustainable, and the degree to which they ever took effect, are complex questions. It must be said, there is little evidence that the dominant Anglican elements in the South took exception to the notion of land-based aristocracy, a model with which they were entirely familiar. In other words, the Reformist tendencies that lie behind American achievements in the direction of democracy and—John Winthrop's term, of course—liberalism, have Puritanism in New England as fons et origo.

Someone should write a good book about all this, one that would make distinctions historians seem never to make: between Puritan North and Anglican South, between the period of Cromwell on the one hand and the rest of the colonial period on the other—that is, between times when the colonies were necessarily self-governing, and when they were compelled to renew their royal charters, and, more generally, when the laws in force in any case were British and when they were colonial. Historians describe the harsh legal practices of Virginia as "colonial," when in fact they were simply British. At the time of the Restoration, Peter, condemned in London as a traitor, was made to watch, and the next day to suffer, an execution so appalling I can't bring myself to describe it. It was cruel, yes, but it was not as unusual as one might wish, since Elizabeth the Great had introduced it as a punishment for recusant Catholics.

Ah, well. In any case, Winthrop's sons were active in the English revolution. Cromwell had once considered moving to

Connecticut. Books like the ones Edwards quotes from were widely known on both sides of the Atlantic. Ties between England and Puritan North America were many and strong.

One question. Were there no witch trials in the colonial South? They went on in Britain well into the eighteenth century, so in terms of social and religious culture there is no reason I know of to exclude the possibility. The South itself has not appeared immune to outbursts of public violence. I mention this because the trials in New England, a strange departure from custom, have been treated as uniquely Puritan. With the generally lurid exploitations of the phenomenon, they add an aversive energy to the void of unknowing that has engulfed this interesting civilization.

And one comment. Thank God for the publishers, whoever they are, who keep this once famous, enormously influential literature in print, in blurry facsimiles, at best, though sadly enough sometimes abridged and modernized. The Reformation was all about the power of books. In this case, books that were once suppressed by law, even burned, are very nearly suppressed by the curious compounding of ignorance and aversion that is so important to our sense of our own history. It is appropriate and remarkable and melancholy that their continued life is owed to the fidelity of these printers of books, the descendants, perhaps, of the unacknowledged heroes of the Reformation, and of the Renaissance as a whole.

•

The writers Edwards cites were exploring the human psyche, individual human nature in its capacities as moral agent, in Edwards's terms, and as soul. Their vision of humankind was directly related to their thinking about the kind of political society that would be suited to its flourishing. It is a given of their thought that the soul can be, and is meant to be, ravished and transformed by an experience—something more than an insight or a vision—of the divine. While it is a given also that an experience of this kind is purely a gift of divine grace, they were intent on predisposing in one another and themselves a receptivity to this divine and supernatural light, which Edwards with great subtlety finally distinguishes from light, making it utterly different in kind from even this most rarefied earthly thing. He escapes the constraints of particularity his analogy might otherwise imply, and establishes a sense of the singularity of the high order of perception for which the senses barely supply analogies. The soul was made ready for this experience by the conscience, a human faculty the English Puritan John Flavel says is inferior only to God. Conscience lays bare the sinfulness and unworthiness that make clear the absolute dependency of any soul on God's grace. Those who pass through this experience and are changed by it are presumably true saints. Those who are part of the church and make a good account of themselves while awaiting the experience are also called saints, or godly persons.

We are familiar with a superficially similar version of this set of beliefs, and Edwards was, too. The difference might be said to be one of emphasis, though it is in fact a profound difference. For Edwards, the authenticity of the experience is proved, to the converted themselves, in the right conduct of life. For those he criticizes, the experience itself is assurance of salvation without reference to conduct of life. In *Some Thoughts Concerning the Present Revival of Religion in New England*, Edwards describes at length what he calls the "degenerating" of these experiences, with which we are familiar as well. In *All Things for Good*, Thomas Watson says, "Christians must keep a decorum; they must observe what is comely," and "Take heed of a morose, supercilious behaviour. Religion does not take away civility, but refines it." In his *Works*, Edwards says, "At length the experience of some persons, who began well, come to little else but violent motions of carnal affections, with great heats of the imagination, a great degree of enthusiasm and swelling of spiritual pride . . . The unhappy subject of such a degeneracy, for the most part, is not sensible of his own calamity; but because he finds himself still violently moved, has greater heats of zeal, and more vehement motions of his animal spirits, thinks himself fuller of the Spirit of God than ever." Edwards considers this embarrassing. "Persons will find themselves under a kind of necessity of making a great ado, with less and less affection of soul, till at length almost any slight emotion will set them going; and they will be more and more violent and boisterous, and will grow louder and louder, till their actions and behavior become indeed very absurd." He says zeal "may degenerate more and more into human and proud passion, and may come to bitterness, and even a degree of hatred."

It is in this declined form that unsympathetic history sees the whole tradition of what Edwards calls experimental—that is, experiential—religion. What history ignores is the extraordinarily fine-grained and humane attentiveness to perception and experience that follows from the high Puritan conception of the soul—we must grant them the word—as suited to the reception of ultimate truth and ultimate beauty. Their emphasis is suggested by the titles of their books—*The Tender Heart*; *The Bruised Reed*; *The Art of Divine Contentment*; *A Treatise of the Soul of Man*; *Conscience, with the Power and Cases Thereof.* The great old writers of Edwards's tradition placed a most sacred and delicate mystery at the center of human inwardness. Perhaps this fact and its consequences elude us now because our approach to the study of the psyche could hardly be more different from theirs. In fact it can no longer be assumed that the words *psyche* or *soul* or *mind* can be taken to correspond to anything real. Whether this matters, putting aside the fact that either of these conceptions, theirs or ours, is of a kind to be judged broadly true or broadly false, depends on the importance a value-laden vision of human nature has in sustaining a democratic society, even a humane society. In any case, this is an important instance of the fact that these voids I have mentioned produce a sort of warping of perception that makes things the opposite of themselves. It would be impossible, in an environment without distortion, to make the case that Puritanism was harsh or cold or rigid.

•

Nothing I have read forbids my taking Edwards to be pre-Revolutionary, that is, to be feeling the tremors before the great upheaval he did not live to see. It came abruptly enough when it came to suggest that there were signs of imminent rebellion building for years, perhaps for a hundred years. There had been Puritan religious excitements before and throughout the Cromwell period, and Edwards might have believed the Great Awakening to be what it was in fact, the precursor of another revolution. Considering that New England was a population largely made up of near descendants of sympathizers with and collaborators in the first modern revolution, greatly augmented by refugees from the oppression that followed its collapse; considering that they had maintained the religious and intellectual culture of the revolutionaries, including extraordinarily high levels of literacy and an active press; considering that the population had grown so prodigiously from this base that it would inspire Malthus's theory on the subject; considering that every Bible in English would remind them of the signal achievements of their ancestors—in light of all this, a breach with England, when it came, could only be about much more than the price of tea. The New Englanders had an illustrated martyrology depicting the ghastly deaths of many men and women they revered as saints and heroes. Oddly, their interest in this enormous volume, which in an earlier version influenced Shakespeare, is treated as another of their creepily unwholesome obsessions. It is in fact a carefully documented history with relevant source materials in Latin and Greek and in translation, which might usefully be consulted to establish the idea content of Puritanism, as it was once meant to justify and preserve it.

Why did Edwards bring so much attention to these classic Puritan writers in *A Treatise Concerning Religious Affections*? In his preface he alludes to a time when Satan "prevailed against New England, to quench the love, and spoil the joy of her espousals, about an hundred years ago." This would be the Cromwell period, when the Commonwealth made England new, or when New England experienced a virtual independence from a government that was sympathetic in any case, or when it seemed that Puritan New and Old England, "both the Englands," as one Cromwell period writer called them, would be, in effect, wed. The parliamentary government, therefore the Revolution in England, collapsed in part because of sectarianism. Cromwell and his Congregationalists fought two major battles against the Presbyterians. He won, of course, being Cromwell, but in such circumstances there is only loss. Edwards can see the fissuring that is taking place already within the present revival, accusations and animosities over how conversion is prepared for and experienced and how it should manifest itself in subsequent behavior. And then there are the skeptics, Bostonians and others, who are also Puritans, and who must be persuaded of the authenticity of these conversions and, more generally, must be made to accept that God is acting in bringing about this awakening. Edwards feels this revival to be of exceptional, historical significance, as his allusions to early Christianity, the struggle with Rome, as well as his use of the language of actual warfare make clear. So his intentions are, as he says, to address the question that most concerns both mankind as a whole and every individual person, the nature of true religion. Factionalism is for him both the degeneration of religion within the individual sensibility, and the collective effect of this degeneration on groups of individuals, for example, in the tendency of people to conform their behavior to the behavior of those around them. He identifies no adversary except, glancingly, Satan. He will not pass judgment on the spiritual state of individuals no matter what he thinks of their conduct. The covenant of grace leaves that mystery to God. Even one despairing over his own spiritual state must remember that "life in the winter is hid in the root," in the words of Sibbes. This high Puritanism does not offer any final assurances. They did not believe in salvation by works, but they did believe that the effective will to lead a generous life was an indication that one was saved. In *All Things for Good*, Watson says, "The mercies of God work compassion to others. A Christian is a temporal saviour. He feeds the hungry, clothes the naked . . . Charity drops from him freely, as myrrh from the tree."

•

Granting the impossibility of judgment in individual cases, including one's own, Edwards does believe hypocrisy, self-deception, and the influence of Satan are active in this and any revival, tending to destroy the revival and to discredit religion. The only response is to make each person an honest and competent judge of the integrity, the graciousness, of her own experience, of his own soul.

I have no idea what the relation of the British authorities to the colonial press was when Edwards wrote. I know that in the nineteenth century, during the Chartist movement, which was the nearest Britain ever came to another civil war, a stamp act was used to put dissident publications out of circulation. An expensive stamp had to be affixed to each copy, so the readers to whom they were addressed could not afford to buy them. This seems more the sort of thing that would have offended the New Englanders than any mere tax on comestibles. A free press was characteristic of Reformed societies, notably Geneva, the Netherlands, and England during the reign of Edward VI and the Protectorship of the Earl of Somerset. Edwards's allusion to the Commonwealth period, surely a touchy subject from an English point of view, is oblique. More generally, the question that comes to mind, reading the preface, is what is he trying to prepare his readers for? Cromwell's great military success was largely due to his attracting an army of, in his words, "plain, russet-coated fellows," ordinary, self-disciplined, reliable men who were unmoved by danger and hardship, godly men, in a term of the time, meaning Puritans in all their varieties. Edwards's ideal is clearly much closer to such figures than to the enthusiasts whom he sees as in love with themselves and their "affections" rather than with God. He justifies his criticisms, which he knows "may be reproached in these captious, censorious times," by summoning the voices of the Puritan golden age. His hope is to poise the awakening on the knife edge of zealous restraint. He quotes Flavel: "The more rational any gracious person is, by so much more is he fixed and settled and satisfied in the grounds of religion: yea, there is the highest and purest reason in religion; and when this change is wrought upon men, it is carried on in a rational way. Is. I:18, John 19:9."

•

The great inducement to what Edwards would consider a true and ideal frame of religion, and the great standard of having reached it as well, is aesthetic experience. Puritanism is commonly thought of as averse to beauty because they rejected iconography, ornamentation, and personal display. This is a consequence of their seeing elements of idolatry in the religious use of images, of reaction against the costliness of churches in a world much afflicted by poverty, and of rejection of the sumptuary laws that made social status apparent in dress. These were responses to popular criticisms current since the fourteenth century at least. Simultaneous with this outward austerity, if that is the right word, is a celebration of the intrinsic beauty that is the signature of God in creation. Shepard says, to find God, "O, pass by all the rivers, till thou come to the spring head; wade through all creatures until thou art drowned, plunged and swallowed up with God." It is crucial that the unmediated perception of the divine, that most glorious and most inward human privilege, is an aesthetic experience. Edwards says, "He that sees the beauty of holiness, or true moral good, sees the greatest and most important thing in the world, which is the fullness of all things, without which the world is empty, no better than nothing, yea, worse than nothing. Unless this is seen, nothing is seen, that is worth the seeing: for there is no other true excellency or beauty. Unless this be understood, nothing is understood, that is worthy of the noble faculty of understanding." And he says, "God is God, and distinguished from all other beings, and exalted above 'em, chiefly by his divine beauty, which is infinitely diverse from all other beauty. They therefore see the stamp of this glory in divine things, they see divinity in them, they see God in them, and so see 'em to be divine; because they see in them wherein the truest idea of divinity does consist. Thus a soul may have a kind of intuitive knowledge of the divinity of the things exhibited in the gospel . . . the argument is but one, and the evidence direct; the mind ascends to the truth of the gospel but by one step, and that is its divine glory." This experience gives the person who receives it a "spiritual knowledge" that "primarily consists in a taste or relish of the amiableness and beauty of that which is truly good and holy; this holy relish is a thing that discerns and distinguishes between good and evil, between holy and unholy, without being at the trouble of a train of reasoning." It shapes the conduct of saints in the world: "There is such a thing as a divine taste, given and maintained by the Spirit of God, in the hearts of the saints, whereby they are in like manner led and guided in discerning and distinguishing the true spiritual and holy beauty of actions; and that more easily, readily and accurately, as they have more or less of the Spirit of God dwelling in them." Conduct so derived and guided will be sweet, humble, meek, and charitable. Edwards's purpose is to protect a tradition of Protestant inwardness that, on the strength of the exalted human capacity it recruits to a direct perception of this most sacred beauty, can claim to participate in essential cosmic reality. This is the definitive experience, over against which all other religious experience is exposed as false or feigned or misguided. It is based in a discipline of self-scrutiny that would shield it from every pressure, including the tendency toward enthusiasm and degeneracy Edwards sees around him.

A striking difference between the kind of thinking about human nature and experience that one finds in Edwards and his tradition on the one hand and modern thinking on the same subjects on the other is that the older thought invites assent. Readers are implicitly invited to consult with themselves as to the persuasiveness of the description of the inward life that is offered to them. The forcefulness of the prose in these passages is meant to stir recognition. Is it possible to assent to the idea of a beauty that exceeds any conception we have of beauty? Is the moral and religious sense an aesthetic sense, as unmediated in its reactions as taste? The meaningfulness of the questions themselves would await affirmation by individual responses to them, and the differences of response would themselves be meaningful. That we live in and with our minds differently from one another is a given of Puritan theology. That we can experience our own minds differently from one moment to the next is also a given. In the understanding of Edwards's tradition, these things are true because the mind is in intimate relation to God, stirred by conscience, accepting or resisting grace. The Puritan scheme can be deeply sensitive to shadings, variable responses to the essential and immutable. In *The Bruised Reed*, Sibbes says, "We must acknowledge that in the covenant of grace God requires the truth of grace, not any certain measure; and a spark of fire is fire, as well as the whole element. Therefore we must look to grace in the spark as well as in the flame. All have not the like strong, though they have the like precious, faith . . ." A glimpse of incomparable beauty has all the authority of a vision of it.

In any case, we do indeed differ in the character of our experience, person to person and moment to moment. Our modern anthropologies have no language to account for complexity and mutability, nor for conscience or aesthetic sense as experience. If a theory of consciousness cannot address primary aspects of consciousness, it should not claim to have supplanted a more sufficient conceptual language, certainly not by treating the complexity that conceptual language reflects as if it were nonexistent. That these richer terms have always implied a metaphysics raises other questions to be dealt with in their own right, but which do not in any case impinge on the question of the meaningfulness of words like *conscience*, *mind*, and *self*.

This recent anthropology is an instance of the phenomenon I spoke of earlier, the emergence of devouring voids, with their potent tendency to generalize emptiness. The center of Puritan individualism was the conscience, so sacred that it was the foundation of their definition of freedom. The much-revered William Ames, Shakespeare's contemporary, says, "Conscience bindeth according as it is informed of the will of God: for in itselfe it hath the power of a will of God, and so stands in the place of God himselfe," and "Conscience bindeth a man so straitly that the command of no creature can free a man from it," and "The conscience is immediately subject to God, and his will, and therefore cannot submit itselfe unto any creature without Idolatry." Flavel says, "View the conscience and thoughts with their self-reflective abilities, wherein the soul retires into itself, and sits concealed from all eyes but his that made it, judging its own actions, and censuring its estate; viewing its face in its own glass, and correcting the indecencies it discovers there: things of greatest moment and importance are silently transacted in its council-chamber between the soul and God; so remote from the knowledge of all creatures, that neither angels, devils, nor men can know" what is transacted there. The conscience is enlightened by acceptance of the Gospel, according to Ames, but a Law of Nature or a Law of God "is naturally written in the hearts of al men." His essay, he says, is offered "that I might do something, whereby the unlearned, and such as are destitute of better helpe, might somewhat be helped." This suggests Shakespeare's audience, the literate unlearned, that remarkable population to whom Shakespeare as well as these popular theologians could speak so brilliantly and with such confidence. I have been reading the classic Puritans to understand Edwards's spiritual and intellectual world. But clearly they are at least as relevant to an understanding of the whole literature of the English Renaissance. The workings of the conscience are a primary interest of Shakespeare's drama, where the word *conscience* recurs frequently. He can always reasonably be supposed to share and address the interests of his audience, without presuming to identify his religious thinking or his politics.

Let us say that *conscience*, like *soul* or *mind*, is socially constructed, the product of a particular cultural history. Or let us say it has the kind of reality conceded when a certain part of the brain lights up in an experimental subject who summons a guilty memory. In either case, there is nothing in the experience that anchors it in unequivocal meaning. Ames, in his treatise on the conscience, says that "conscience, though erroneous, bindes alwaies so, that he that doth against it, sinnes. The reason is, because he that doth against conscience, doth against Gods will: though not materially, and truley; yet formally, and by interpretation: because what the conscience doth declare, it declareth as God's will." So even while the fallibility of the conscience is granted, its sanctity as a mediator between the mind and God is so great that one sins in doubting or disregarding it. To bring such seriousness to the negotiation of one's moral and ethical life might interfere with good times as currently defined. But on the one hand it invites the highest degree of interest in and respect for the singular experience of oneself and one's circumstances, and on the other it can somewhat supplant the fear of hell as an inducement to seeking a relationship with God. Shepard says, "It is not a slavish fear of hell" that converts people, who "abhor to live like slaves in Bridewell, to do all for fear of the whip." He goes on to describe the terrors inflicted by an offended conscience, true. But a troubled conscience is one's own, defending one's integrity and moral competence, perhaps rescuing one's soul. It had a central place in the strenuous drama of Puritan life.

Whether the conscience is or was indeed only a social construct is the kind of thing that will never be established finally one way or the other. But for purposes of argument, let us say this is a correct understanding of it. We know it can require different behaviors in different cultures, and we know that the Puritan conception was supported by an antiauthoritarianism that made them dissenters, nonconformists, and revolutionaries. It is the lynchpin of the kind of spiritual autonomy that came with the rejection of priestly confession and absolution, together with other rites and mediations of the Catholic Church. These rejections had been current in suppressed popular religious belief in England at least since John Wycliffe in the fourteenth century, so their implications were well thought out by the seventeenth century and were central to a tradition whose heroes of conscience are memorialized in John Foxe's *Actes and Monuments of the Martyrs*. It is clear that the concept had a powerful formative history for Puritans, which would differentiate their understanding of it from others in fundamental ways. To this extent it is certainly socially constructed.

In all its variant forms it has had great importance in Western civilization, as have mind, self, and soul, which, despite their great potency as ideas, are now regarded as mere constructs.

If we grant the plausibility of this view of things, then in doing so we acknowledge not only that these concepts can be, as it were, deconstructed but also that other concepts of mind and self can supplant them, new constructions that grow out of presently authoritative models of reality. For Freud the conscience, or superego, is the internalization of an oppressive father figure. For the neo-Darwinists it is a part of the system of self-deception that for whatever reason hides our inevitable selfishness from us. Models like this radically undercut the old assumption that a human mind has a faculty oriented toward truth and ready to offer testimony against the mind itself when it is erring, misguided, or corrupted, though the mind, or the subjectivity, or whatever we call it now, is assumed always to be erring, misguided, and corrupted, which makes the word *truth* meaningless, since our own perception and acculturation are obstacles to our determining the truth in any case—which in turn means, by these lights, that truth itself cannot be said to exist. All this can sound very sophisticated, except when it comes from the mouth of a politico who says we are beyond fact-based reality, or an undergraduate who declares a staunch preference for his own truth, also not fact-based.

We have stepped from a metaphysics into a void. Whether the state of things we have entered was inevitable or whether we could have constructed something out of culture and history that would have borne our weight and shown us a serviceable enough true north no one can say. But here we are. Do we owe good art or good information or freedom of conscience to a humankind that cannot be assumed to have any natural affinity to the true or the good? We are gazing these days at an abysmal No.

However the fact is to be understood, traditions of thought do pass down through time, the traditions relevant here being so-called modernism and the endlessly consequential anti-history that abolishes context and fosters incomprehension on subjects of such intrinsic interest that on this basis alone they should be acknowledged and studied. This consuming ignorance is beyond any account I can offer for it, but it does feast, black-hole fashion, on the humanist heritage preferentially, as it did when the classical tradition gave way to the Dark Ages. The ways we think do themselves deserve thought. For example, if concepts with religious history such as soul and conscience can be sufficiently redescribed in other language, this in no way diminishes their reality. If they might be redescribed and are not, then we should wonder why they are not, how their exclusion from the vocabulary of self-declared humanism is rationalized, and what the effects of the exclusion might be. If they cannot be redescribed in a nonreligious language, then we need to consider what is threatened or lost when religious language is lost. For the Puritans, conscience as a concept put the mind or soul in relation to God. It made the self an object of scrupulous contemplation. And it created a sanctity around the individual that assured important liberties.

Our sample of existence—that is, the growing sum of whatever we can observe, test, describe, derive, or know in any meaningful sense—is too small and untypical, too contaminated with error and assumption, too prejudiced by accident and limitation to yield a metaphysics. Yet we need a metaphysics, an unconfirmable parallel reality able to support essential concepts such as mind, conscience, and soul, if we are to sustain the civilization culture and history created for us. To quote Flavel, "The soul of the poorest child is of equal dignity with the soul of Adam." All men are created equal. Nothing about these statements is self-evident. Yet they can shape and create institutions, and they can testify against them when they fail. They have only their own beauty and the beauty of their influence to affirm them.

Considering the Theological Virtues

The Laing Lectures at Regent College, Vancouver, B.C.:
February 8, 2017

FAITH

I have been asked fairly often over the years why I choose to identify myself with religion. It is an unusual choice now for a novelist who writes for a general, nonsectarian readership. But what is "usual" is not really any kind of constraint. It is the merest cobweb waiting to be brushed away, insofar as it makes itself felt at all. There are a great many fine books in the world, more every year, so if some readers are turned away from mine by my choice of subject, they are at no risk of deprivation. The answer to this question is, of course, that religion is a very central interest of mine, and I have never seen any reason to look away from a subject to which I am so strongly attracted.

Several things are going wrong here already. The word *interest* does not really describe my tropism toward the vast field of experience and thought and expression I call *religion*, for want of a better word. Nor is *subject* an appropriate term for something so minutely rich and so cosmically enveloping. I have adopted myself into an old Protestant tradition, once important in England and America, now relatively unknown in the world at large and in America as well. On the one hand, it has a rich and brilliant theology and a remarkable history, and on the other hand, it is so small a part of Christendom that I can be comforted and reassured that it is indeed only a part of this vast and various world presence we call the church and the great religions. While my thinking is Christian, it has led me to a kind of universalism that precludes any notion of proselytizing. It would shake my faith in the goodness of God if I were to believe that his particular favor was reserved to members of my denomination. This is to say, I feel no conflict or contradiction between religion broadly considered and religion narrowly considered. Furthermore, I know from experience that very secular people can take a generous interest in religion and be highly sensitive to the beauty of it—that is, when its exponents are also aware of its beauty, as too often they seem not to be.

So it is conventional among contemporary writers to exclude religion from their work, however religious the writers might in fact be. This reticence seems to be regarded by many as a courtesy, an acknowledgment of the fact that the subject can be painful or private or can stir prejudices or hostilities. Such scruples are respectable, certainly, but they tacitly reinforce the assumption that religion is essentially and inevitably divisive. So this assumption is rarely tested. It has not been my experience that the response to my books among Catholics or Jews or Muslims is in any degree less generous than that of readers whose traditions are closer to mine. The feeling of an overplus of meaning in reality, a sense that the world cannot at all be accounted for in its own terms, is a profound bond and understanding between and among religious people. It is universal in religions to grant the meaningfulness of metaphysical thought: They all query Being itself.

Granting conflict. But there is always conflict, and to treat it as something peculiar to religion is simply uninformed. Most of us must know that religion uniquely denounces and condemns violence—to what effect we cannot know, since history is infused with religion and might well have been much darker without it. In any case, to be able to acknowledge this profound and beautiful shared assumption, that there is indeed an overplus of meaning, would be to respect something very near the hearts of people we are too ready to think of as alien in every sense. Religion could quiet our antagonisms if we let it be what it is fundamentally and at best.

It is because of the strange state of religion, and of the conversations surrounding it, that I feel obliged to account for the fact that my preoccupations are the subject of my work. To me this seems simply appropriate. If they had narrowed my audience, no matter, I really never expected an audience. When I discovered I did have one, I took this to mean that I had their permission to write as I chose. My mind and my books have passed through life together, in conversation, so to speak. This pleases me. The resistance I have been warned to expect is not real, so far as I can tell. The warning seems to be no more than an instance of a dogged tendency to resent injury in anticipation, undeterred by the fact that the injury never comes, or that it has only the long life and broad application of anecdote, or that it is so slight as to be negligible if it is even real. People live and die stifled by fears of hostility or ridicule, the elves and ogres of contemporary consciousness. These dreary and trivial anxieties encourage dark prejudgments of people at large. They seem to be particularly characteristic of people who call themselves Christian, though they discourage faith, hope, and love, which in this particular case would certainly drive out fear.

I think and write about religion because I am religious. It occurred to me early in life that I wanted to align my life with things that seemed true to me. My always important brother once told me that according to Jonathan Edwards we should never allow ourselves a thought we would not entertain on our deathbeds. Stark as this standard is, and unattainable as it is, thank God, it does suggest the importance of our thinking— not primarily in light of ultimate judgment but as something appropriately disciplined by the brevity of all lives, and by acknowledgment of the extraordinary fact of one's being a consciousness capable of shaping and orienting itself.

The mind, that most luxuriant flowering of the highest possibilities of the material world, likes to natter and mope and trivialize itself. We let an astonishing fertility run to weeds. I realize this statement is meaningful only if it is first granted that some thoughts, our own and others, are relatively worthy of us, or unworthy on grounds of triviality, or flatly destructive. Not much in contemporary life encourages us to make this kind of distinction. Pathology invites medical or legal intervention, of course. Short of this, we are offered strategies for making ourselves more useful to the economy, for coping with stress or warding off dementia. We have no current language for the culture of the mind, which another generation might have called the care of the soul.

There are things in reality whose limits will never be found—notably mathematics, language, and the human mind whose creatures these are. I find this fact interesting and suggestive. No doubt we will never know or find words for any meaningful fraction even of the aspects of reality that are available to our strategies of comprehension. But if this is true, it is true in fact, not in principle. High civilization, and humankind itself, may not last long enough to begin to discover what is potential in us, in our capacity for knowledge and understanding of the physical universe, including, of course, the things of this world. This potential is splendid and amazing, in itself more wonderful than anything it might discover, even if it were free from the limits our own choices set for it.

I have found considerable resistance these days to "mind" as a concept. There is the brain, with its modalities. No more is granted. If it is objected that we are highly individuated, that we assimilate and interpret a great range of experience in ways that are distinctive, perhaps unique to us as individuals, well, the self has gone the way of the mind. It would seem that a new vocabulary should be supplied to acknowledge the experience of—so to speak—selfhood, but none is forthcoming, so far as I know. Absent the self we would be free of some familiar miseries—embarrassment, anomie, alienation, not to mention self-consciousness—and we could disregard every notion of gift or calling, which do often make us restless with our actual circumstance, bent on defining ourselves in ways that dismiss or override expectation.

Such experiences are excluded now from learned accounts of human Being. I take this to be the case because mind and self are irreducibly complex. And this is true in part because they exist in time. They unfold, eventuate, in ways that are distinctive even when they are predictable. If we attach meaning to this existence in time, which implicates aspiration and retrospect, self-fulfillment and self-betrayal, growth and decline, then we are not captured in any moment in which, say, self-interest is enacted, or any series of such moments. We pass through time like pilgrims, always changed and somehow always the same. We have identity through time, not only in the sense that, as Wordsworth said, the child is father of the man but also because dreams recur and memories abide whether or not they are welcome. Periods of trial and of insight interact in our minds not simply as memory but as things to be pondered, whose meanings modify one another over time and whose value changes in light of further experience. I used the word *mind* because this kind of inwardness is not accommodated by the word *brain* as it is presently understood—that is, by the exclusion of our experience of it, though it does preside over and effectively constitute our experience.

If I am granted the word *mind*, I think I should also be permitted the word *soul*. I make my claim for its meaningfulness on the following grounds: First, mind as I have described it lacks ontological mooring. If it is like other things on earth, if animals have minds, if sensibility is a quality general among living things—possibilities I am ready to concede—then our usual conception of the nature of Being is seriously defective. Second, if we extrapolate from a false notion of fundamental reality, if we say human beings must be assumed to be of a kind with everything else, and we then proceed from an impoverished view of everything else, we can only arrive at an impoverished view of human beings as well. These exclusions of concepts like mind and soul are intended as rigor and objectivity, but if they are based on fixed assumptions that are false as well as fixed, then they are only rigorous in the manner of the lesser forms of dogmatism.

All this is to say that I am aware of the arguments brought against the kind of worldview faith proposes. I have given these arguments considerable thought and study because they are important now, as they have been since at least the eighteenth century. It seems to be in the nature of religious concepts, notably God and the soul, to trigger skepticism. People have always tested these claims of ultimate truth against their own models of reality. Nothing is proved by the fact that these two things never align, except when religion is wrenched into conformity with human understanding and effectively ceases to be religion. If this absolute reality remains aloof from our attempts at comprehension, then it is like every deep truth about the nature of things. This proves nothing, of course, but it puts faith and doubt on the same footing, a useful beginning place for a discussion like this one.

In their various articulations these agnosticisms and atheisms have amassed prestige over time and acquired a general familiarity as well. Ground has been granted to them, uncritically, as a concession to the advance of knowledge, though often enough faith as imagined by its debunkers has little to do with faith as experience, and nothing to do with the intellectual and aesthetic traditions of religion. And the supposed "science" that has been used as leverage against it over the centuries is too flawed, even quaint, to count as knowledge. This may in fact be where the problem arises. Those who think always in objective or positivist terms imagine God as someone somewhere—an old man enthroned on a cloud, an imaginary friend. For those who think of him metaphysically and experientially he is the Creator always creating whom we know through divine attributes we can feel in ourselves—love, faithfulness, and compassion among them. I note here that these are attributes modern studies of the human mind do not attribute to us, at least not without converting them first into forms of self-interest—desacralizing them, in effect. I concluded long ago that reverence for ourselves and reverence for God are mutually dependent, inextricable. Of course nothing is ever so absolute as this sounds. I never mean to imagine limits to the grace of God. But I am struck by the consistency with which the traits that bind us together, that we value in one another, and that might therefore be assumed to promote survival are excluded from this "science" of human nature. These are, as I have said, attributes also ascribed to God.

It is certainly striking that the project that so often claims to have emptied the heavens should at the same time, conceptually, at least, have stripped humanity of minds, moral natures, and selves—though there seems to be no necessity behind the simultaneity of effects. This suggests to me that our conception of the human self was as much theomorphic as our conception of God was anthropomorphic—that we discovered godlike gifts and qualities in ourselves even as we attributed them in a vastly higher form to the Creator.

To characterize God as loving or patient, aggrieved or angry has been treated as a naïve projection of our hopes and fears onto an indifferent cosmos. This view of things can be neither proved nor refuted, since belief and interpretations of experience influenced by belief on either side are quite reasonably excluded. It must be said, however, that when human nature is thought of as analogous to the nature of God, the consequences are extraordinary.

For purposes of comparison with this traditional view we have all the modern anthropologies. Various as they are, they are entirely of one mind in avoiding the slightest suggestion that human nature has anything divine in it. In fact, it seems to be a project of theirs to minimize radically everything human in it. By human I mean, of course, everything singular about us among the species, including our bias toward error and our gift for destruction—traditionally marks of our alienation from God—as well as our reason, imagination, and creativity. We must be shorn of a great many attributes before we can begin to seem more ape than angel, even when that angel is Lucifer.

The word *soul* authorizes a scale and seriousness in the conception of the human being that has no equivalent when the subject is broached in any other terms. First of all, it uniquely invests each individual person with an absolute dignity and significance. One by one we live out a passage through the world that, however opaque, is meaningful in cosmic terms. The immortality of the soul makes us all participants in an ultimate reality that transcends and in every way exceeds this transient earth. This understanding places great value in the individual and, at the same time, finds great significance in the moment-to-moment conduct of mortal life. There is clearly a reciprocal relationship between the idea of immortality, of an eternity that exists with reference to humankind, and the belief in the singular value and significance of human life. Each implies the other. And if we simply and utterly perish with the beasts, the conceptual universe contracts sharply.

The conclusions we draw about the appropriateness of one vision or the other must be called intuitive. They are the decisions of faith. Doctrine and practice can shore up belief, even stand in the place of it, when the deeper leanings of the soul tend not to sustain it. This must mean that there is also a deeper faith behind a seeming lack or loss of faith. But the plausibility of the soul as the defining human attribute ultimately depends on our experience of ourselves and one another—and the world as well, with its power to instruct, which corresponds so tantalizingly to our prodigious ability to learn.

Here is an old account of creation and our place in it.

The palaces of princes are not beautified and adorned, to the intent men should pay their respects and honors to the walls, but to shew the grandeur and magnificence of the king, to whose person their honor is due . . . The world is a glorious and magnificent pile, raised designedly to exhibit the wisdom and power of its Creator to the reasonable creature man, that from him God might receive the glory of all his other works . . . This creature man, the masterpiece of all the visible world, [was] therefore crowned king over it the first moment he was made.

Humankind was formed of "vile and despicable dust," and "the consideration is humbling, and serves to tame the pride of man, who is apt to dote upon his own beauty." Yet it redounds to the skill and wisdom of the Creator, "who out of such mean, despicable materials, has fashioned so exact and elegant a piece."

But "the soul is the most wonderful and astonishing piece of divine workmanship; it is no hyperbole to call it the breath of God, the beauty of men, the wonder of angels, and the envy of devils. One soul is of more value than all the bodies in the world."

This is from *A Treatise of the Soul of Man*, written in the mid-seventeenth century by the English Puritan John Flavel. I found Reverend Flavel in a footnote to Jonathan Edwards's *Treatise Concerning Religious Affections*. I have both felt and sought out the influence of this tradition of Christianity, partly for its wisdom and loveliness and learning, partly because it illustrates endlessly that very much of what we think we know is in fact only the husk of old polemic. Puritans are said to have hated life, the flesh, the world—as heretics were always said to. Their writings, far from supporting this notion of them, are rich with humanist thought and with celebrations of human perception and experience. Crucially, for them beauty is a mode of divine address, a signifier of divine intention. The world is filled with sunlight, the heavens are filled with stars, our bodies are exact and elegant, and in all this the sacredness of creation is manifest, there for us to see because our senses and minds are formed to apprehend it and glory in it. For purposes of comparison, modern anthropologies are silent on the subject of beauty except in those cases where, by their lights, it rationalizes the selection of mates. What they do not acknowledge they always exclude. In Edwards, the sense of beauty is the profoundest experience of consciousness, capable of a vision of the divine that is pure of any sense of self. He says, "God's nature, or the divinity, is infinitely excellent; yea 'tis infinite beauty, brightness, and glory itself. But how can that be true love of this excellent and lovely nature, which is not built on the foundation of its true loveliness? How can that be true love of beauty and brightness, which is not for beauty and brightness sake?" And, "A true saint, when in the enjoyment of true discoveries of the sweet glory of God and Christ, has his mind too much captivated and engaged by what he views without himself, to stand at that time to view himself, and his own attainments: It would be a diversion and loss which he could not bear, to take his eye off from the ravishing object of his contemplation, to survey his own experience . . ."

So, my Puritan tells me, humankind is the masterpiece of the visible world. This is an aesthetic judgment, though it refers to all our gifts and competences. And the soul is the beauty of men. We see sacredness in one another in a particular beauty that, in the manner of sacred things, is identical with a great truth. This thought is beautiful and true to our best experience. I do not propose to argue for the truth of religion by storming the heavens, by arguing from design or offering ontological proofs. These things are meaningful only to those who are predisposed to finding them meaningful. There is a much stronger argument to be made, beginning from Calvin's descent into the self, where, he says, one will find unmistakable marks of divinity. The soul, being both radically individual and universal among human beings, is an inexhaustible revelation of one's own nature and of the nature of every other soul who has lived, lives, and will live. The concept of the soul is the profoundest possible bond among us, an unshakable basis for compassion, recognition, and love, which, acknowledged, would enable us to love enemies, welcome strangers, and all the rest.

And then there is the dignity and joy, the heightening of consciousness, that comes with the thought that each of us participates so deeply in ultimate reality. Flavel says this about language:

> Other creatures have apt and elegant organs; birds can modulate the air, and form it into sweet, delicious notes and charming sounds; but no creature, except man, whose soul is of an heavenly nature and extraction, can articulate the sound, and form it into words, by which the notions and sentiments of one soul are in a noble, apt and expeditious manner conveyed to the understanding of another soul.

Something true is said here. Surely all of us have, at some moment, been moved by a bad poem, or the memory of an old song, or by a confession of guilt or love, even when we might not entirely trust the speaker. Theories that see language as basically functional do not account for its complex power, its ability to touch the soul, so to speak.

These theories tend to be based on speculations about the motives and behavior of our remotest ancestors, of whom we know very little indeed and are liable to misinterpreting the very little we do know. The approach may or may not make sense, but it certainly means these speculations are unconstrained except by the preferences of their formulators. In any case, a supposed original simplicity tends to be interpreted in such contexts as meaning that simplicity persists as the essential character of whatever is in question. Language is "really" a system of signals used to maximize self-interest. High achievement of whatever kind is "really" a ploy for attracting mates. Human beings are "really" primates with hypertrophic brains. Presumably the manifest complexity of all these things is an accretion of simplicities, which never yields qualitative change.

This makes complexity epiphenomenal, a distraction from primary reality. But in fact complexity is totally pervasive. Consider the nucleus of an atom, or rather, consider as we can whatever it is we have tagged with names like nucleus and atom. A void is scintillant with matter and antimatter. Simplicity exists only as an idea, the abstract of a cursory reading of the given world. So by what miracle could it be essential to anything? Early evolutionary theory was bolstered by European encounters with simple people speaking simple languages, so they thought—a catastrophic error of interpretation that lives on in these theories about the primal origins of human traits and behaviors.

How to find a way to reconceive virtually everything. How to rid our worldview of a systematic fault in our thinking, which leads us to disallow the universe of things its terms will not accommodate. This is a difficult problem. I propose that we consult earlier writers, that we consider a cultural moment more inclined to hyperbole than to reductionism. For those who can do so in good faith, I propose a return to theist realism, by which I mean attention to the world as it is, without reductionist translation and transvaluation. To do so would be to reanimate the aesthetic vocabulary my Puritans made such free use of. If we adopt their view, that through our minds and senses we participate in absolute reality, then beauty, elegance, or charm, which we perceive as attentively as any other information, and which we replicate with remarkable nuance and fluency, is acknowledged as an active element in creation. Beauty is a conversation between humankind and reality, and we are an essential part of it, bringing to it our singular gifts of reflection and creation.

Which terms, in these few sentences, would the prevailing model of reality disallow? *Minds*, first of all. *Singular gifts*, certainly. *Reflection* by this or any other name is not a thing I have seen mentioned in the literature. Surely experience is the test for the meaningfulness of such language. Do we reflect? My Puritan considers a lovely image of the fusion of body and soul and rejects it in order to intensify it. Until death, he says, body and soul are even more indissoluble than light from space. Does the brain process this image? Or does the mind reflect on it? I have lived from birth with space and light, as we all do, and had never considered how they exist together. My mind is gratified by this new perception, just arrived from that distant star, the seventeenth century. Of course my particular mind has had a long training in attentiveness to figurative language and to Renaissance and Reformation thought as well. It has done the autonomic business of retaining, shelving, and discarding, which predisposes any mind to distinctive interpretation of any body of knowledge. The mind has proclivities, and a history. In fact, the mind *is* a history. In excluding it from acknowledged reality, the prevailing anthropology excludes our most defining experience of ourselves. This is consistent with the growing consensus that we have no selves. It is amazing how we disappear.

My theistic realism is vastly more capacious, and notoriously anthropocentric. I will quote at some length from Flavel, to demonstrate Christian humanism in full flight.

> The soul has in itself an intrinsic worth and excellency, worthy of that divine Original whence it sprang: view it in its noble faculties, and durable powers, and it will appear to be a creature upon which God has laid out the riches of his wisdom and power.
>
> There you shall find a mind susceptive of all light, both natural and spiritual, shining as the candle of God in the inner man, closing with truth, as the iron does with the attractive loadstone; a shop in which all arts and sciences are laboured and formed; what are all the famous libraries and monuments of learning, but so many systems of thoughts, laboured and perfected in the active inquisitive minds of men? Truth is its natural and delectable object; it pursues eagerly after it, and even spends itself and the body too in the chase and prosecution of truth, when it lies deep, as a subterranean treasure, the mind sends out innumerable thoughts, reinforcing each other in thick successions, to dig for, and compass that invaluable treasure, if it be disguised by misrepresentation and vulgar prejudice, and trampled in the dirt under that disguise, there is an ability in the mind to discern it by some lines and features, which are well known to it, and both own, honour, and vindicate it under all that dirt and obloquy, with more respect than a man will take up a piece of gold, or a sparkling diamond out of the mire: it searches after it by many painful deductions of reason and triumphs more in the discovery of it, than in all earthly treasures; no gratification of sense like that of the mind, when it grasps its prey for which it hunted.

He goes on with his praise for the mind, then of will and conscience, the passions and the affections. He identifies the mind with the soul and celebrates its intellectual capacities and integrity as proof of its "divine Original." In this he follows Calvin, elaborating on a famous passage in *Institutes of the Christian Religion*. Putting theology to one side, insofar as the passage permits, is he saying something true here? Is he saying something we can confirm from experience, as individuals and as sharers in the life of civilization? Is the vast conceptual space he claims for the mind necessary if a true account is to be made of it? I personally am impressed by the fact that we have sent a little spacecraft beyond the solar system. Whatever unnamed truth lies behind his words—in the next paragraph he describes the study of the heavens, as Calvin did also—his account of the mind is highly consistent with human history and culture. By comparison with this or with virtually anything that lives, the human being of the modern theoretical imagination is static as a mummy, encased in its tiny, simple repertoire of motives, oddly incapable of meaningful evolution. Again, can accretions of minor calculations of self-interest, reduced as far as theorists can manage, add up to the assertions of intellect and intention Flavel describes, assertions we see continuously throughout recorded history? Is he evoking an excitement we recognize, which is different in kind from even the most cunningly concealed motive of practical self-interest?

If our own experience of consciousness is meaningful as a basis for evaluating statements about consciousness—and why wouldn't it be?—then recognition is an important test of any model that is presented to us. Among the remarkable human traits Flavel does not mention, and which would not set well with his rapturous humanism, is a vulnerability to accepting low valuations of ourselves as individuals and groups that then become predictive. As a girl, I expected to be terrible at math and I was. This might have been true in any case. But many studies confirm this effect in many settings. We can actually stupefy ourselves and one another. Recently an undergraduate at a major university wrote about the many voices telling his generation that they would only "live, work, and die." I have encountered this sort of thing among students any number of times. I'm sure it has many sources, but I see no reason to ignore the effects of the kind of teaching they receive that undertakes to describe their own nature to them. Some instructors like to shock students out of a complacency that has effectively been gone from the world since they were students themselves. Without wishing to seem judgmental, I must say I find this sort of thing brutal and destructive, a little stupid, calculated to produce a cheap effect, an iconoclasm that amounts to no more than stomping the dust of icons long shattered. No doubt this annoys me more because the pretext for it is indefensible as science. In any case, there are studies showing that positive attitudes and circumstances can be enabling, and where legitimate it is surely the role and obligation of educators to provide them. Flavel and Calvin were both expressing the vision of the Renaissance, a period notable for intellectual fruitfulness.

Be that as it may.

Is there an intermediate position between the exaltation of Flavel and the extreme reductionism of contemporary theory? Flavel's faith assumes a brilliant Creator God whose attributes dignify and sanctify the creature made to share them. Neither language nor imagination could exceed the grandeur of human nature or the worth of the individual soul. Of course they bear the marks of the Fall, "lovely and excellent" as they are all the same, "but what shall we say, how shall we conceive of it, when all spots of sin are perfectly washed off its beautiful face in heaven, and the glory of the Lord is risen upon it!" and holiness and righteousness are "super-induced upon this excellent creature!"

Do we deserve this? Can we know? The most unambiguous proof of our significance is too disheartening to be dismissed as self-aggrandizement. We should probably stop denying that we are exceptional among the creatures, now that most of us can make a list of ways we might well put an end to it all. I am not competent to speak about religions in general, but it is certainly true that Christianity has a very potent sense of the human capacity for evil. Its humanism is anchored in the doctrines of Creation and Fall, not at all paradoxically, since as an image of God the essential dignity of humankind is uncompromised by acknowledged sinfulness. This is very much more complex, therefore truer to experience, than is allowed for in the entity offered by the theorists, the unmind and unself incapable of either good or evil. And here again the participation of humankind and of the human self in ultimate reality, assumed in religious tradition, is tacitly rejected. We know that very straight lines can be drawn between human choices and the fate of the living world. Yet nothing in this anthropology suggests that there are issues of better and worse to be engaged, choices to be made that are quite starkly moral, if anything at all is of value. I note in passing that the individualism, even solipsism, sometimes associated with experiencing oneself as a soul is a conception that entails an ethic of love and service in a world of souls, an ideal as fully excluded from modern anthropologies as is the metaphysics that supports it.

We distract ourselves from powerful, ancient intuitions of the grandeur and richness of being, and of human being, with a reductionist theoretical contraption endlessly refitted in minor ways to survive the collapse of old scientific notions that have sustained it and to present itself once more as the coming thing, with the whole history and prestige of science behind it. Those intuitions, which figure in the highest thought and art civilization has produced, are faith.

HOPE

Once a minister at my church asked the congregation to reflect on their understanding of Christian hope. A lady so tiny with age that when she stood up her hat was just visible above the pew said, "The first thing I'll do when I get to heaven, I'll run and find my grandma. She loved me so much!" Her small voice crackled with anticipation. This hope of hers was almost too confident to be called hope. But our modern understanding may have impoverished its meaning somewhat. In New Testament Greek, the word translated as *hope* seems to have meant something closer to *expectation*. In any case, some homely, profoundly beautiful thing had befallen her many decades before, and so the great drama of immortality in which she trusted was for her chiefly the occasion for one highly particular hug, scented, no doubt, with laundry starch. She imagined herself running like a child through the New Jerusalem, taking no note of its splendors, avid as a child would be for one voice, one face, one touch.

Her vision is fraught with theological difficulties. What about *judgment*? We do give this word a darker meaning than is appropriate to it. It can mean "vindication," "praise," "reward," as when the master in a parable finds a servant to be good and faithful. Nevertheless, Christians more or less assume that it is not a thing to be evaded.

The grandmother's day of judgment might have taken into account the fact that she had figured so graciously in a child's life that the memory had been cherished through long years, keeping her, child and woman, loyal to the hope of heaven. When the grandmother was younger and capable, by whatever tender human arts, of giving the child such utter confidence in her love, she probably had no idea that she was creating in the child a memory that could take its place among our conceptions of celestial things, even outshine them. Her reward might be—allowing as one can for the mysteries of time and timelessness—the extraordinary, endless moment of love given and returned.

Aha, says the skeptic. A clear case of projection of human hopes onto an indifferent cosmos. That this is a projection of human hopes is clearly true. However, that the cosmos is indifferent is not a thing that can be asserted with equal confidence. The skeptic's language implies that human beings are wholly anomalous, the universe of Being an anechoic chamber in which their songs and prayers and laughter and lament are as if nothing, a sound in their own heads, talk in a dream. If this is in fact the case, the next question must be how this verbalizing that goes on among us relates to our collective intelligence, and then why our intelligence gives us our strange, progressive access to the workings of things, notably the cosmos. Einstein and others have said that the universe is most remarkable in being comprehensible by us. And they have left the matter there. But the converse must also be true, that we are most remarkable in our ability to comprehend it. We are anomalous in being able, sometimes, in some degree, to think like the universe, so to speak, which is to say that we are bound to reality otherwise and more profoundly than our biological kindred, the beasts of the field, the birds of the air.

That we see this as making us alien within it is a choice, by no means inevitable or even logical. From an evolutionary point of view, our high intelligence is peacock feathers, a fluke that somehow eluded the threshing and sifting of the demands of survival until it became instrumental in our survival. There seems to be a suppressed teleology in this, wholly at odds with evolutionary theory, as if the big head and long helplessness of the first fully human infant prepared for the day, millennia in coming, when the capacities potential in her or him were sufficiently realized to compensate for these extreme vulnerabilities. There is no need to account in evolutionary terms for the very many things that are singular about us—by the lights of this schema, which is very rigorous except when it is not. By its mode of reckoning, everything about us that can be interpreted by them as promoting the survival and propagation of the individual organism is acknowledged and accounted for, while whatever remains—for example, our tendency to wonder about our place in the universe—is somehow extraneous. And what is evolutionary theory but one major branch of the great human project of pondering just this question? Its exponents should have some insight into the impulses that drive us to expend our energies and resources mulling such things, and some insight into why these theorists assume that they can unriddle, meaningfully reduce, such a high order of complexity. This would certainly be the task of attributes their anthropology cannot describe.

•

I return so often to this modern school of thought because it is very widely influential and because it is such a profound deflation of the idea of the human that where it is assumed, there are no terms for speaking meaningfully about our epochal species, individually or as a whole. One reads that by its lights we have neither minds nor souls. Consider what we mean by the words *mindless* and *soulless*, and how reduced a human being would have to seem in our eyes before we could begin to justify the use of such language. If we began to realize that he was in fact capable of grief, or loneliness, or loyalty, we would be ashamed of the estimate we had made of him. Yet we are told that humankind altogether is to be thought of in just these terms. As a consequence, we have become inarticulate in speaking and writing about the mind as the stream of reflection and emotion that it is. At the same time that we rejected the conception of a God who could be called loving or passionate, we ceased to attend to like qualities in ourselves. Even to speak of God as "living" is to imply attentiveness with its consequences, qualified by righteousness and by love. The modern anthropology cannot capture the vital individuality of a human being. Absent the great analogy, that we are images of God, we hardly seem to know what we are.

•

To stand apart from what we are and consider ourselves. This is definitively human. It is also definitively human to be grossly wrong, about ourselves first of all. Modern thought is represented as having escaped, and renounced, the errors of the past. This means, whatever else, that our propensity to err, even catastrophically, is conceded. The concession does not in any way reduce our liability to further error, a fact far too seldom taken into account. Early Darwinism was the handmaiden of racial science. Early genetics was the handmaiden of eugenics. I will not mention nuclear energy, and its crude and naïve beginnings, whose consequences will play themselves out literally forever. The horrible children of half-baked science are the result of misplaced optimism, confidence so insistent on its own justification that it scorns reasonable doubt. This while it prides itself on rigorous skepticism.

But my subject is hope, the theological virtue, which I would distinguish very sharply from what I have called optimism. Hope implies a felt lack, an absence, a yearning. Come quickly, Lord Jesus. The father of the prodigal son hopes for his return. We know that he watches for him. Nothing in the parable implies that he has any grounds for confidence that his son will return, certainly nothing we know about the young man's character or affection for his family. In fact the father's hope is based solely on his love for his son. He yearns for a wholeness only his son can supply. If his son, finally returned, is no better than he was when he left, his father will hope for some glimpse of a sign that this is not only or always or essentially true. Hope is loyalty. It seems that earthly love is always compounded with hope.

Skeptics say the religious project their feelings onto an empty heaven. It is important to consider what these feelings are, how they exist in the world of things, as they certainly do. Love is in its nature projected, a spontaneous assertion of one's own perception on an earthly reality, a reality that could as well be called empty, at least indifferent. This is the sociopathic view. It is entirely possible, in fact very common, to love where there is no trace of reciprocity, and no prospect of it. If the rebel Absalom had returned to his father, David, and asked his forgiveness, this would have answered a hope of David's, certainly. If Absalom had only survived his insurrection, David's most desperate hope would have been fulfilled. Neither of these things happen, and David's love for his son is undiminished. If love is greater than hope, as Paul says it is, this may be true in part because love is prior to hope, a condition of it, and is fulfilled when hope falls away, fulfilled, if in fact it ever is fulfilled. Again, I am speaking of hope the theological virtue that ranks with faith and love, not of any transient, casual state of mind that might be called by the same name. That tiny lady I mentioned, whose expectations have been long since put to the test, had built her conception of heaven around a hope of restored and renewed love. I believe this is often the case, whether the object of love is a person or an idea or God himself. Love never ends, the apostle tells us. Projected forward it is hope. What it would be, fully realized, we can imagine only because we experience hope as absence. Blessed are you who hunger and thirst after righteousness, for you shall be filled. Blessed are you who mourn, for you shall be comforted.

I mentioned the sociopathic view of things, which sees the world as valueless, as exciting neither affection nor loyalty. Then there is the sort of person who loves and is loyal, even, so it might appear to others, in defiance of common sense—King

David, the father in the parable. And, by implication, God the Father. In human terms, who has the better sense of reality, the man who knows about love only by report, or the man who, in the face of a terrible betrayal, will still say, "My son, my son"? Granting that this is the father we would all wish to find waiting for us, does this mean the hope is baseless, a delusion to which we are attracted, or subject, because we are aliens in the universe? But what possible grounds do we have for saying that we are, in fact, aliens? If nature, in the reductionist sense, is all there is, then we can only be fully as much a part of it as a mollusk or a stone. If reality is to be thought of as saturated with a strange brilliance, as science that does actual research continuously tells us it is, then we are very much a part of that. And if we are an exceptional expression of a pervasive brilliance, a creature uniquely suited to knowing—that is, to science—then we should feel a certain respect for our means of knowing, fallible as they always are. Our ideas are subjective, inescapably influenced by circumstance, *but we are not absolutely trapped in our subjectivity because our minds project an expectation, an estimate or a hypothesis that seems plausible to us, imposing it on everything we perceive.* Over time we may unlearn our first projections through experience and instruction or by contextualizing them among ideas that seem more plausible or that we accept as confirmed. This is a normal strategy of consciousness, the opening engagement of inquiry with its object.

The important point is that projection is the other side of subjectivity, the bringing to bear of intuition, induction, and existing knowledge on whatever we perceive, in the always wider sense that the word *perceive* must be granted. Scientists say now that the emergence of the planetary system occurred in a much shorter span of time than had been assumed, in perhaps three million years rather than hundreds of millions. The chain of reasoning that lies behind this spectacular revision downward began with evidence of magnetic polarization in a meteor. Only recently has it been possible to find such evidence. Our powers of perception continuously deepen and expand, leaving us always with the familiar problem of understanding our discoveries in light of existing knowledge and reasonable interpretation, knowing, of course, that both of these will be modified, perhaps radically.

Let us say that religions explore the ancient human intuition that there is an energy behind experience, something not sufficiently like the reality accessible to us to be captured in the language that has developed to accommodate ordinary experience. Projection is our method of inquiry, the grounds of speculation and hypothesis. For millennia no one would have imagined that we might sometime literally read the history of the universe in a stone. Given time and the basic integrity of civilization, there is no way to set any limit to what we might sometime know about physical reality. Nor will there be any way, if the project is carried on for a million years, to know what will still be unknown, which it is prudent to assume will be almost everything. If science sometime answers the question of the existence of other universes—and the answer is not no, which could never be more than a tentative conclusion, since their nonexistence might look exactly like their inaccessibility—then every question opens again about their physics and chemistry, not to mention their origins and duration. If three or five are proximate in some sense of the word, how many are there at, so to speak, a further remove? Are the ones we might access typical of their kind? With what confidence could we generalize from our sample? These are all reasonable questions that our scientists may sometime be in a position to address. First they would project on these new systems of Being everything experience taught them to expect. Then they would modify expectation as circumstances required, and as their resources permitted, though, we may assume, never sufficiently.

My point is simply this. We can easily imagine that our brilliance and ingenuity are so great they will finally find their way to their own limits. Then let us assume a reality of another order in which all this glory and mystery and force is comprehended, as ancient Hebrews and as Christian metaphysicians have done. The voices of the Bible magnify the Lord. He is enthroned on the praises of Israel. For millennia these voices have prepared the way for our grasp of this exuberantly limitless universe in which as a planet we are minute to the point of disappearance and as a species we are as passing as a breath. If we did not know our nature and situation, they would seem flatly implausible. But here we are. We are in fact proof that plausibility is a meaningful standard within special circumstances only. Yes, we cannot resist the pull of gravity, and no, we cannot really take in the fact that our cluster of galaxies is flying at 392,000 miles per second toward something called the Great Attractor, driven in part by pressure from an expanding void. Reality on its grandest scale bears no analogy to daily life here on our singular, weather-swaddled little earth. But there it is, and here we are, the great rush of the cosmos silent and impalpable to us. And within our starry calm exotic things can flourish that are unimaginable without it—history, memory, hope and doubt, love and loss, good and evil, and, less abstractly, tiny old women who are vesicles for all of them. We might praise the fruitfulness of the ground and the general constancy of the seasons more rapturously than even the psalmist did, knowing what he could hardly know, that reality is overwhelmingly of another kind, and that this earth is so minor an exception to the generality of things that it is insignificant in any account of the universe, unless, of course, it is the very quintessence of significance.

If the second view of it is granted, and, more broadly, this view of the special circumstances that make it fecund and allow for its endless effusions of elegance and variety, including among them humankind, then the so-called indifferent cosmos—vast and cold and fiery as it is, ancient as it is, enthralled as it is by forces we as yet can't name or describe—seems the wrong place to look for evidence of divine interest in our world. This is not to say that the whole cosmic arrangement is outside the reach of Providence. It is only to say that the world is indeed a stage. Things happen here, under this roof, fretted with golden fire—improvisations on themes of hope and fear, dread and hatred and love. Curtains rise on lives and civilizations, things happen, and curtains fall. Centuries seem like a stately dramatic convention over against the wheeling eons that roar beyond this strange little theater, where words and actions are bracketed by the assumption that they can matter. How can this be true? But it is. How can passions and emotions script our brief hour? But they do.

Of course the old conceits about the indifferent cosmos and the empty heavens are condescensions. They impose crude notions of the worship of a sky god on cultures of remarkable subtlety and brilliance, which happen also to be a great part of our heritage. Those who dislike religion assume that it is primitive, the kind of error or nostalgia people who are modern and enlightened should be ashamed to persist in. And many don't persist, a testament to the power of shaming. But a truer reckoning, one that looked at the life we so ironically call mundane, would vindicate the wisdom of every soul who ever said a grace over her supper.

•

Religious hope is often thought of, even by religious people, as an evasion of plain, brute death. Death is truly a fearful thing. Then again, traditional Christianity has taught that survival beyond death also has its perils—judgment, hell, Purgatory in Catholicism. And narrow is the path. Many people who believe that omniscient scrutiny will be brought to bear on their earthly lives would actually prefer extinction, to avoid what must be called embarrassment. Christianity would have softened its worldview instantly by offering extinction as one possibility. It would also have weakened the essential thing implied by the teaching of endless damnation—that what we do or fail to do really, really matters. How this fact could be underscored more boldly can hardly be imagined, except in Jesus's saying that he is hungry with the hungry, imprisoned with the prisoner, and is himself denied whenever they are denied. Then the day of judgment is any day, every day. We choose between self and Christ as individuals and as citizens continuously, a truth that should either sanctify the world to us or give us a bad scare. Probably both.

This has everything to do with hope. It means Christ is in the world and we actually can do right by him. How can this be true? I know I look on the more glorious assertions of my religion with confidence enhanced by the shallowness of arguments against them. I believe an assertion that is simultaneously an ethos and an aesthetic is true in every important sense of the word. It means that a profounder communion than Communion itself is offered to us, because in the least of these, however least is reckoned, Christ is present, body and blood. It means that, as godliness is the height of our aspirations, complicated by our fallibility but sometimes approached by God's grace, so our moments of deepest vulnerability cannot reduce us to less than utter sacredness. The crimes we suffer and the crimes we do are all assaults on holiness. Knowing this, if we could ever really know it, would make us Christians, respectful of ourselves and reverent toward the world.

If so very much is at stake, what follows? That absolute values are invested in the world, and that, because they are shared by God, they are absolutely real, as our possessions and attainments, our suffering and sorrow, are circumstantial and transitory. We can hunger and thirst after righteousness, hoping to be filled, because righteousness will outlive greed and oppression, and we will live in the unclouded radiance of God's most gracious justice. Like David, like the father in the parable, like the lady in my anecdote, we can hunger and thirst for love, too, whether it is scorned and frustrated, or still only possible, or deeply remembered, because, we are told, God is love. I said we can hunger and thirst. I mean we do hunger and thirst, because we bear a likeness to God. We are a part of this ultimate reality and by nature we participate in eternal things—justice, truth, compassion, love. We have a vision of these things we have not arrived at by reason, have rarely learned from experience, have not found in history. We feel the lack. Hope leads us toward them.

•

Scripture tells us that we can ourselves vindicate hope by our loyalty to the more profound reality with which the world is invested. When Jesus says we are to love one another, he is telling us to serve one another, to feed and clothe, to visit, to bless—to be aware of other's hopes and to honor them. Who is my neighbor? We know, two thousand years on, that this question is by no means rhetorical. There are whole political parties ready to tell us how much harm can come from the indiscriminate sharing of loaves and fishes. Meanwhile, hopes of just the kind to arouse God's compassion somehow don't stir ours. King Lear, cast out on the heath, feeling what wretches feel, calls on "pomp," wealth, to "shake down the superflux and show the heavens more just." This gives rise to an alarming thought. Greed, even indifference, imperils God's good name among, for example, workers whose pay is stinted or the poor to whom justice is denied. Then a kind of blasphemy is added to the flouting of law and gospel. "Let your works so shine before men that, seeing them, they praise God." Then, what if men see no works, or if such as they see are stingy or grudging? The hopes that moved Christ, that a child or a friend or a brother might live and be well, are disappointed day after day, because we stand between grave need and gracious heaven. We are dishonest stewards. But we all know this. If we are God's stewards, that means he has placed his hope in us, his loving hope for the well-being of that population always present to him, widows, orphans, strangers, laborers—the whole nation of the poor, one by one. Scripture calls him a living God. The thing that can give hope a kind of bitterness is that it is also living, constantly and intensely vulnerable, an opening to the possibility, or probability, of disappointment. Scripture is full of divine disappointment—"Can you not watch with me one hour?" The most indubitable proof of human freedom is that in general we prefer to sleep, and do sleep.

As I have said, this sort of thinking is ordinarily dismissed as anthropomorphic, the projection of human traits onto an empty heaven. Of course there is also the important projection of human preferences onto an ancient text. It is instructive to note how very far these differ from the God of light and hope, exactly as if that very human question "Who is my neighbor?" were never answered. Still, if we imagine an injured man lying by the road, we will imagine also the hope that would arise in him when he heard voices or footsteps, and the sinking away of hope as they approached, then passed.

Life is largely an instruction in emotions of this kind, generally slight and transient enough to inoculate us a little against the greater shocks that will surely come. Perhaps if all the hope in the world, large and small, were made visible, creation would appear as tense as a strung bow. We may all live in anticipation more than in present time, worry and dread pulling us out of the moment, too, but hope giving us better purpose, the imagination of what might fall into place, to our benefit or satisfaction. Hope shapes intention. It leaves improbable possibilities open, which means that it influences the unfolding of future time. No one knows what time is, of course, but insofar as it is a stream of events influenced by earlier events—giving this word its broadest meaning—then, say, leaving the light on and supper in the oven might mean that anger would not end in alienation and all its consequences. In this instance the future would be different from what it might have been. Say a thousand small accommodations of hope were made in any city in any one day, as no doubt they would be, and many more besides. Then the sun would rise again on an ordinary day, different in a thousand unremarked particulars from the ordinary day it would have risen on otherwise. There would be hope vindicated and rewarded, hope waiting or lingering, hope thwarted. Each of these would have its consequences, threaded imperceptibly through ordinary time, changing time as I have defined it here. This is to say that whatever the future is, we have a certain purchase on it, far less by intention than in the unself-conscious expression of our nature. Hope is our capacity to predispose events to take a certain turn, by preparing for it or by recognizing tendencies favorable to it. This sounds like a cheering commonplace. But if futurity, time that is not yet present but will be, is an aspect of cosmic reality, like the decay products that will displace radioactive isotopes, then our acting on the future intentionally or not puts us in an effective relationship with an aspect of cosmic reality. So how alien from it can we actually be?

I absolutely do not wish to suggest some power of positive thinking. Hope is profoundly vulnerable to disappointment, as I have said. I am simply considering how a human capacity interacts with the given world. Most of what we do, we do with reference to an hour from now or a year from now. No matter whether we do what we intend to do well or badly, whether or not we are actually preparing what we intend, we are giving future time its character, its burden. One of my old Puritans proposed that we might be judged twice, once at our death and once when the full effects of our lives had played themselves out, specifically when every crude or false or slanderous thing we have said is gone from every living mind. This is another way of making the same point. Slurs on vulnerable people affect the future of whole societies, as surely as they did their past. On this little ball of earth, where action and inaction, speech and silence all have consequences, we are, I would say, a special instance of cosmic time. We inhabit it differently from creatures who are without our strange efficacy. We exist in it differently from the wheeling constellations. In a remarkable degree, for the purposes of this planet, we create it. Religion is an intuition that in this respect the cosmos, for our purposes, is neither indifferent nor inhuman. This means what we really ought to know by now, that our moral choices, the resort to violence, exploitation of the vulnerable, our allowing populations to experience loss, despair, and bitterness, such things impact reality profoundly and irreversibly. Time for human purposes might more closely resemble a mind, a vast memory, or a troubled, self-protective conscience than "the ticking of eternity," to quote Edna St. Vincent Millay. The modern theories of the self take no account of history. Their dehumanization of Being is total. So our impact, our history, cannot be acknowledged, though it could bring virtually every form of life to an end.

Again, while it is no doubt true that if we encouraged better hopes in ourselves the whole thing would last longer, this is not the point I wish to make. My point is that the ancient intuition that creation has some profound business with us, that we are by no means aliens in this world however eccentric our presence in it, in fact *because* we are an eccentric presence in it, is sound. If this is granted, many things follow, one of them being the presumption of the validity of categories of human experience, for example, beauty, meaning, good, and evil. Another being the essential, irreducible interest and value of the human person and of human life. There is no baseline reality over against which human reality can be called less real, however radically unlike they are, and because they are radically unlike. Our errors and illusions can have all the potency of floods and famines. Truth can never really be said to come naturally to us, yet we as a species seem to be alone with the concept of truth. This little Eden, earth, is an exception to the universe, still and temperate amid unimaginable extremes of heat and cold and barrenness, where great rivers of matter pour through spaces so vast that their inconceivable velocity seems to change nothing. And we, on earth, are again exceptional, a simple fact that should not be omitted from any account of us simply because it makes us indescribable in the terms we propose, rightly or wrongly, for the understanding of other creatures.

I propose that a radical anthropocentricity amounts to nothing more than facing facts. I know some people take this as grounds for callous assertions of our dominance over the biosphere—in defiance of that very human thing common sense, not to mention human moral standards, which we are clearly free to ignore but which generally restrain most of us. This is an absurd leap, which lands anthropocentricity in the same place as the notion that we are beasts among the beasts, loyal only to our genes. That so many of us are strongly inclined to gain the whole world while losing our own souls is a bias of our nature, which can rationalize itself without the help of any particular theory.

I have not forgotten my tiny old lady and her enduring love, which is the basis and substance of her hope. Let us say that in the sphere of Being that allows us life, where, remarkably, what we do matters, it is also true that *we* matter, that our little world of evening and morning is as providential as it has seemed to other generations on far slighter grounds than our science has provided to us. *Providential* means both "free" and "arbitrary."

Let there be and there was. Paul says love will not pass away. John says God is love. At best, hope is an intuition that this could be true, with the kind of essential truth affirmed in eternity, in the Being of God, who is in infinite ways more anomalous even than we are, more improbable even than we are, judged in the terms of a reductionism that is infinitely less useful in his case than in ours. Say that in our difference from everything else we and God are like each other—creative, knowing, efficacious, deeply capable of loyalty. Say that in his healing and feeding and teaching, Jesus let us see that the good that matters to mortal us matters also to eternal God. Then we have every reason to hope.

LOVE

God is love. These words, which appear twice in the First Epistle of John, are dauntingly vast in their implications. Clearly the writer intended that they should be. His letter begins with a theological or metaphysical statement very like the opening passage of the Gospel according to John, but even by that standard, luminous with a singular witness. "That which was from the beginning, which we have heard, which we have seen with our eyes, have looked upon and touched with our hands——." This John, perhaps the disciple in his old age, writes with astonishment that Jesus was seen and touched, that these most ordinary things were true of him. If his words recall the accounts other disciples made of their encounters with Jesus after his resurrection, this would only make the point that the Jesus who lived was the Jesus who was resurrected——"the life was made manifest, and we saw it, and testify to it, and proclaim to you the eternal life which was with the Father and was made manifest to us——."

On the basis of his friendship with Jesus, John makes an absolute statement about the nature of God. At the same time, he very powerfully evokes the fleshly humanity of Jesus, in whom, through whom, this statement is justified. Some scholars say John was writing to counter Docetism, an early heresy that understood Jesus as purely spiritual. There is a tendency among scholars to interpret a text by placing another narrative beside it that makes its language and content evidence of a rhetorical or polemical strategy. So John is writing to reinforce a tenet of the new faith. This is clearly true. Still, the implications of this kind of scholarly interpretation are more important than they appear. John might well be responding to an early misunderstanding of a claim that is never readily grasped, perhaps never really grasped at all, though familiarity can dull anyone's

sense of the strangeness of it. Then again, he might be expressing his own abiding wonder at his friend's presence through all
those silent years before his life became remarkable enough to
leave an account or a record, the years when Jesus, his voice as
yet unheard in the street, lived the humble life that brought
him to his epochal death.

A theory set beside a biblical text or any text might be true
enough in its own way and yet distract from the actual significance of the thing it is meant to explain. Imagine a caller to
911 saying, "Help! Help! My house is on fire and my dog and
my Picasso are both inside!" The responder could say, with ac-
curacy, that the caller had employed familiar rhetorical strategies, including repetition and volume, to convey an anxiety
about the potential loss of items of material and emotional
value characteristic of calls of this genre (engaging in hyperbole, perhaps, since it is unlikely that he owns a Picasso) as well
as his desire for urgent attention to this problem, also typical.
But this would involve a substantial loss of meaning. To read
John's testimony as essentially controversial, an insistence on a
point of doctrine, a shoring up of orthodoxy, rather than as a
record of his own amazed remembrance, is among other things
a retrojection of later concerns of the church onto its earliest,
formative generation, as if it would already be alert to threats
to itself as an institution. That fault lines began to emerge early
is not surprising, considering the rapid spread of the faith into
distant cultures where its original basis in Judaism would not
have had the strong influence it had in Judea. (I know Judaism
in the modern sense did not exist before the destruction of
Jerusalem in 70 C.E. But it seems as good a term as any for the
religious culture that would become Judaism.) That these de-
partures from Johannine, Pauline, and Petrine teaching took
form as competing doctrines might be expected as well. This
does not mean that John is addressing them here. The striking
thing about John's letter is not simply the assertion that he and

others who had known Jesus could attest to the fact that he was indeed a human being. It is that someone John had known as a brother and teacher was also a profound, direct revelation of God, and this enabled John to speak of God with utter confidence and authority, and joy as well. It is not the divine attributes of Jesus—his teaching, his healing, his miracles, even his resurrection—that must be insisted upon and that are remembered as things to be wondered at. It is that Jesus could be seen and touched. Very God had been embodied in a human being, a human life, one so fully human that he could and did pass in the street unremarked.

Clearly the Jewish world of the time was full of pious young men. By pious I mean good. It is a peculiarity of our time that I am obliged to make this clear. Jesus, in the tradition of the prophets, attacked self-righteousness and hypocrisy. This should not obscure the fact that even imperfect or occasional or, for that matter, merely habitual obedience to the Law of Moses that required love of the neighbor, love of the stranger, justice and generosity to the poor, days of rest, and so on would sustain a culture vastly gentler than most, ancient or modern. Then there is the fact that Judaism was under pressure from military occupation by the world's greatest power and from the influence and prestige of Hellenism, so that the best way for them to protect the life of their faith was to live their faith. While this is always true, their circumstances would have strongly encouraged the choice. To do this would have required learning and reflection of the kind Paul boasts of having experienced as a young Pharisee. Paul is himself evidence of sometimes inappropriate zeal, of course, no doubt driven by exactly these pressures.

At the synagogue in Nazareth Jesus is given the book of the prophet Isaiah to read from, the greatest of all prophets of justice and liberation. So we know that his fellow Jews maintained their faith in a God who cared for the afflicted and the brokenhearted. Jesus, as he tended to do, widened the circle of God's compassion, noting that according to their own scriptures mercy had been shown to foreigners and pagans. Instantly the people turned from praise to violent hostility, thinking quite reasonably that the oracle of rescue and restoration was a promise made to them, to embattled Zion. There is an irony in this kind of response, after the hearing of this tender and beautiful poetry, that is a thumbnail history of the reception of Scripture in every generation. Nevertheless, we learn from this moment that Jesus, a pious young man with no learning and no status, was teaching in the synagogues, and that the voice of God being heard there was full of tenderness and love, a singular truth that was always the treasure of the children of Abraham. Cf., as they say, Baal or Ishtar. So let us say that Jesus could have been very virtuous, living consistently by the light of the law and the prophets, and yet have drawn no particular attention to himself.

I must say I am pleased by the thought that youths moved by loyalty and patriotism, and justified anxiety as well, would be diligent students of love. It is important to remember that the two commandments Jesus names as most important were given that status by Jewish scholars before him, so no scrupulous adherent could overlook them. Cultures differ radically in the things they permit and the things they forbid, even tacitly, and ours has made it very difficult to speak about love. What does it mean to love an enemy? What meaning can the word have when it is applied so generally? Though Jesus widened the circle to embrace enemies, those who, by definition, were a clear threat to the community, or to his hearers as individuals, even those who rejected this teaching would no doubt know better than we do what it would mean, what it would require. Presumably if he or she decided to accept Jesus's restatement of the law, she or he would be able to fulfill it more satisfactorily than we can.

All this is to say that perhaps Jesus was born when he was because at that moment Judaism was in a state of intense life, as a body of learning and an ethic, that made Jesus's teaching important and comprehensible—to a very few, of course, and to them very imperfectly, and yet as fully as it would ever be comprehended anywhere on earth.

•

I know that many Christians make a distinction between "the God of the Old Testament" and "the God of the New Testament," very much to the detriment of the former. The name of this heresy is Manichaeanism. It is widespread and well established now. It posits two gods in perpetual conflict, one good and one—the Creator God—evil. However modified in deference to monotheism, this idea is embedded in much modern scholarship. A great many among us feel an emphatic moral superiority to the God of Abraham, Isaac, and Jacob. This is surely bizarre, since to say the least Jesus shows no impulse at all to dissociate himself from him.

There is, however, a great realism in the Old Testament. It looks with a clear eye and, often, with a broken heart at the agonies of history, and it insists on wresting them into a frame of meaning. To make the Testaments equivalent as theologies of history, we must consider what the New Testament would be if it went on to chronicle the Crusades and the Inquisition, and did so with comparable honesty and realism.

There are problems of translation that are the persistence of words whose meanings have changed since they became classic or at least conventional. One of these is, of course, *love—agape* in Greek, *caritas* in Latin, and then, in English, *charity*, a word which, sadly, has acquired a meaning having no inevitable connection at all with love. Then there is *jealous, jealousy. Jealous* and *zealous* come from the same Greek word, in the pre-Christian translation of the Old Testament called the Septuagint. They were once synonyms. Jewish translations render the corresponding Hebrew word as *impassioned* or *passionate*, which was an early meaning of the word *jealous*, and is still sometimes used in phrases such as "jealous of one's reputation," meaning intensely aware and protective of it. We see the word in Scripture and assume that the Old Testament God is governed by an emotion we are ashamed to find in ourselves. I am entirely sympathetic with attempts to preserve the classic language of the Bible, but when it is gravely misleading, not only with reference to the Hebrew Bible but even as it might have been read in English two or three centuries ago, then it should be changed. *Jealous* in its modern sense is deeply disparaging. It seems to justify the conception of the God of the Old Testament as crude and primitive, as many writers on the subject now assume that he was—and this, besides distorting Christianity, mightily encourages disrespect for Judaism.

There is solid evidence that love was central to Judaism before Jesus, which is in turn evidence of their conception of God. You shall love the Lord your God with all your heart, mind, and strength, and your neighbor as yourself—both of these greatest commandments turn on that word *love*, so obedience to them would require a very real understanding of its meaning. In the Gospel according to Matthew, when a young man asks Jesus what he must do to have eternal life, Jesus quotes from the Ten Commandments and from Leviticus: "Thou shalt love thy neighbor as thyself." The young man says, "All these I have observed," obviously long familiar with them all. Later in Matthew, Pharisees and Sadducees intend to "entangle [Jesus] in his talk." A lawyer asks Jesus what is the greatest commandment. Jesus answers the question a little differently here than in other places. He names "the great and first commandment," and then the second, which he says is "like it." In the Gospel according to Mark, Jesus quotes these commandments in response to a question put to him by a scribe. This again occurs in a context in which Pharisees and others try to "entrap him in his talk," speaking to him as men of learning might speak to someone less favored than they. The scribe who has put the question tells him he has answered well, elaborating on Jesus's straightforward answer, perhaps with a certain pedagogical intent. Jesus approves the scribe's words from a higher plane than learnedness. He says, "You are not far from the kingdom of God." This assertion has the effect of a striking reversal of authority. His questioners go away, not daring to question further. In Luke, again a lawyer tests him, asking him what he should do "to inherit eternal life." Jesus replies with a question: "What is written in the law? How do you read?" The lawyer replies with the two commandments, and Jesus says, "You have answered right." This exchange leads to the question "Who is my neighbor?" and the Parable of the Good Samaritan.

These could all be versions of one moment, or of separate moments. That they recur in three Gospels reflects the importance of this construction of Scripture in Jesus's time. Clearly there is a "right answer," an interpretation already established among the religiously instructed before Jesus has repeated it and endorsed it. Otherwise it would not be so consistently represented, and remembered by his tradition, as a test of his understanding. It should be noted that the fact of Jesus's affirming the status of this commandment on the basis of his unique authority means that the scribes, Pharisees, and the rest had indeed arrived at a true understanding of the essence of Scripture.

From the point of view of Scripture, his answer is not obvious. The first commandment comes from the great assertion of God's nature—he is one—and of his profound relationship with Israel. This great commandment is given at a dramatic and definitive moment in the history of their faith and nation. What in every instance is called the second-greatest commandment is really only a part of a verse, Leviticus 19:18, which appears without special emphasis in a list of the kind one finds in Leviticus. Here is the whole verse: "You shall not take vengeance or bear any grudge against the sons of your own people, but you shall love your neighbor as yourself: I am the Lord." In its entirety, it seems to suggest that the love it commands might be selective, intended for "the sons of your own people" and amounting to a ban on revenge against them. So the stripping of the verse down to one phrase, making the commandment general or universal, is an interpretive choice already made before Jesus's ministry began, and is already authoritative. Two things should be noted: First, the other laws that provide the verse's immediate context are compassionate provision for the hired laborer, the poor, and the sojourner, without any narrower definition. And second, another verse in the series, Leviticus 19:33–34, says: "When a stranger sojourns with you in your land, you shall not do him wrong. The stranger who sojourns with you shall be to you as the native among you, and you shall love him as yourself; for you were strangers in the land of Egypt: I am the Lord your God." When the same language requires the same response to neighbor and to stranger, which here clearly means foreigner, this might well encourage the more generalized reading the verse by itself does not sustain. The lawyer asks, "Who is my neighbor?" On the basis of the first verse he might have taken the word to mean a son of his own people. But this reading is never implied. Jesus's parable expands the word *neighbor* to include foreigners, presumptive enemies—anyone, in effect, toward whom one acts lovingly, which ought to be anyone at all. When he does this, he appears to be carrying further a kind of interpretation already made of this commandment.

The one thing to be noted above all is that Scriptural interpretation in this period had settled on one phrase in one verse out of the hundreds and hundreds of laws in the Law of Moses, and set it beside the mighty, defining "Hear, O Israel," spoken by Moses after he has given them the Ten Commandments, and in anticipation of their entry into the promised land. Jesus again approves the pairing of the two, saying that the second of them is like the first, when on their face, in the matter of their provenance and the rhetorical emphasis given to them in the text, the two are radically unlike. Yet here we have Pharisees, Sadducees, scribes, and lawyers all of one mind in virtually equating them. Christian interpretation of the Judaism of the period tends to treat it as legalistic in a negative sense, minutely scrupulous about inessential things. It would take attentive scholarship, certainly, to have singled out the commandment to love one's neighbor in Leviticus and to have decided what was essential in it. No doubt considerable consultation would have been required to have arrived at a consensus about its singular importance. And Jesus says that on these two commandments hang the law and the prophets. All this is to make three points: that Jesus shared and participated in this tendency in Jewish thought, which may go back no further than to his much older contemporary Hillel; that the pressures under which Judaism lived in this period drove its thought toward the center of its faith rather than toward ceremonial peripheries; and that the richness of such thought supported the teaching of Jesus, his disciples, and their movement.

What were they all talking about? First, that one must be consumed in the fullness of one's humanity by the love of God, and second, that one should extend the fullest possible love to other people—an undefined group larger than the circle of those whom, in best cases, it is simply natural to love. The placement of this commandment, its pairing with the highest and most solemn of all laws, precludes any reading of it that would make it circumscribed or trivial. The questions with which we are left are: What does it mean to love God, and what does it mean to love another human being? John makes it clear when the claim to love is spurious. He says, "If anyone has the world's goods and sees his brother in need, yet closes his heart against him, how does God's love abide in him?" The Samaritan of the parable shows very practical consideration for the needs of the stranger he finds by the road. That is, he very impractically sets no limit to his own generosity. After providing for the stranger's immediate care, he says he will return to pay any costs that exceed the amount he has left with the innkeeper. Would he know the innkeeper could be trusted? Certainly the parable suggests that prudence, that is to say, considerations of self-interest, should not be brought to bear when demands are made on one's kindness and generosity. How we have struggled with this! Far more than with the sins we are so much readier to renounce, denounce, dramatize, scorn, conceal, and confess. And this sin, the withholding of kindness and generosity—*love* is the crucial word in this context—structures entire social systems and philosophies. In his letter, James says, "If a brother or sister is ill-clad and in lack of daily food, and one of you says to them, 'Go in peace, be warmed and filled,' without giving them the things needed for the body, what does it profit?" The pious inflection he mimics would have been familiar at any point in history. The Law of Moses makes specific, ongoing provision for the alleviation of poverty, rarely noted. The Hebrew prophets are passionate on the subject, also treating it as the standard by which faith can be tested, and the offense by which the favor of God can be lost. Ezekiel 16:49 says, "Behold, this is the guilt of your sister Sodom: she and her daughters had pride, surfeit of food, and prosperous ease, but did not aid the poor and needy." This is a good illustration of the fact that there are certain sins as well as certain texts we choose not to dwell on.

Is any of this relevant to our times? It is always relevant to any time. Thomas Aquinas quotes Ambrose: "It is the hungry man's bread that you detain; the naked man's cloak that you store away; the poor man's ransom and freedom that is in the money which you bury in the ground." And, "He who spends too much is a robber." And, "It is no less a crime to refuse to help the needy when you are able and prosperous than it is to take away someone else's property." Economic polarization was perhaps more visible in his world than in ours, for those of us who live in wealthier countries away from the war zones, though it is certainly here, too. There is now a great deal of prestige associated with being far wealthier than anyone ought to be.

I haven't wandered from my subject. I am simply pondering the fact that in Scripture the proof of loving God is so typically material generosity toward those in need, together with the fact that the burden they are taken to be always feels new and onerous to us. A particular, tender solicitude is characteristic of God, from the Law of Moses, where he insists that the poor man should have a garment to sleep under; to the prophecy of Isaiah, which foresees a blessed time when there will no longer be infants who live only a few days; to Jesus's promise of rest to those who labor and are heavy laden, and his explicit identification with the hungry, the naked, the thirsty, the imprisoned. While the Code of Hammurabi includes some humane laws among many others, it was claimed by that king as his work, his wisdom. *Divine* origins are claimed for the Law of Moses, which is therefore a revelation of the divine nature. "Thou shall not suffer a witch to live" is a problem from this point of view, supporting a dark vision of the Old Testament God. And it is also, of all these laws, one Christendom embraced and applied over centuries with notorious zeal, oblivious to those limits on punishments, notably for theft, which would have saved hundreds of thousands of European lives, or those laws against theft of human beings, which would have saved millions of African lives. Selection and emphasis are of obvious significance, and, as I have said, Judaism in the time of Jesus had chosen from the mass of the Torah, and identified as the essence of it, a single sentence from a single verse: "You shall love your neighbor as yourself."

•

The movement that came to be called Christianity is reflected in its earliest days in the Epistles. It spread into the ancient world before the Gospels were written. So the letters to these early congregations give us a sense of what first attracted people to the movement. The letters are very highly ethical. Their ethos is summed up by Peter in two words: "Honor everyone." James gives these instructions: "If you really fulfill the royal law, according to the scripture, 'You shall love your neighbor as yourself,' you do well. But if you show partiality, you commit sin, and are convicted by the law as transgressors." By partiality he means favoritism toward the rich. He is emphatic on this point. By the scriptures he means the law and the prophets, since the Christian Scriptures would not have existed at this point. His egalitarianism and his ethics are based in the divine image, which makes the honor owed to God and that owed to men simultaneous. He says of the tongue, "With it we bless the Lord and Father, and with it we curse men, who are made in the likeness of God. From the same mouth come blessing and cursing. My brethren, this ought not to be so." The Divine Being and human beings participate in one holiness. That this can be true, that it is true, is a great part of the meaning of the Incarnation of Christ and the human life and death of Jesus of Nazareth.

It must have been wonderful to live in the newness of the faith, when John's words could still remind his hearers what it was to see with their eyes and touch with their hands those likenesses of God among whom *they* were passing *their* lives. I didn't intend to write an essay quite so dependent on Scripture as this one is. I know there are a great many people for whom the Bible has far less interest and authority than it has for me, many people now to whom it seems alien and incomprehensible. All this is compounded by the fact that there is a large, loud faction who represent themselves as Christians while speaking and acting with such contempt for this "royal law," this most difficult commandment, that they have erected a sham moral system based on the principled rejection of it. My intention here has been to trace the word *love*, to consider what it might have meant when it came into our moral and metaphysical language, in the early Scriptures and in traditions of Christianity that are often said to be compelling to the point of entrapment, but which are consulted and invoked very rarely now, as are most things that have a place in our intellectual heritage.

Consider these passages from another classic text, interpreting the commandment to love one's neighbor. In our service toward others, we are "to look upon the image of God in all men, to which we owe all honor and love . . . Therefore, whatever man you meet who needs your aid, you have no reason to refuse to help him . . . Say 'He is contemptible and worthless'; but the Lord shows him to be one to whom he has deigned to give the beauty of his own image. Say that you owe nothing for any service of his; but God, as it were, has put him in his own place in order that you may recognize toward him the many and great benefits with which God has bound you to himself. Say that he does not deserve even your least effort for his sake; but the image of God, which recommends him to you, is worthy of your giving yourself and all your possessions," and much more to the same effect, concluding that, however wicked men may be, we are "to look upon the image of God in them, which cancels and effaces their transgressions, and with its beauty and dignity allures us to love and embrace them." This is from *Institutes of the Christian Religion*, by John Calvin, who is often said to be the godfather of the church of the hard heart and the closed fist, when he could not be less suited to that role. I quote Calvin because I have him at hand. He is a fascinating instance of the fact that the lens of history inverts. He says, "It is very clear that he lives the best and holiest life who lives and strives for himself as little as he can, and that no one lives in a worse or more evil manner than he who lives and strives for himself alone, and thinks about and seeks only his own advantage." American culture is often said to be Calvinist. Maybe once it was, and maybe our once considerable generosity was owed to the fact.

In any case, to honor and to love are virtual synonyms in all these contexts. I have read that some people feel we are entering a post-humanist era, and that this is a good thing because it will encourage us to be more sensitive to the rights of animals. I agree, at least that our civilization has lost that old impulse to value the other, and the self as well, for the beauty of human life as a phenomenon. To expect the decline of one sensitivity to enhance the rise of another one is a considerable leap of faith, certainly. I have seen no evidence of it. And in fact much of the human world is engulfed in suffering. Be that as it may, it is not unusual now to hear that humanism, the centrality of the human in our culture and civilization, is a destructive error, species-ism. This kind of thinking has an audience only because our respect for humankind has declined already.

What has it consisted of, over all those years since the Renaissance? It had beginnings in classical antiquity. "Certain philosophers . . . long ago not ineptly called man a microcosm because he is a rare example of God's power, goodness, and wisdom, and contains within himself enough miracles to occupy our minds, if only we are not irked at paying attention to them . . . For each one undoubtedly feels the heavenly grace that quickens him. Indeed, if there is no need to go outside ourselves to comprehend God, what pardon will the indolence of that man deserve who is loath to descend within himself to find God?" This is Calvin, writing in the sixteenth century.

And this is Shakespeare, writing in the seventeenth century, and expressing something of Calvin's exasperation at the brilliance and sublimity of what the human creature is, and yet somehow refuses to be: "What a piece of work is a man! How noble in reason, how infinite in faculty! In form and moving how express and admirable! In action how like an angel, in apprehension how like a god! The beauty of the world. The paragon of animals." Hamlet says this as he absorbs the fact that Rosencrantz and Guildenstern have attempted to deceive him, that he has irksome Polonius to deal with. And here is John Flavel, a seventeenth-century English Puritan preacher: "The mind passes through all the works of creation, it views the several creatures on earth, considers the fabric, use and beauty of animals, the signatures of plants, penetrating thereby into their nature and virtues . . . It can, in a moment, mount itself from earth to heaven, view the face thereof, describe the motions of the sun in the ecliptic, calculate tables for the motions of the planets and fixed stars," and so on. These varieties of brilliance are certainly not less characteristic of humankind than they were when the Renaissance celebrated them, when the Reformation cited them as marks of the divinity in man. Finally, these lines are Emily Dickinson's. She begins: "The brain is wider than the sky" . . . "The brain is deeper than the sea," then, "The brain is just the weight of God, / For, lift them, pound for pound, / And they will differ, if they do, / As syllable from sound." Our own earlier tradition is largely lost to us because we have forgotten the humanist content of both the Renaissance and the Reformation.

Can we love and undervalue at the same time? Among those of us for whom the commandment has authority, are we fulfilling it when we are forgetful of the incomprehensible complexity—spiritual, intellectual, and emotional—of anyone we encounter? Are we indifferent to the gifts that tradition calls their likeness to God? Has our conception of God himself changed to a point where we do not see in him the brilliance that made our brilliance imply sacredness?

During Dickinson's lifetime the antislavery movement in America made much use of this language of humanism to argue for the sanctity of every person. American historians have inflicted grievous harm on American history. The Dickinson family moved in abolitionist circles and were friends of friends of the very radical John Brown. You heard it here first. Of course, shorn of her cultural heritage and shorn of the cataclysmic history taking place around her, it might be a reasonable exercise of the imagination to see her poetry as dealing with scorned love or something of the kind, I suppose. In historical perspective, one of the great projects of our time appears to be diminution.

The sanctification of the individual—not the love of humankind in the abstract, which would be much easier, much less irksome, but of the singular neighbor, as encountered—implies to writers who embrace it radical human equality and dignity. There are traditions that would give the self priority here, since self-love is the basis and measure of love of neighbor. I prefer Calvin's view, that the encounter is, ideally, a moment of profound recognition, in which all considerations of self would be forgotten. I see certain Christians now ready to forgive themselves and their allies for transgressiveness that amounts to nothing else than injury and insult to that sacred other. This behavior is encapsulated and denatured or sentimentalized in the little word *sin*. By these lights, the suffering of Christ bought his followers the right to cause suffering in their neighbor, then to repent at leisure. The universality of the divine image would encourage another reading of the verse: "Against thee and thee only have I sinned."

It is true in any case that, lacking a humanist amazement and joy at the astonishing creature one is by virtue of being human, all those miracles of thinking and dreaming and perceiving and creating, of offering generosity and love and also accepting them—lacking all this, there can be no appropriate honor given to the other, of whom these very things are also true.

There seems to be little attention given these days to God as creator, in terms of his having put the mark of his character on his creatures. Insofar as religion is considered naïve, this is often by its association with notions of the world's origins that are in conflict with modern science. But science can be one of those parallel narratives I spoke of earlier, true in a way, but a distraction from the main point. No doubt there are reasons, actually or potentially articulable in scientific terms, for things to be as they are. These theories, so influential now, can sound convincing—so long as human experience and the mind's response to experience are left out of account. But there really are no intellectually respectable grounds for leaving them out of account, and no grounds for accepting as exclusively valid a parsing of us that has no language to describe or engage them.

For what should we honor and love ourselves and one another? For heart, soul, mind, and strength, for the astonishing richness of human being that enables us to enjoy our gifts and to shape them and explore them and to make more of them than we would ever have thought possible. God wants this from us and from our neighbors, whom we love when we give them courage, grant them sacredness, sustain them in thinking, inquiring, and imagining, and assure that they have the needs of the body, which frees these powers in them beloved by God.

Integrity and the Modern Intellectual Tradition

The Annual Charles Gore Lecture at
Westminster Abbey: March 7, 2017

I place the origins of modern intellectual tradition in the seventeenth century for the purposes of this discussion, granting that assertions of this kind are most useful when they are understood as provisional. The *modern*, however the word is understood, has been going on for a very long time, has in fact grown old in the course of its pilgrimage from the late Renaissance to the day before yesterday. Here, in brief, is my theory of how the modern period arose and how it has become another era, and in need of another name. The term *postmodern* doesn't serve—it only connotes namelessness. The fact that it has not been improved upon is interesting in its own right, of course.

The modern, the era of science, arose when the Renaissance and the Reformation brought acute and positive attention to human subjectivity. The mind became a sacred space where God communed with the individual in ways that enabled thought and perception in the discovery of empirical fact. While it is difficult to imagine a purer statement of subjectivity than Descartes's "I think, therefore I am," his subjectivity is not entrapment because God permits him his perceptions, and God would not lie. Scientific inquiry in its beginnings was one mode of interaction between the human and the divine that arouses those gifts of the mind which were thought of then as proof of a human and divine bond and likeness.

Scientific method proved powerful, empiricism allayed philosophical worries about subjectivity until they were in effect forgotten, and the assumption became general that science could and sometime would explain everything, including the mind itself. So over time the mind was desacralized and the world as well, metaphysics was put aside, and science, brilliant as it was, took on the character of dispeller of myth and agent of disillusionment. There was nothing inevitable about this. In the first place, the remarkable capacities of the mind, in the Renaissance often celebrated in terms of its ability to understand the movements of the stars and planets and their relative size and distance, were spectacularly demonstrated in the emergence of vast new areas of knowledge. Yet somehow that central mystery, the ability of the mind to deeply know the physical world, ceased to be acknowledged, even as its impact on thought and culture grew continuously. The most remarkable thing about the universe, as Einstein and others have said, is that it is accessible to our understanding. Then the converse must also be true—the most remarkable thing about *us* is that our understanding is of a kind to find the universe accessible. A good Renaissance humanist, a Pico della Mirandola, would seize on this as proof of our central place in creation. But as science developed it put such thoughts aside. It dropped the great Renaissance fascination with our singular character as creatures who learn, devise, imagine, create. Brilliant science celebrated itself, rightly enough, but it ceased to marvel over the gifts of the singular species that invented science and has persisted in it. Humankind has fallen in its own estimation, while the notion emerged and still vigorously persists that this utterly human project is somehow inhuman. Among other things, it is usually taken to be aloof from the errors we are prone to.

Religion came to be reckoned among these errors. It began to be regarded as a crude explanatory system, an attempt to do what science actually *could* do, that is, account for the origins and the workings of things. And on these grounds religion came to be treated as though it had been discredited by science. Scripture, the Church Fathers, and classical theology have far other interests, yet Christianity has been earnestly and ineptly defended by some as if it really were battling science for the same terrain, as if it really were a collection of just-so stories all along, rather than the body of history, poetry, ethical instruction, and reflection—and metaphysics as well—that had deeply informed, dignified, and beautified Western civilization for so many centuries. Science has not produced social ethics or poetry. It has very little to say about history, has induced little in the way of philosophical reflection. This is nothing against it, of course. It is about other business.

But to put science in place of religion as if it were an equivalent framing of reality must necessarily entail the loss of many things that have indeed been lost. There are some transformations that are worth pausing over, simply to appreciate their strangeness. Christianity, which had shaped literatures and cities and regimes, had structured time and consecrated the passages of life, began to be tendentiously misrepresented, and very few seemed even to notice what was happening. This is as true now as it has ever been. And there are still the would-be loyalists who will forever insist that the Bible *is* in fact a collection of utterly veracious just-so stories, reinforcing the arguments of their supposed adversaries.

It is a pity that Europeans took to tramping around in the non-European world when they did, corrupting every kind of evidence while imposing their assumptions on the lives and languages of the people they found there. Notably, in their response to indigenous religions, they interpreted what passed through the dense filter of their incomprehension as primitivity, which primitivity was then widely asserted and assumed to be the basis and essence of all religion. This kind of thinking lives on among scholarly syncretists, who propose that the God of the Hebrew Bible is a composite of local gods, a little El, a little Baal, a little Marduk. These mythic eminences left literatures that are a more than sufficient refutation of the notion that they contributed attributes to the God of Israel. But where a core primitivity is assumed, their very unlikeness authenticates them.

In any case, in the course of all this there has been a radical transformation of the West's conception of humankind. No one now would say of us "in apprehension, how like a god!" A Shakespeare returned from the grave would be astounded to learn what that apprehension has been up to, how far it has penetrated into inconceivably distant reaches of the universe, for example. Writers of his period generalized instances of brilliance to characterize man in the abstract, the human species itself. We detach human achievements from humankind, whom we are then free to consider in whatever reductionist terms might suit our purposes, recently as economic units who can only act rationally in terms of self-interest, in every interaction minimizing cost to themselves while maximizing benefit, whether consciously or unconsciously.

How like an angel.

Wars, plague, punishments designed to terrorize and appall, lethal poverty—every kind of horror was commonplace in Renaissance England. If we think we have grounds for doubting the sacredness and splendor of our species, they had better grounds. At the same time, the best that we have done, the sheer mass of it, would surely confirm them in their high estimate of human capacities. This is to say that there is no necessity behind the extreme declension our species has suffered in its own eyes.

In defense of this lower valuation, our moral failures will be enumerated. There are a great many of them, as there are in any age or generation. We may be more aware of them than earlier periods were of their own crimes and vices. If this is true, and if the case we wish to bring against ourselves might be called moral, it is interesting that we can at the same time be receptive to a model of human nature that is morally blank at best. Self-interestedness is not a trait well thought of in traditional moral systems, however demotic. That it is presented to us as uniquely and inevitably our governing motive puts an end to all the old struggles of the soul, and moots old considerations like honor or loyalty or compassion. I do not wish to imply that people are no longer moved by such considerations. But I am impressed by the authority of an idea of self and others that strips everyone of individuality and of seriousness, and of the possibility of actions that are original and free. What will Western liberalism finally mean if there really is no more to respect in citizen and stranger than this?

So if we say that the age of science began with a Renaissance awe at the power and agility of the human mind, endorsed by the faith that its brilliance was to be enjoyed and marveled at as engagement with God and likeness to him; if we have now arrived at a point where the mind and the self are frequently said not to exist, according to contemporary theory following God himself out of the universe of credible things—then it is clearly an understatement to say a tremendous inversion has taken place. The exalted mind of early science has given way to a flattening of experience that, on no actual grounds, is called modern and also scientific—this while science has made tiny earth a seraphic eye that turns every way, looking always farther and deeper into the strange, surging cosmos.

·

I have presented a list of historical errors that have affected Western life profoundly, and the rest of the world as well because of the assertiveness and prominence of Western culture. The modern period has been shadowed by gloom, nostalgia, disillusionment, anomie, deracination, loss of faith, dehumanization, atomization, secularization, and assorted other afflictions of the same general kind. It has become an iron cage. And so on. Objectively, there is very little in late modern experience to account for all this moaning. By the standards of earlier centuries we have been very fortunate. These days most people see their children live to adulthood. It would be hard-hearted to consider this a small blessing. There are related facts, also nontrivial. For example, far fewer women die in childbirth, leaving far fewer orphans. In Western countries, at least, most people can read, a major enhancement of life. All this is definitely something to work with, in terms of our having lives we can enjoy and make meaningful. And a great many people do precisely this. Nevertheless, as a matter of curriculum, which is our substitute for catechism, we learn that something has gone very wrong, that our human modifications of the world make it impossible to live a truly human life. The horizon open to us is that "patient anesthetized upon a table." An implication behind it all is that the disillusioned know something the uninitiated don't know. The importance of that unnamed thing is granted, and the gloom it brings with it is given place, in books, on canvases, in plays and installations. And everything that reflects its scale and coloration, which to my eye looks like resentment, desolation, and self-pity, is ipso facto modern. So it has been for more than one hundred fifty years. Enormities have befallen the West during those years, which were wholly enormities committed *by* the West, induced in part by the sense of threat and failure, and nostalgia as well, that has cursed late modernity, both culture and period. I generalize. But in my experience there is an alienation between science and the humanities that discourages humanists from acquiring more than a minimal awareness of science, poorly digested, while at

the same time they assume that their own work is marginalized, even a little humiliated, by the triumph of science. Unaccountably, in this brilliant period the workings of the mind,
which uniquely express and describe the mind, whether as
poetry or as microbiology, have ceased to be of interest in
themselves.

The thought has been prevalent for a long time that the
human project, whatever that is, has failed and left us stranded
and bewildered. The myth is that this is the effect of modernity with its disillusionments, the sad burden of all we now
know. But in fact our errors have brought us here, the inver-
sions and misconstructions that arbitrarily, though as if by
necessity, enforce certain conclusions about what life means
and how it can be experienced by us. Intellectual integrity can
be and often is understood to mean that one enters boldly into
diminished reality, even kicks the rubble around a little. But it
should mean examination of received notions, for example, that
reality is indeed diminished. Intellectual integrity is not
possible so long as we give ourselves over wholly to cultural
consensus, however broad, however long enshrined.

At the beginning of the modern period, God was a given in
the field of thought that was the seedbed of science in our sense
of the word. This aspect of the thinking of figures like Descartes, Locke, and Newton is regularly treated as a tip of the
hat to prevailing powers, or a carryover from a kind of thinking they were themselves finding the means to leave behind. It
looks to me, from my reading in the period, as though the
Reformation in England, which radically isolated the individual in the fact of asserting his or her immediate relation with
God, found consciousness—that is, experience—a very rich field
of theological exploration. Their exploration took the form of
a parsing of the mind according to its functions and capacities,
with the understanding that it is, and is made to be, the inter-
mediary between God and the soul, granted, of course, that

anyone might choose to reject this awareness of God's intimate awareness of him, and might turn away from the knowledge of God implicitly proffered to him. Adam figures in all this as the archetypical human being in whose creation we are all created and whose attributes we receive, fallenness famously, but also the ability to know God as Adam did.

I confess I am perfectly happy to accept this view of things. However, I can hardly recuse myself from a discussion in which, so far as I know, I am the lone participant. So having given fair warning of my biases, I will consider certain consequences of conceiving of the mind thus theistically, putting aside the question of God's existence, simply admitting his existence with its effects into the discussion as Einstein did the cosmological constant, not as anything demonstrated, only as something somehow necessary to making the rest of the system work.

First of all, to do this re-situates the discussion of the nature of the mind in our *experience* of the mind, our own and others', rather than in theoretical speculations about the brain as a product of evolution, or the brain as a lump of tissue responsive to stimuli. Wherever any kind of brain is studied, except a human brain, the questions are what can it do and what does it do. Researchers in London have demonstrated that a bee can learn to perform behaviors that are unlike anything a bee is called upon to do in the normal course of life. A very tiny brain is sufficient to produce behavior that might appear to justify the word *intelligent*. This is consistent with Darwin's observations of ants in his garden. So reductionism in the case of an insect is inappropriate because, elegant as its suite of instincts clearly are, they do not preclude its having the ability to react to novel circumstances, to appraise and adapt, within limits we will never establish since we will never know how to test for them exhaustively. Appraise and adapt—I use anthropomorphic language here, lacking any other, therefore lacking any way to suggest a distinction between human and insect purposiveness. Despite Darwin, it has been usual for a long time to make reductionist accounts of human behavior and consciousness, likening them to those of ants or crickets to demonstrate, in effect, that anthropomorphic language is not really appropriate in our case either. But better science undercuts the old notion that tiny-brained creatures are automata running solely on instinct. It appears they can sometimes decide when instinctive responses would not be useful. I go further here than the science does in inferring self-awareness. In any case, as we learn that intelligence has been lavished on the living world at large, we should be less reluctant to acknowledge our share in it.

It is increasingly clear that there is no baseline simplicity to which our own essential nature can be reduced. Mysterious intelligence is mysteriously pervasive. Bad science has for a long time assumed a not so great chain of Being, an apparent rising complexity that is in fact only a compounding of simplicities, explainable top to bottom in terms of a fundamental primitivity. In fact we are an extraordinary instance of a pervasive complexity. Science has not proposed any way of accounting for this fact, not having been aware of it as a fact until quite recently. A theistic vision of the world is freer to see the world whole, as it is in itself, so to speak. "The world is full of the grandeur of God. It will flame out, like shining from shook foil," in the words of Gerard Manley Hopkins. Within this great given, that Being is an astonishment, any aspect of Being can be approached with an expectation of discovering wondrous things. The slime that comes up from the depths of the sea in fishermen's nets is a ruined universe of bioluminescence. Microorganisms live in clouds, air moves in rivers, butterflies navigate the earth's magnetic field. The matter cosmologists call "dark," which makes up most of the mass of the universe, seems to be nonatomic. Wonders never cease.

Over against this we have a constricted empiricism, the building upward from the seemingly known or presumptively knowable, its expectations based on limited technology and on the old idea that science is a process of deromanticization, demystification. To speak as the theists did of lavishness, elegance, artfulness is to introduce language capable of acknowledging that there is more to the world than its intricate economies of survival. Locke, a theist, saw Being as a great, boisterous ocean that will always remain essentially unknown to us. The more we learn, the truer this seems to be. To apply too broadly a paradigm drawn from narrow experience is an error that entails cascading errors. Classical religion brings assumptions of vastness and relation, and beauty, and wonder and humility before its subject, all very useful in giving reality its due. I do not wish to imply that secular scientists do not often bring these gifts to their work, or arrive at them in the course of their work. It is in the study of humankind that these things are consistently absent. It is as if we can only be granted a place in the universe if we are made vastly less extraordinary than we clearly are. This is the kind of persisting bias and error that intellectual integrity would forbid. The old theists looked at extraordinary humankind, the quintessence of dust, to consider the nature of the universe. This makes perfect sense. We do, after all, demonstrate in our being what is potential in matter and time.

If we approach the mind with my cosmological constant still factored in, we can say the mind is morally competent—Adamically speaking, that is—in its design, allowing for all deviations from the ideal or the norm. I am not the first to note that modern thinking about the mind has often proceeded from the study of pathologies, real or not. It seems clear enough to me why Victorian women might have been prone to hysteria. I look back at the comparatively mild limits and prejudices I escaped by grace of the civil rights movement as if I had found myself two steps clear of a falling rock. In the American South, the intense depression observed in slaves sold away from their families was diagnosed as an illness to which their race was oddly prone. In such cases, assumptions about the nature and life experience of certain human beings obscured the obvious, and science built on the sand of engrained error. I suspect this may be why the study of human consciousness is so markedly different from science in general. It very typically confirms or defends theories about social roles. The fact that it does not view the human person with particular respect as consciousness or, to use an old phrase, as moral agent has a long history of grave and shameful consequences. The great anomaly here is that the science of the human brain, if *science* is indeed the right word, does not take account of what the brain actually does. I have been invited from time to time to lend my brain to science, that is, to pass it through an fMRI while using it creatively. Even if I had not seen an article about how this machinery had been taking hair from the heads of experimental subjects due to faulty calibration, the thought that I could attempt anything remotely similar in such circumstances to what I do when I am writing fiction is simply bizarre. This is surely a grand instance of the application of faulty methods to a faulty question. The science of the mind, as it is practiced now and has been practiced for generations, has no place for human inwardness, the reflective settling into oneself that somehow finds and yields structure and meaning, not all at once but as a kind of unwilled constellating of thoughts and things to which some part of one's attention may have drifted any number of times. It is in the nature of the mind to distill, to do its strange work over time. No snapshot, no series of images, could capture its life.

Walt Whitman wrote a beautiful little poem about a spider, and about the workings of consciousness:

A noiseless patient spider,
I mark'd where on a little promontory it stood isolated,
Mark'd how to explore the vacant vast surrounding,
It launch'd forth filament, filament, filament, out of
     itself,
Ever unreeling them, ever tirelessly speeding them.

And you O my soul where you stand,
Surrounded, detached, in measureless oceans of space,
Ceaselessly musing, venturing, throwing, seeking the
     spheres to connect them,
Till the bridge you will need be form'd, till the ductile
     anchor hold,
Till the gossamer thread you fling catch somewhere,
     O my soul.

This could be a description of the making of coherency
from experience, as the mind does autonomically. It could describe the making of a poem, or the process of reaching beyond
the isolation of subjectivity by means of these gossamer threads
of inquiry and speculation to arrive at a kind of insight we
might call scientific. None of these readings would exclude the
others. That the spider serves so well as a metaphor for the soul's
musings places both of these silent creatures in the same
"vacant vast surrounding," places the soul in the world experientially, without condescension to the world and without rar-
efaction of the soul. I note the importance here of the complex
psychology intrinsic to the self theistically understood. The
speaker of the poem watches himself watching, understands
that there is purpose in his attentiveness, that it is itself a gossamer thread finding a hold in the delicate strategy of exploration he sees in the spider. He beholds himself in his essential
humanity, as solitary, as one given to musing and to discovering analogy and elegance where his attention rests.

Science tells us we have no souls. And science gives us no name and no way of accounting for the phenomenon of self-awareness that makes our thoughts, doubts, dreams, memories, and antipathies so interesting to us, and our frustrations with our faults and failures so acute. Granting that "the soul" as an idea might be culturally particular enough that it gives self-awareness a character not intrinsic to it. The classic soul is more ourselves than we are, a loving and well-loved companion, loyal to us uniquely, entrusted to us, to whom we entrust ourselves. We feel its yearnings, its musings, as a truer and more primary experience of ourselves than our ordinary consciousness can offer us. Traditionally souls are spoken of as saved or lost, being the immortal part of humankind, even though they are also thought of as unoffending, indeed as offended against when we misuse our worldly agency. Freud's superego bears a superficial resemblance to the soul, the great difference being that the superego is the internalization of strictures and demands that are not one's own or friendly to one's well-being, and that intervene in the formation of a primary self. The old song says, "It is well with my soul." No song says, "It is well with my superego." That would describe a state of utter capitulation to a harsh authority enforced by a submerged but dreadful guilt.

It is interesting to consider what we have received in exchange for the theistic worldview of our ancestors. Psychological complexity is acknowledged in modern theories of the mind—in Freud's tripartite psyche, in notions of an unevolved reptilian brain coiled at the base of consciousness, in bicameralism, and recently in the brain as a sort of calculator making continuous and presumably accurate estimates of the organism's relative advantage, "cost-benefit analysis" in the terms of economics, the discipline whose prestige seems to have overwhelmed what remained of humanist impulses in this field. Complexity enters this schema because some undescribed mechanism intervenes to conceal our selfishness from ourselves, to allow us to believe that our generosity actually is generosity and so on. Why, if self-interest is the unique and universal motive, any shame or blame would attach to it is one question. Another is, what would this system of concealment look like as biology or neurology, and would its complexity, its physiological cost, be repaid by concealments that hardly seem necessary in the first place, given the selfishness thesis? In any case, all this complexity takes place in isolation within the standard human skull, which is not a very pleasant place to be. I suppose this is both a source and a consequence of modernist malaise.

"My soul by grace of God has fared / Adventuring where marvels be." These are lines from the poem "Pearl," written in the fourteenth century. The voice of the poem describes a dream vision of a girl child who has died. The speaker sees her as a lovely young woman by a river, in a paradise he cannot yet enter. The poem speaks beautifully and tellingly of such loss, acknowledging a depth of grief that is, finally, embraced in the consolations of a cosmic order that is as tender and profound as such sorrows would require. We might call this wish fulfillment, the projection of human hopes on an empty heaven. Or we might call it a vision of Being that is large and rich enough to accommodate the experience of human love and grief. How else to do justice to them? "Pearl" movingly evokes a young child's translucent loveliness, and pearls adorn the sleeve of the cosmic Christ. The garden where the child is buried is a faint but real promise of the paradise where her soul flourishes. The beauty we see in this world is a sign and portent of an ultimate beauty, and we are rightly enthralled by it. Beauty has no place in modern theories of the mind, nor do the pleasures of memory, thought, or perception, or the aesthetic pleasures. Endorphins are not adequate to filling this void. They only mean that pleasure happens, as I hope we all know, even without the word.

My argument is essentially that the universe of theism is

large enough not only to admit of the great range of human emotion and imagination, pathos and grandeur, but to enhance these things, to value them even when they are never noticed or valued or, for that matter, expressed in the whole of a mortal life. Unless it is to distinguish itself very sharply from theistic tradition, I have no idea why the various psychologies are alike in disallowing the more ingratiating human traits. Religion is represented as a repressive system from which modern thought is a liberation. Yet all these psychologies are bleakly determinist, and so poor in their view of the possible that it is impossible to guess what their version of a free act would look like. The notion that all behavior is essentially self-interested might liberate selfishness, but that would be no more than a slight deviation from a pattern of behavior that is inevitable in any case. If decency is merely feigned, the enabler of selfishness, it might be no deviation at all. I grant the problems associated with the doctrine of predestination, and I find it a vastly deeper problem to be asked to subscribe to the idea that meaninglessness is irresistibly implanted in human nature, that the superego will wrestle the id to a draw, that the reptile will not hiss and draw embarrassing attention to itself, that the hand in the collection plate will appear to be putting something in and not taking something out. A better modernist anthropology might change my sense of all this, but as it is I think it is entirely appropriate to evaluate what there is on offer.

In case there are doubts, this really is a lecture on the subject of intellectual integrity, a thing many of us have felt to be sorely lacking these days. Why is it so difficult to find the language to approach this subject? Well, these psychologies I mention imply or say outright that there is no mind. Then how do we speak of intellectualism? These psychologies imply or say outright that there is no self. Then how do we speak of integrity? The notion has caught on very widely that there are no facts, only interpretations. Truth itself is dissolving as a concept in an acid bath of idle cynicism. So to what standard are the ethically inclined to hold themselves? Who knows to what extent the "thought" of a period is what we take it to be. But modern thought especially has been made a curriculum and a catechism. There are no grounds for doubting its influence. Again in the matter of intellect or ethicalism, it is conspicuously lacking in terms to address these things or to value them.

For a very long time it has been assumed that intellectual integrity in the modern period demanded the rejection of religion. As corollary there is the assumption that we must adopt the worldview of the modern period. This subtle coercion, to embrace certain ideas on other grounds than their merits, might explain their survival despite their being, from a human point of view, desiccated things, deeply unsatisfactory. And this while brilliant science continuously sets before us a vaster, more cryptic and spectacular cosmos, the brilliant human mind being mirror and alembic of all this grandeur, as it has always been. The modern science of the mind is to science in general as a blighted twin is to a living body—mimicked life and thwarted development. I propose that this is true because it epitomizes "the modern" as a concept. It is first of all a worldview. The methods of the science that sponsors it presuppose its validity—the soul will never reveal itself to an fMRI, and poetry, prayers, painting, and architecture are inadmissible as evidence. These theories of the mind change, to the extent they do, as cultural styles change, not in the way of hypotheses that are winnowed and refined in the ordinary course of inquiry. (I use the word *mind* because their attentions to the brain yield, by their lights, insights of global validity into human nature, the kind of inwardness implied in a deceptive valuation of one's own motives, and so on. To say they learn this from scrutiny of the brain would be false. The idea goes back at least to Freud.)

Most of you probably know that Einstein's great mistake, the constant he added into his theory to make the equations work as he wanted, and which he regretted ever afterward, has turned out to be no mistake at all but an anticipation of the effect of dark energy as antigravity. I skirt specifics because I don't understand them. But there is a point to my analogy. If a theoretical account of the order of things does not describe what reason or intuition propose to the understanding, then the factor that would correct for its deficiencies should be looked to, pondered. The modern world, insofar as it is proposed to humankind as its habitation, is too small, too dull, too meager for us. After all, we are very remarkable. We alone among the creatures have learned a bit of the grammar of the universe. Einstein was known to mention God from time to time, which need not imply theism in any traditional form, only the sense of a universe more intrinsically orderly, capacious, and finally unknowable than theory and formula could capture. For him the Lord seems to have been another cosmological constant, an undemonstrated given necessary to allowing the reality he wished to describe its full character. We have in ourselves grounds for supposing that Being is vaster, more luminous, more consequential than we have allowed ourselves to imagine for many generations. No idea is authenticated by the fact that it hurts our feelings. Intellectual rigor is not inevitably reductionist. Intellectual integrity cannot oblige us to deny what is manifestly true.

Old Souls, New World

The Ingersoll Lecture on Human Immortality,
Harvard Divinity School: April 27, 2017

The long-prevalent belief that what is proposed as truth or reason can only be credited in the degree that it is consistent with the strata of physical reality by any means available to our experience is mistaken. It is mistaken in its conception of the nature of the physical and, therefore, in the nature of everything else. It has insisted that what it offers as the sole model of reality is exhaustively pertinent to every meaningful question about reality, dismissing as not meaningful every question to which it is not pertinent. But for some time now science has been fetching back strange reports about the radical apparent discontinuity between volatile reality at the subatomic level and the stolid lawfulness of reality at the scale of our experience, for example. The fathomless anomalies of the infinitesimal present as any ordinary day, any transient thought. We know now that physical being as we experience it is wildly untypical in cosmic terms. Reality as we know it now does not yield or legitimize a narrow or prejudicial vocabulary. Science has given us grounds for a liberating humility. We need not continue to encumber our thinking with strictures it has long since put aside.

We should instead be finding language that is capable, capacious, and responsive. The expectations induced by any fixed approach should be relaxed, in pondering history as surely as in considering human nature or the depths of physical reality. Ideology has been a terrible mistake, theory another one. Both mimic positivism in their stringencies and exclusions. There is no writer, and so on. Why should any given thing have happened? No theory, no convention or prejudice, should take precedence over the fact that if it did happen, it arose out of the endless complexity of human life, human lives. The Puritan Thomas Shepard, generally credited with founding Harvard, remarked that a man with a wooden leg could trim his foot to fit his shoe, but in the case of a living limb this would not be advisable. By all means those who think about history should avoid such trimming, since they deal with living flesh, specifically those human swarms whose passage through the world is the sum and substance of history.

We have not yet absorbed the fact that history has fallen into our laps, and we hardly know what it is, let alone what we should do with it. We have been busy destroying the landmarks that might otherwise help us orient ourselves. We have impoverished ourselves of every sense of how over time a society emerged that we and most of the world have considered decent and fortunate. Could we save this good order from a present threat? If it collapsed, could we rebuild it? These are real questions.

The stringencies and inadequacies of positivism in all its forms have sent me to the literature of early modern, pre-positivist thought, where its attritions were not yet felt. I have been reading some old sermons and treatises by sixteenth- and seventeenth-century English and Anglo-Americans. I have been reading the Puritans. I confess to being drawn to orphan figures, movements, and periods. My reward is in the discovery of their frequently remarkable value and significance. It was no doubt inevitable that I would come finally to the Puritans, among the most effectively dismissed of all historically consequential movements. They are seldom mentioned except as a pernicious influence on our civilization, both early and abiding. Few grounds are offered to support this view of them, and those that are offered are ill-informed. That name "Puritan," affixed to them polemically, has singled them out for a particular dislike that we have learned to share. Arthur Golding, in the Epistle Dedicatory to his translation of John Calvin's commentary on Galatians (1574), remarks wistfully that there are those who "are in the eyes of some persons not only to be despised but also blamed; verily as who should say it were a fault to endeavor to be faultless." It is curious that the desire to live a scrupulous life should be anyone else's business. And what were the transgressions of which Puritans were particularly aware? Errors in their own thinking. Hypocrisies and idolatries. They are supposed to have frowned upon the joys of life, to have had a special, dark obsession with sexuality, to have hated all things beautiful. None of this is true.

There is a strong tradition of piety in Europe, reaching back to the twelfth century at least, that is always denounced in just these terms whenever it becomes visible enough to seem to authorities to pose a challenge. Notably these groups were the Albigensians or Cathars and the Waldensians in southern France and northern Italy and Spain, the Lollards in England, and after them the English Puritans. The earlier groups were all seen as heretics. They were violently suppressed. The writings of the Cathars were burned, and what records we have of them are testimonies made under torture, so it is difficult to know much about them. We do know that they were the civilization of the troubadour poets and the courts of love. Oddly, they and the other groups were and are all associated with an aversion to sex. Considering the struggles the dominant traditions themselves have had with this aspect of human nature, it is strange that this notion about dissenter groups should serve as an aspersion against them. Nevertheless, it was and is employed consistently and effectively against supposed heresies, despite every change of moral climate. Where the aversion to sexuality is strong, the status of women is generally low, particularly in matters of religion. Albigensian teachers and clergy were male and female indifferently. Lollards denounced priestly celibacy as a disparagement of women. Puritans idealized marriage and educated their daughters. I have looked further into the matter than most people, and I have found no evidence of special anxiety on this subject, in fact very little mention of it at all. Puritans had a serious interest in sin, and they also had their own definition of it. From what I have seen, the great sin in the Puritan understanding is religious hypocrisy within their own churches and within their own minds—evangelical hypocrisy, in the words of Shepard. Their rigors were felt inwardly, among themselves and within themselves. Self-scrutiny was mastered as a discipline.

The association of Puritanism with sexual repression in Anglo-American cultural history has significant effects. Any writer who is a little salacious now and then, or who translated Ovid, say, could not have been a Puritan, even though that translator, Golding, also put many of the Latin and French works of Calvin into English. In fact, in his preface to Calvin's commentary on the book of Daniel, Golding says of him, "As I do profess myselfe to be one of his scholers, and do prayse God for the same more than any earthly matter: so do I not of arrogance alter or change any thing in his writings." Golding was making his translations in the 1570s and '80s. Since his translation of Ovid's *Metamorphoses* is a major source for Shakespeare's plays, there is no reason to assume he would not have picked up others of Golding's books. The commentary on Daniel deals at length with a question of great interest to Shakespeare and his period: what a ruler's legitimacy consists in, and why and how it can be lost. The imposing of an inappropriate test on the vast literary output of the English Renaissance, which was also the English Reformation and which encompassed the rise of Puritanism, very effectively minimizes the influence of the movement, and mischaracterizes its focus, its temper, and its worldview.

There is a stigma attached to this influential strain of early modern thought that generally forecloses the possibility of interest in it or respectful attention to it. It is no help at all to say Puritans were Calvinists, since every aspersion cast on them is cast on him as well, on no better grounds. These stigmas have created dead zones in British and American historical thought—around Geneva, around the English Civil Wars, around early New England, and even around the English Renaissance, a period celebrated and pondered endlessly—within limits that seem unaccountably narrow unless the power of stigma is taken into account. The influence of Geneva as a republic governed by elected councils, the importance of the English Civil Wars, which, in crucial respects, were a model for the French Revolution, and the formative first century and more of our own civilization all tend to be badly dealt with or effectively ignored. Even great Shakespeare has been caught in these snares.

·

I have been using the word *Puritan* without defining it. There was no church or institution by that name, no membership in any formal sense. The word in England was applied to nonconformist or dissenting Protestants—Presbyterians, Congregationalists, Baptists, Quakers, and anyone else—who did not accept the legitimacy, or in any case the claims to exclusive legitimacy, of the newly created Church of England. The affinity of these groups is demonstrated in their years of military effectiveness and in their sustaining a parliamentary government for a decade, more or less, until Oliver Cromwell died, leaving no competent successor. Before battle, or when there were important decisions to be made, their soldiers would separate according to their various sects to pray, then come together again to plan or to debate. The unity among them was not untroubled—the Presbyterians and the Congregationalists fought two major battles against each other around the issue of monarchy, which was less acceptable to Congregationalists than to Presbyterians. But over the course of years of warfare the population did divide along the lines of Puritan or Parliamentarian and Anglican or Royalist. This division justifies the use of terms that by themselves do not do justice to the complexity of either side. The best of the Puritan writers are now claimed for the Anglicans, which can be confusing. But if they were forbidden to preach, jailed, forbidden to come within five miles of a city, or inclined to making long stays in Rotterdam, or if they emigrated to New England or thought about it, it's safe to say they were Puritans.

The stream of Puritanism that landed in New England and flourished there, and was greatly supplemented by the arrival of refugees fleeing the consequences of the collapse of the revolutionary government and the restoration of the monarchy in England, had a highly characteristic intellectual culture. Its theological stronghold was Cambridge University. It was based on the paramount authority of Scripture, for them understood as an ancient text in three ancient languages, counting Aramaic. Their clergy were trained in these languages as well as in Latin so that they would be competent interpreters of a text that was never definitively rendered in any translation. This by itself marks a great difference between their religious consciousness and that of all our modern supposed literalists. There was a great, treasured difficulty at the center of Puritan culture that enlisted them in the study of history, of antiquity in general, and of the natural sciences, which by their lights gave insight into the nature of God as Creator and as Presence. For all these reasons they needed a Harvard and a Yale, a Princeton and a Dartmouth, a Grinnell and an Oberlin and a Mount Holyoke, and, while their influence lasted, scores of other schools, private and public. We can and do dismiss this intellectualism as elitist, congratulating ourselves for the distinct modesty of our own aspirations. But the American Puritans maintained a historically high level of literacy in their population. In England and Europe their immediate forebears had struggled and died to create a Bible in English, which could be understood by the unlearned. This became the basis of all later Bibles in English, including the Authorized or King James Version.

From the time of John Wycliffe forward, England had a population they called the unlearned, who were literate in English or knew someone who was. Learnedness meant competence in Latin and French, later perhaps in Greek and Hebrew. When the press made books relatively cheap, translators made history and theological and classical literature accessible to readers of English, removing an important cultural barrier. Golding omitted Calvin's occasional brooding over a word in Greek or Hebrew out of consideration for what he called the unlearned reader, assuming at the same time that the reader would be interested in a work of theology. Writers in this period often quote passages in Latin, and then, unfailingly, they translate them. This was the period of the chronicle histories, a narrative of national life that could be read by the literate unlearned. Shakespeare's and Marlowe's use of translated classics and of histories written in English might be thought of as a part of all this, offering Aeneas and Antony, Edward II and Richard II to audiences avid for a kind of aesthetic and intellectual experience that had always before been closed to them.

The lessons and sermons of Puritan preachers propagated the kind of learning required of their clergy and were printed and circulated in Britain and America. Again, their learnedness might have been welcomed because it was also a breaking down of these same exclusions. In *The New England Mind*, the American historian Perry Miller describes a Puritan sermon as a "closely knit, carefully reasoned, and solidly organized

disquisition." The preacher "argues his way step by step, inex-
orably disposing of point after point, quoting Biblical verses,
citing authorities, watching for fallacies in logic, drawing upon
the sciences for analogies, utilizing any information that seems
pertinent." Miller says, writing in 1939, "[The Puritan preacher]
demands a degree of close attention that would seem staggering to modern audiences and is not to be paralleled in modern
churches." Or, I would say, in modern universities. The rigor
the preacher demanded of himself, like the brilliance Shakespeare allowed himself, reflected confidence in his hearers and
deep respect for them. The pious would take away a meaningful education from their hours in church. There were no women
in the universities, but there were women in the pews. In the
Wycliffite manner, the Puritan elite worked to close the gap
between themselves and people at large.

Let us say that their early culture in America assumed the
appropriateness of educating the general population ambi-
tiously. Granted, their instruction was always fundamentally
religious, as it would have been anywhere in the Western world.
I know that early New England is very usually described as
"theocratic." So is Calvin's Geneva. What this can have meant
at the time, when rulers in England and throughout Europe
felt justified in imposing religious conformity by means of the
most extreme violence, I have never understood. The norms of
the West then certainly made New Englanders liable to practices that we might consider oppressive, though at the moment
we seem to be tending away from enlightenment ourselves.
Still, the word *theocratic* is applied to them as if tolerance flourished elsewhere and they alone resisted its sweet influence. This
is profoundly at odds with history.

Meaningful comparisons are available. The Massachusetts
Body of Liberties of 1641 is largely a list of protections of citizens of the colony, notably those who are accused or convicted
of crimes. It forbids double jeopardy, provides for representa-

tion and appeal, and forbids "bodily punishments" that are "inhumane, barbarous, or cruel." It includes protections of women, children, servants, foreigners, and strangers, and of animals, forbidding "any tyranny or cruelty towards any brute creature which are usually kept for man's use." And it concludes with a list of twelve capital crimes, with the biblical verses cited that permit and/or require this punishment. This code is attributed to the American Puritan minister Nathaniel Ward. It was revised seven years later, in 1648, in the somewhat more pedestrian and punitive Laws and Liberties of Massachusetts.

Dale's Laws, named for Sir Thomas Dale, the deputy governor of Virginia in 1611 when the code was approved by the colonial council in England and enacted in that colony, is a very different thing. It begins with a list of infractions to be punished by death, beyond those commanded by Moses, which are there also. These capital offenses include speaking impiously or maliciously against the Holy Trinity or any of its Persons, blaspheming the name of God a third time, speaking traitorous words against the king's person or authority, speaking derisively of God's holy word, being absent three times from twice-daily divine service, stealing from a church, speaking derisively a third time of the king's council that governed this "pious and Christian plantation," taking food from a garden, or, surely the most understandable of crimes, running off to the Indians. Newcomers were to present themselves to a minister to give an account of their faith, to be instructed if necessary, and to be flogged each time they failed to submit to instruction. Notably missing from the Virginia laws is the slightest legal protection for people vulnerable to even extreme punishments. Notably missing from the Massachusetts laws are compulsory church attendance and compulsory religious instruction, or laws against disrespect of clergy or of Scripture. In other words, these ungodly and unbiblical laws imposed on the Virginians from London were theocratic as the word is usually understood. The laws of the Puritans, with their insistence on two or three witnesses in capital cases, their restraints on the severity of punishments, their protections of servants and widows derive very largely from the Old Testament. The verses that authorize them could as well be cited as are those that authorize capital punishment. So I suppose these laws might appropriately be called theocratic, if the word were ever used with a little precision.

Severity is so utterly associated with Puritanism that I feel compelled to emphasize my point here. Dale's Laws are Anglican. The church whose doctrines are enforced in them by flogging is the Church of England. The Puritans and the Church of England were adversaries, within years of engaging as adversaries in two wars that would destroy a larger percentage of the British population than any other war the British have engaged in. So it is with civil wars. In any case, I have learned from my attempts to do them a little historical justice that when I so much as mention harshness or oppression people will hear the word *Puritan*, or, possibly, *Calvinist*. Those who comment on the Massachusetts codes always remark on how closely they anticipate the American Bill of Rights, how modern they are. I've gone looking for that English common law they are often supposed to have been based on. Sir John Fortescue, Sir Thomas More, Sir Edward Coke—no luck at all. Advice would be appreciated. Oddly, there seems never to be any mention of Moses.

Be that as it may. There are problems with the comparison of these two codes. Dale's Laws is older by a crucial generation or two, pre-Revolutionary, while the Massachusetts laws were formulated during the period of the Commonwealth and rule by Parliament. This fact would have meant both that England was engrossed in its own struggles, giving the colonies new latitude, and that the tendency of society away from the monarchical order would encourage a more local, communitarian ethos. The Laws and Liberties begins "To our Beloved Brethren and Neighbors the Inhabitants of the Massachusetts." The preface to Dade's Laws says that they reflect the king's interest in advancing "true religion" and "the glory of God." There is a stated intent to bring the light of the Gospel to those barbarous Indians.

The Virginia colony struggled bitterly, though it was considered to be in a much more favorable location than Massachusetts. It approached starvation and anarchy. This would account in some part for the seemingly desperate severity of these laws. At the same time, the severity of the laws might have stood in the way of any sense of a common interest. John Winthrop's speech on the importance of mutual charity to the survival and success of his settlement appears to have been borne out. Also, there was an unusual degree of consensus among the Massachusetts colonists to support civic order, while Virginia had the advantage and misfortune of a military presence to enforce submission.

•

Certain peculiarities in the long moment of American Puritanism must be considered. It was, so to speak, a branch that fell from the trunk of Anglo-European civilization during the storms of religious contention and societal disruption. That is to say, it was a culture already formed around certain ideals and practices, and already preoccupied by matters meaningful in the context of the old civilization. The conflicts that severed them were long-standing, a fact that accounts for the maturity and stability of Puritan institutions. New Englanders did not grope for a new social ethos or order. They knew who they were. American Puritanism did not simply come into being ex nihilo, or as if spontaneously generated by the contact of certain somber English persons with a remarkably frigid shore, though history tends to treat it this way. It was in its general outlines an old presence in English life, long suppressed, briefly dominant, then suppressed again. Under Queen Mary particularly dissenters had fled to Europe, where there were cities, in Germany, France, the Low Countries, Switzerland, Bohemia, and elsewhere, which had already organized themselves in accordance with Reformed social thought and which Reformed English saw as models. Puritanism is an English name for the local expression of a movement that was in fact actively international. The term has been effective in creating the impression that people to whom it was applied were narrow, eccentric, and naïve, though they printed and translated each other's books, studied and taught in each other's universities, afforded each other shelter in times of persecution, and fought in each other's wars, as many English did on behalf of the Dutch Republic. Colonial Puritans traveled to Britain and involved themselves deeply in British affairs, including the Civil Wars and the Commonwealth government.

The English Puritans were so prone to writing and printing that there is no special difficulty in reconstructing their forgotten history, once one is aware of their forgotten literature. One vast work, highly popular in England and America, is sufficient by itself to demonstrate their understanding of themselves and their origins. This is *The Actes and Monuments of the Martyrs*, by John Foxe, which covers, in truly incredible detail, the history of the church, in his view the true church, from its earliest origins in the beginning of the Christian era to the time in which he wrote. The true and primitive church, for him, is the dissenting tradition.

This might seem a naïve undertaking. But Foxe's book is in fact heavily documented with early treatises in Greek and Latin and their translations, letters to and from popes, disputations on theological subjects which are long dialogues in Latin and then English. Golding, in translating Calvin, uses the word *historiography*, which otherwise I might have considered an anachronism in this context. Foxe's work, which grew to three huge volumes, is by far the most sophisticated historiography I have encountered—ever, I suppose. Obviously it is not without bias. Nothing of the kind could be. I am in no position to authenticate the hundreds of documents the volumes contain, though I have seen nothing—in the letters of Mary Tudor to her half brother Edward VI, for example—that is at odds with what I have seen elsewhere. The theological disputations stand on their own, without tendentious interpretations. There is careful attention to the reigns of kings, including those who figure in Shakespeare's plays. The chronicle histories draw on Foxe. Where in the world all this material could have come from I have no idea. The books were printed, meticulously, by John Day, an important publisher of dissenting works. They are illustrated with engravings famous for their depictions of martyrdoms, and more appropriately famous for their quality. I have read that Foxe's adherence to the truth has been questioned in some particulars. Clearly I am the last person in the world to believe in the infallibility of any history. But, granting that there surely are errors in such an enormous work, not to mention questionable assumptions and interpretations, and that it was produced to champion one side in a passionate debate, it can nevertheless tell us a great deal about who the Puritans believed they were, and about the legacy they embraced.

Puritans felt they were in a line of descent of defenders of an original Christianity, by which they meant those who lived before, or rejected what they took to be, historical accretions: the papacy, the sacrifice of the Mass, transubstantiation and communion in one kind, priestly celibacy and celibacy of women religious, auricular confession, purgatory and prayers for the dead, pilgrimages and crusades, and the use of icons among them. From what we can know about earlier suppressed movements in England, in all these things they did anticipate the Reformation. Over years and generations there was a furtive traffic in forbidden texts that is demonstrated by the punishments of those found in possession of them.

•

I will argue that Puritanism in Anglo-American tradition took a distinctive character from a particular constellation of events of the fourteenth century—the brief flourishing of a high literature in English, the Black Death, Wycliffe's career as a professor at Oxford, the translation by him or under his influence of the whole Bible from Latin into English, and the rise of Lollardy. I know I am entering contested territory here. It is usual to say that English Protestants retrojected Protestantism onto this moment opportunistically. *Protestantism* is an inexact word here. *Puritanism* would be much better. In any case, ideas have origins, and influences are real and constitute a lineage of true legitimacy and importance. Historical figures are historical because they set in motion change they themselves could not anticipate and might not endorse in every particular. These writers whom it is supposedly wrong to regard as proto-Puritan articulated ideas that could only have shaped Puritanism in the very fact of their appropriation, even if it was granted that there is no more direct relationship among them. I will note here that stigma is again a factor in all this. *Lollard* is usually said to refer to slurred speech, associating this movement with the lower classes. According to the *Oxford English Dictionary*, its first meaning is "A name of contempt given in the 14th c. to certain heretics, who were either followers of Wyclif or held opinions similar to his." A great part of the work of bad history is done by these terms of contempt. In light of this scorn, it might seem odd that the Puritans' claim to this "heretical" movement should be rejected. But, as it happened, the first great period in English literature was somehow associated with it. Geoffrey Chaucer was, like Wycliffe, a friend of John of Gaunt, uncle to King Richard II. William Langland may have been a Lollard himself. John Gower, a friend of Chaucer, was active at the time, writing his odd, didactic poetry. Wycliffe is ranked among these great early writers in English for his prose. So there is enormous prestige attached to it all, however uneasily.

An interesting and remarkable thing about Lollardy or Wycliffism is that the movement had impeccable intellectual origins and, in its early phase, attracted the support of people of rank. This is true at the same time that it was essentially a movement meant to liberate and elevate the impoverished and oppressed by giving them a Bible in their own language as well as sending out poor priests to instruct them in understanding it. Wycliffe was a man of good family, a scholar, philosopher, and preacher of very high standing, known and admired by the powerful figures of the period, enjoying the loyalty of his colleagues. According to the article about him in the eleventh edition of the *Encyclopaedia Britannica*, the essence of his teaching was "the immediate dependence of the individual Christian upon God, a relation which needs no mediation of any priest, and to which the very sacraments of the Church, however desirable, are not essentially necessary . . . [He] divorces the idea of the Church from any connexion with its official or formal constitution, and conceives it as consisting exclusively of the righteous." Radical as all this was at the time, Wycliffe is most remarkable for his having sponsored, at least, the creation of his Bible in English, its first version completed in 1382. To that time, of course, Latin and French were the languages of the upper classes, universities, government, and church. Sigmund Freud called Americans Lollards, intending no compliment. Still, he might have had a point. There was in New England a virtual aristocracy of learning and at the same time a commitment to making learning general that structured their institutions— churches, schools, and press. This looks more like Lollardy than like other social orders of its time. By comparison, neither public education nor printing were characteristic of the Anglican South, in the colonial period or after it. The high populism of the Wycliffites, who after 1400 were burned for their efforts, their writings burned as well, put knowledge and therefore autonomy of a kind into the hands of ordinary people, the peasant, the plowman.

In 1348 the Black Death had struck England, diminishing the population of laborers so abruptly and severely that those who remained were able to negotiate for better wages or to travel to find better employment. Their standard of living rose, landowners took harsh steps to reverse these gains, and finally in 1381 a powerful insurrection broke out called the Peasants' Revolt. Wycliffe and his teachings were blamed for this uprising. That he did inspire it in some degree is not unlikely. He provided a vivid instance of that intuition broadly shared by religions, and at times even by the religious, that human beings are sacred by nature. In this case as in many others, human sanctity is taken to imply basic human equality, or at least a basic right to fairness and respect.

Wycliffe wrote his thoughts on social conditions in language that could be understood by those who suffered under them. And he was furious. He said lords "should know God's law and study and maintain it, and destroy wrong and maintain poor men in their right to live in rest, peace and charity, and suffer no men [under their authority] to do extortions, beat men, and hold poor men out of right by strength of lordships." Instead, lords, prelates, and rich men "waste in pride and gluttony . . . the treasure of poor men, the while they be in much pain and wretchedness in body and soul," that they "despise [poor men] and sometime beat them when they ask their pay. And thus lords devour poor men's goods in gluttony and waste and pride, and they perish for [hardship], and hunger and thirst and cold, and their children also; and if their rent be not readily paid . . . they [are] pursued without mercy, though they be never so poor and needy and overcharged with age, feebleness and loss of [possessions] and with many children." These lords do not help a poor man to his right "but rather withhold poor men their hire, for which they have spent their flesh and their blood. And so in a manner they eat poor men's flesh and blood and are man killers . . . Wherefore God says by the Prophet Isaiah, that such lords are the fellows of thieves and their hands are full of blood." Wycliffe's writings were seized and burned for more than two centuries, and yet I can read to you from a stout volume of his English works. His tradition never was successfully suppressed. In 1523, when Martin Luther's writings had begun to appear in England, Bishop Cuthbert Tunstall wrote to Erasmus that "it is no question of pernicious novelty, it is only that new arms are being added to the great band of Wycliffite heretics." The similarity is more than coincidence, since Wycliffe's Latin writings circulated widely in Europe. If Lollardy was indeed a part of the identity and memory the Puritans brought with them to America, the evidence is clearest in the nature of their spirituality—Lollards said, "Lord, our belief is that thine house is man's soul."

Another piece of evidence is again a difference between colonial Massachusetts and the colonial South. Even after the Restoration, London seems to have had relatively little interest in New England. The South was another matter. King Charles II commissioned John Locke, of all people, to produce a document called the Fundamental Constitutions of Carolina, at the time a general name for the South. "Out of his grace and bounty" the king granted these laws so that "we may avoid erecting a numerous democracy." Presumably this is a comment on the recently ended Commonwealth period or New England, or both. This constitution is meant to erect instead a land-based aristocracy, descending ranks of narrowing privilege, a hereditary nobility owning by inheritance land they cannot divide among heirs or otherwise alienate, so that the ranks and orders will remain as they are forever. These ranks have fanciful names: the palatine; beneath him landgraves, from the German; beneath him caziques, from the Haitian. Baronies figure somehow. Seldom mentioned are the leet-men, but conclusions can be drawn. Item twenty-two specifies that leet-men are subject to their particular lord without appeal: "Nor shall any leet-man or leet-woman have liberty to go off from the land of their particular lord and live anywhere else, without license obtained from their said lord, under hand and seal." Here is item twenty-three: "All the children of leet-men shall be leet-men, and so to all generations." This model was not realized, but the fact that the royal government would have been supportive of a colonial neo-feudalism through all the years that passed between Charles II and George III, from 1669 to 1775, can be assumed to have had an effect. In light of this the distinctiveness, indeed the radicalism, of the Massachusetts codes and social order can be seen as highly intentional. Item 110 of the Fundamental Constitutions of Carolina says, "Every freeman of Carolina shall have absolute power and authority over his negro slaves, of what opinion or religion soever"—in other words, Christian or not. The Laws and Liberties of Massachusetts says, "There shall never be any bond slavery, villienage, or Captivitie amongst us unles it be lawful Captives taken in just warres," or people who are indentured. These are regrettable exceptions, but the code specifies that "these shall have all the liberties and Christian usages which the law of god established in Israell concerning such persons doeth morally require." Again we see the liberalizing influence of Moses.

With all respect to the great Southerners who contributed so much wisdom and eloquence to independent America, New England had already made a long experiment with—by the standards of the world at the time—liberty and equality. The impositions of the royal government being limited in their case, they were relatively free to honor the old Lollard passion for ordinary people—first of all, as any good Wycliffites would do, by providing for their education. When John Eliot made his translation of the Bible into the Algonquin language, published in 1663, he was attempting to do what Wycliffe did when he put it into English.

I have not addressed every accusation made against the Puritans. Many have no basis in fact, or they fail to take into account English and European standards of the time, which very often make their severities seem mild. And the polemic against the Puritans has simply been done to death, a cultural tic that is mindless yet full of consequence because it leaves us without any sense of the origins of elements of our culture that we should be aware of, so that they can be valued and perpetuated, and so that the impetus behind them can be understood. It is true that the laws passed in the Southern colonial assemblies—when they were allowed to meet—were more rational and humane than those imposed on them from London. Still, they are no model for a free society. We need to give the Puritans their due.

•

New England was a long moment, an accident of history. The earliest immigrants meant to land in Virginia. If they had succeeded, no doubt many things would have been different, for them and for us. That some of them did make it through the first winter and the disasters that followed seems again almost accidental. But they did, and they became a small but growing society. They were very strongly shaped by events, past and present, on the other side of the ocean—the Thirty Years' War and then the English Civil Wars and the Commonwealth and its collapse, which brought a flood of refugees of just the kind to reinforce an identity already formed. This is a singular history. If New England in the nineteenth century did not rise to what we considered—just a few months ago—to be civilized standards in its response to immigration, it is fair to consider the standards of those times and our own vulnerability to the appeal of nativism, for which, as an exercise in honesty, we should shoulder the blame ourselves. In any case, the influx of people with very different histories, together with the pull of the opening continent, brought the Puritan moment to an end.

This does not mean that its influence has ended. There is still some point in speaking about this country in terms of its Puritan origins. They originated an understanding of law that made it a system of liberties rather than of prohibitions. They educated one another and themselves fervently and wrote and printed with a passion to be expected of people whose ancestors might once have been accused of heresy for knowing the Ten Commandments. We still educate very broadly, though we seem to be forgetting where this impulse came from, that it was at its source a sharing out of the riches of civilization, prompted by that old belief that the mind was meant to be God's dwelling place. Education was, and I would say it still is, by far the most generous approach that can be made to the mysteries of mind, self, and soul, all of which know themselves as they create themselves. I approach tautology here, but this seems to be in the nature of the subject.

•

Recently I wrote an essay on Jonathan Edwards's *Treatise Concerning Religious Affections*—that is, on the inward experience of religion. I was struck by how suspicious he was of these affections, how prone the religious were, in his opinion and no doubt in his own experience as well, to self-deception, arrogance, and hypocrisy. By itself this treatise might read as profound alienation from or disillusionment with his tradition and community. But Edwards provides lengthy footnotes, which cite great Puritan writers of the previous century, most of them English. They and he take the same view of the matter. The discipline of the mind to avoid presumption or any other abuse of the capacity to enjoy the knowledge of God is a great subject among them—before, during, and after their Revolution. So far from expressing alienation, Edwards was invoking classic Puritanism and also carrying the tradition forward. No doubt his cautionary severity was called up by the passions of the Great Awakening, but he had major authorities ready to hand to second him in his warnings, which address tendencies in the human mind toward self-deception, hypocrisy, and the rest. It would be a crude reading of all this to assume that Puritans must have been more inclined to these faults than the generality of Christians. Since they were for them a primary sin, and a cause of sins, they may have managed to be a little less guilty of them than others. In any case, this is an important consequence of their exaltation of the mind and its processes, which had to be used well and scrupulously.

This is not a teaching of popular religion now. It has become commonplace to see those who pose as moralists and as exemplary Christians exposed in some particularly squalid act or practice, and to see them driven back, not by conscience but by exposure, upon the mercy of Jesus, who, it would seem, died to neutralize the consequences of scurrilous behavior. So far as their coreligionists are concerned, they demonstrate the benefits of having been saved, which include using Christ as a strategy of concealment in the first place, with that great mercy always up their sleeves, in case things sometime get embarrassing. Edwards says this about a style of piety flourishing among us now:

> As the love and joy of hypocrites, are all from the source of self-love; so it is with their other affections, their sorrow for sin, their humiliation and submission, their religious desires and zeal: everything is as it were paid for beforehand, in God's highly gratifying their self-love, and their lusts, by making so much of them, and exalting them so highly, as things are in their imagination.

'Tis easy for nature, as corrupt as it is, under a notion of being already some of the highest favorites of heaven, and having a God who does so protect 'em and favor 'em in their sins, to love this imaginary God that suits 'em so well, and to extol him, and submit to him, and to be fierce and zealous for him.

Far better to have a lively fear of hypocrisy, granting that it is a subtle adversary, an endless temptation, as all those old divines agree, and given the fact that Jesus himself denounced it. From Wycliffe forward, the dignity of the individual was assumed to involve his or her being capable of responsibility for his or her thought and understanding, which meant a serious familiarity with the Bible, and the kind of self-awareness the powerful pious in his time and others so utterly lacked. Faith is as close to, and different from, presumption as virtue is close to, and different from, hypocrisy. These subtleties fascinated the New Englanders, who seem never to have doubted that they were an issue for any mind in any moment.

•

It has been usual to treat the great school of writers who emerged from American Puritan culture in the nineteenth century as having put aside the constraints of the old faith and stepped into a larger conceptual world. But in fact the striking kinship among them suggests they found source and stimulus nearer home. Whatever else might be part of a Puritan world-view, the exalted mind is central for them as it is for all these writers. Emerson, Thoreau, Whitman, Melville, Dickinson, share a fascination with the commonest elements of life as they are mediated and entertained by perception and reflection. The Puritans spoke of their religion as experimental, that is, experiential. Sacredness is realized in the act of attention because reality is communicative and the mind is made, grace assisting exquisite effort, to experience its meaning. Dickinson and Melville propose minds brilliantly critical of their own perceptions, opening a vastness of suggestion in every shortfall, like a Puritan sermon. Emerson, Thoreau, and Whitman see through all convenient or dismissive categories to the actual, the vital and essential. In every case their protagonist is the perceiver. The beauty they achieve has the character of acuity rather than refinement. It equalizes. The absence of shrines and rituals and processions that interpreted the world and guided understanding of it in England and Europe reflected, as absence, a sense of immanence that gave theological meaning to anything in itself in the moment of perception—a buzzing fly, a blade of grass. The exalted mind could understand the ordinary as visionary, given discipline and desire.

The seventeenth-century English Puritan John Flavel wrote in *A Treatise of the Soul of Man* that "the soul of the poorest child is of equal dignity with the soul of Adam." He said this about a human being: "It is a most astonishing mystery to see heaven and earth married together in one person; the dust of the ground, and an immortal spirit clasping each other with such dear embraces and tender love; such a noble and divine guest to take up its residence within the mean walls of flesh and blood. Alas, how little affinity, and yet what dear affection is found betwixt them" while breath "sweetly links" them. Whitman's addresses to his soul might have had thoughts like this behind them. Whitman and any of his contemporaries might have read Flavel. He, or someone of similar mind, might well have come up in a sermon.

Perhaps we have given ourselves lives and expectations that are too small to sustain the customs and institutions the Puritans left to us. Or perhaps we will recover languages that can acknowledge the great mystery and dignity of humankind, which is essential to the best they left us. Here, at Harvard Divinity School, is the perfect place for such work to be done.

Slander

Trinity Cathedral, Little Rock, Arkansas:
February 25, 2017

My mother lived to be ninety-two. She spent her last decades, her widowhood, in a condominium in a retirement community near my brother and his family in Charlottesville, Virginia. She had lived a very private, sheltered, small-town life, never employed, devoted to her flowers and her dogs. She was a sharp-minded woman, aware and proud of her intelligence to the end of her life. She was complicated, and my relationship with her was never easy, but it was interesting, which was probably better for me, all in all. With a little difficulty we finally reached an accommodation, an adult friendship. Then she started watching Fox News.

She had a circle of friends who watched Fox News, then gathered to share that peculiar salacious dread over coffee cake. My mother would call to ask me if I thought the world was coming to an end, which put me at something of a loss. I would tell her that, according to Jesus, we would not know the day or the hour, but she would always have just been updated by one of those commentators she and her circle called by their first names, as if they were trusted friends. The authority of Jesus was not quite robust in the light of breaking news. Sharia law! A war against Christmas! Who, she would say, would attack

Christmas?! Just about nobody, of course, but the point of her question was not to doubt that the plot was afoot but to isolate these imagined malefactors from the human and American norm. These instances may sound absurd but they are real, and, like many things of their kind, they estranged and alienated a significant part of the population from those dark forces—I must include myself here—who would and could, for example, put a radical Kenyan Muslim in the White House.

I know I risk raising doubts about my mother's soundness of mind when I say that she was deeply persuaded of the truth of what she heard from Sean and Megan and Bill. But she was at least as acute as any of the millions who watched with her and learned to share the same view of the world, and, crucially, of the country.

Toward the end of her life, my mother began to be tormented by anxieties and regrets. I, her daughter, a self-professed liberal, was one of those who had ruined America. I would go to hell for it, too, a fact she considered both regrettable and just. She did shoulder some blame. She should have been far stricter than she was all those years ago when my character was still forming. A mother less Fox-saturated might have taken satisfaction from degrees and prizes, but to her they were proof that I was in league with the sinister Other; they were enhancements of a prominence I could only misuse. My mother lived out the end of her fortunate life in a state of bitterness and panic, never having had the slightest brush with any experience that would confirm her in these emotions, except, of course, Fox News. She went to her rest before she would have had to deal with the ignominy of my conversation with the president. I saw a clip of some Fox blondie saying that our conversation proved that Obama hated Christianity. Those who have read my books might think me an odd choice of interlocutor if that were the case, but having struggled in the tangled web of my mother's reasoning, I know that the impassioned little commentator might actually have found a way to believe what she said. If not, the polarization she was at that moment exploiting and making worse meant there was precious little chance her listeners would pick up a copy of *The New York Review of Books* to read the conversation for themselves.

•

One mother, one life to live by which she would judge the fruitfulness of her own life, one twilight in which human mortality becomes at the same time mythic and real. I wish it could have ended better for both of us. What a weird intrusion, these loud voices shouting down memory and reflection and assurance, nullifying the most intimate kinship. My mother loved this country and was deeply persuaded that it was in peril, first of all in having tempted the wrath of God with all its liberalism. Again, this was not dementia. She and her friends were actually or virtually housebound. If they had kept their eyesight and their driver's licenses, I have no doubt that some of them would have been out shopping for guns, as so many of the young and strong were doing at the same time for the same reasons.

This is, of course, the age of the weird intrusion. We have voices in our heads that can neutralize experience and displace the world we observe with a much more urgent and dramatic reality, a reality with a plotline and strongly identified characters, with villains bent on enormity and all that is sacred in desperate need of rescue. For my mother and her friends, this was excitement, a big dose of adrenaline, and its appeal in their circumstances is understandable, at least by comparison with its attraction for people who are healthy and mobile and who still enjoy some exposure to the world and some control over their lives. I remember when I was a child, walking out of a

movie theater and finding the world outside utterly bland and
dull. Now we can all impose Technicolor fantasies on that
world, if we are so inclined. Infotainment they call it.

•

The text for today is from the Epistle of James 3:5–10:

> How great a forest is set ablaze by a small fire! And the
> tongue is a fire. The tongue is placed among our mem-
> bers as a world of iniquity; it stains the whole body, sets
> on fire the cycle of nature, and is itself set on fire by hell.
> For every species of beast and bird, of reptile and sea
> creature, can be tamed, and has been tamed by the human
> species, but no one can tame the tongue—a restless evil,
> full of deadly poison. With it we bless the Lord and
> Father, and with it we curse those who are made in the
> likeness of God. From the same mouth come blessing
> and cursing. My brothers and sisters, this ought not to
> be so.

This is very strong language indeed, cautioning against a
sin we seldom hear mentioned and perhaps have no ready name
for. James is not speaking of the lies we tell, although they
would certainly fall within his condemnation, since to speak
the truth is certainly to tame the tongue in some respects, depending on circumstances. He represents speech as literally
inflammatory, as it can be even when what is said is possibly or
arguably true or in fact true. Think of the role of informants
and spies who have shaped history in often grievous ways by
saying something true. Judas kissed Jesus in Gethsemane. The
gesture is false because it is not an expression of love or respect,
and it is true because it singles out the man Judas has promised
to betray to the authorities. We all know people who speak
damaging truth, often by violating confidences or by acting on

an indifference to tact or kindness. James was clearly concerned with more than lying, more even than slander. He is categorical in his denunciation. The tongue is a world of iniquity, a restless evil, full of deadly poison. He offers no rule for the control of it, except that we remember that other human beings are made in the likeness of God and are owed the kind of respect he is owed.

John Flavel, a seventeenth-century English Puritan, considers the thought that we might all be judged twice, once when we die and again when the full consequences of our lives have played themselves out. I find myself turning to this idea often. He says this will not have occurred until no living mind remembers any slander, any injurious word that we have spoken. He was writing in the early days of mass literacy and print, so he would have meant the memory and effect of spoken words. No need for a pulpit or a soapbox now. Any one of us can bully and slander at will. So, in light of history, perhaps we should consider his suggestion very carefully. James says the power of the tongue is utterly disproportionate to the human person, like a bit to a horse or a rudder to a ship. This is truer in an infinite degree now that we have the means to multiply and perpetuate whatever proceeds from it endlessly.

Someone must have been the first to say that Jews poison wells and cause plague. Certain strata of Christendom saw advantage in focusing hostility on the Jews, which became catastrophic when these libels spread. The tongue made women into witches, dissenters into heretics, and for centuries horror swept the world. The tongue called for lynchings. We know that Christians suffered under the same mass aversion in the early days of the faith, that they were stigmatized with rumors of atheism and cannibalism and were persecuted on these grounds. But James is clearly speaking more generally. These conflagrations are not isolated phenomena. They are a pervasive consequence of the misuse of the human power of language. They are not the fault of others who defame the Christian community but potentially and actually their fault, our fault, whenever we speak without respect for the image of God, which is the only form in which a human being can ever present herself to us.

•

I keep returning in my mind to Flavel's proposal, that we might face two judgments. Let us say that God is atemporal and omniscient. Let us say he is attentive to the words of our mouths and the meditations of our hearts. Then he can only be aware of the human context of a thought, the future history of a word. If some resentment or rage is building in a population, any of us might well share in it, justifying it to ourselves on the basis of the very consensus that will make it destructive, even lethal. That the same malice can simmer in a hundred thousand minds might lead us to believe that it must surely be based in something rational, that it is not simply another instance of the potential of ungoverned thought and language to breed firestorms. Surely we are beyond witch hunts and Jew-baiting and their like. Surely.

People enjoy sharing in consensus, especially when it allows us to indulge a guilty pleasure—to be among the despisers rather than the despised, to feel we have permission to express, if only to ourselves, hostilities we might otherwise find shameful. Catharsis can feel so good, and so can the strong sense of identity that comes with knowing who is with you and who is against you—whether this is true or not. The drama depends on your believing you have antagonists, even if a bit of invention is required to make them in any way sinister. But if our words and meditations are present to God's sight, as we so often say they are, and if for him a thousand years are like a day, he might see in any of our thoughts and utterances the impulse that in a year, a decade, or a century will disrupt peace and destroy life. From his perspective, it could be a word spoken by anyone, an acquiescence in some ordinary meanness, that tips a nation toward offense, disgrace, brutality. In other words, we might, at any moment, at every moment, stand before God as in that second judgment, guilty for our part in crimes we do not quite intend and will not live to see.

I am increasingly persuaded that we Christians need to expand our moral universe and to find a way of thinking and speaking that allows us to acknowledge the complexity of a morality deserving the name. I hear people talk of "accepting Christ as their personal savior." This is the threshold of salvation, by their lights, the narrow gate. But who is Christ? According to the Gospel of John, he was present at the Creation and central to it. Without him nothing was made that was made. I keep Greek images of Christ Pantocrator, the great figure of triumph and power, to correct for what seems to me a diminished sense of Jesus in Western religion. A diminished Christ is not Christ, just as a diminished God is not God. To put another object of worship in their place is idolatry.

Lately I have heard more frequently persons who consider themselves religious conservatives saying that those who are redeemed need not take their sins, or the sins of the redeemed in general, or their allies, too seriously. So great was the suffering of Christ, so precious his blood, so loving his nature, so profound his humbling that they can be up to things he specifically condemns, things that expose his name on earth to ridicule and contempt. And it will not matter at all from their point of view—which is to say, insofar as their personal salvation is concerned.

I would propose that this view of things turns on a faulty definition of sin. In the great majority of cases, a sin is injury done to another person, other people, whom, we must assume, God loves at least as much as he loves us. The loving-kindness Jesus models for us is very largely a matter of feeding and healing those in need of such care. The sins denounced by the prophets,

or, if you prefer, by God through the prophets, are sins that
create poverty and exploit and abuse the poor. Thou shalt not
kill, steal, bear false witness. John Calvin says it is theft to fail
to show anyone the honor due him, always implying James's
standard, the honor due the image of God. This standard was
of great interest to the fourteenth century, and again to the
Reformation, but I haven't seen much attention paid to it in the
last few centuries. A great lapse, a great loss. In any case, Jesus
makes it clear that he is one among the hungry, the thirsty, the
naked, the imprisoned, which is very much to the same point.
In the grandeur of his triumph he is also judge of the quick and
the dead. We are never given to believe that he will overlook
the scorn and injury done to the vulnerable. After all, in order
to identify himself with them, he parted the heavens and became a slave obedient unto death.

Those who feel they have crossed a line into assured salvation
look back on the rest of us as essentially deficient in the things
the Lord requires—not lacking in justice and mercy, perhaps,
but lacking in that special assurance that makes justice and
mercy optional and humility a possible sign of weak faith. It is
necessary, by the lights of this theology, that one believe in his
or her redeemed condition, whether it follows from a conversion experience of some kind or is maintained through the
doctrines and sacraments of a church. By extension, they must
also believe that those who have the same theory and narrative
of redemption are also saved. So they become in effect a faction
whose loyalty is to itself, without ethical conditions, putting
aside or radically devaluing the standards of Christian life, which
can be seen by them as distracting from the free and sufficient
act of God's salvation. And so we have scandals in the church,
and we have the collapse of standards in regard to public figures
and organizations who are seen to advance the interests of this
faction. Therefore the great gift of their Christianism to the

country is the disruption and loss of a moral orientation that for cultural and historical reasons has always been Christian.

Putting aside for the moment the subject of truth, of how the word *truth* is to be understood, there is the issue I mentioned earlier, that is, the way we speak of and to one another, and the consequences that follow from the words we speak, as well as from the kind of speech we give our attention to. In Matthew 12:36–37, Jesus says, "I tell you, on the day of judgment you will have to give an account for every careless word you utter, for by your words you will be justified, and by your words you will be condemned." This seems to me to imply that one's spiritual state remains an open question until the end of life, so far as we can be aware. Be that as it may. It is interesting to note that the religious right and the dystopian news outlets arose together. I speculate that this Christianism I have spoken of needed proof of a radical qualitative difference between itself and society at large. So: Secularism bestrides the land like Gog and Magog, and Christians are treated with contempt and hostility. None of this is true, but it is a cherished belief that allows comfortable people to reckon themselves among the martyrs. This need to see unredeemed America as a netherworld has been served by tales of flaming inner cities and raging crime rates. The difference between reality according to Walter Cronkite and reality according to Glenn Beck is to be seen as a measure of decline in the culture, not as the recent exploitation of a burgeoning market for bleak and angry sensationalism. Again, the fact that these outlets are themselves vulgar and bent on inflicting injury is not a problem, since by these means they fuel the excitements of the religious right. This certainly ought not to be considered a benefit to them as Christians, but it does indeed consolidate them as a faction.

Of course Christianity has never been innocent of this sort of thing. I grant that claims to traditionalism going back to antiquity can be made by those prone to unhealthy collective excitements. I am about to write a series of lectures on the Old Testament, a text with which Christian interpretation has always struggled mightily. My impulse tends to be to find my way back to an early stage in the development of an issue, since the trajectory it will follow is often established then. I have just read Saint John Chrysostom's *Homilies on the Obscurity of the Old Testament*. *Chrysostom* means "golden-mouthed," a sobriquet given to him because of the famous eloquence of his preaching. He was the bishop of Constantinople, a prolific contemporary of Saint Augustine and Saint Jerome, a figure of great importance to the subsequent development of the church. To explain the obscurity, from the point of view of Christian readers, of the Hebrew Bible, he mentions the problems that always arise in translation, the difficulty of approaching any experience that is new to one, and so on. But the explanation he dwells on and elaborates is of another kind altogether: The Hebrew Scriptures, he says, are obscure because God did not want the Jews to understand them. Their prophets were actually writing for and in anticipation of Christians. He says, "They [the prophets] forecast many troubles for Jews as well as the fact that whereas they will be rejected, we will be given a place, and the fact that the Temple will be destroyed to rise no more, while Jerusalem will fall and be trampled on by all." And "if they [the Jews] heard this from the inspired authors unmistakably, they would immediately have killed those telling them this," being "frenzied and savage," "bloodthirsty people." He says, "They would also have burnt the inspired books themselves if they understood their contents." He may not have invented the use of anti-Semitism as a hermeneutical tool, but he has certainly provided an explicit early instance of it. If his words have influenced subsequent interpretation, this is surely not their final, gravest consequence. In any case, this virus sleeps in the cells of even very modern biblical scholarship.

Irony of ironies, Chrysostom turns from this diatribe against the Jews to an exhortation against speaking ill of people. There could hardly be a more terrible instance of the power of the evil he condemns than the impact of his own words on the subsequent history of Jews and Christendom. Do we hear comparable slanders now? I suppose that depends on whether or not we believe Hillary Clinton might really have been running a child prostitution ring from a pizza parlor. There seems to be very little limit to how bizarre or scurrilous these rumors can be and yet survive and multiply. As I have said, there are those who devoutly wish the worst to be true. So rumors have a medium conducive to their growth.

When Chrysostom was wise he was very wise indeed, and his comments on evil or merely ill-considered speech are very relevant to our own historical moment. Again, he is speaking to Christians, now in terms of their obligations as Christians, which include that rather neglected virtue, self-restraint. He says, "Just as if we opened the tombs we would fill the cities with pestilence, so if we had no qualms about opening vile mouths we would fill all our associates with a worse disease. Hence the necessity of placing a door, a bar and a curb on our mouth." And, "Let us teach the need to keep a curb on our tongue and not simply to give vent to everything that comes to mind, not to criticize the brethren, not to bite and devour one another. People who do this in words are worse than those biting the body: the latter bite the body with their teeth, the former bite the soul with their words, they wound reputations, they leave an incurable injury." And, "Instead of bruiting abroad others' vices let us cloak them over . . . Let us not bite and chew each others' wounds." This is a ghastly metaphor, worse than the other he offers, of vile talk as flies that land on wound after wound, carrying infection everywhere. Then again, this present time, when we find ourselves struggling to maintain our civic life because of our loss of the ethos

of restraint, civility, and truthfulness, could lead us to consequences we can not yet foresee, when his metaphors will seem
entirely apt. We know this can happen.

It may be the case that Chrysostom's prohibitions against
vile language pertain especially to "the brethren," fellow
Christians. Perhaps it is they who are to be spared these attacks.
Certainly they seem always to have needed to have such restraint preached to them. Paul tells the church at Galatia, "The
whole law is summed up in a single commandment, 'You shall
love your neighbor as yourself.' If, however, you bite and devour one another, take care that you are not consumed by one
another." To the Ephesians he says, "Let no evil talk come out
of your mouths, but only what is useful for building up, as
there is need, so that your words may give grace to those who
hear . . . put away from you all bitterness and wrath and anger
and wrangling and slander, together with all malice, and be
kind to one another, tenderhearted, forgiving one another, as
God in Christ has forgiven you." We in this Christian country
are consuming one another now, bringing disgrace to the faith
with our internecine ferocities, then alarmed that the church's
numbers dwindle. A thing that does tend to be forgotten in all
this is that Clinton is a Methodist, Obama is a member of the
United Church of Christ, as am I. Even if these protections
Chrysostom calls for are narrower than we might wish, they
should at least be broad enough to shelter the three of us. If
Clinton were as notoriously corrupt as—I struggle and fail to
think of a notoriously corrupt Methodist—on what grounds is
she excluded from the flock? Just the same might be asked about
Obama. Chrysostom says of Paul that "when he sees others
also passing judgment on other people's vices," he warns them,
"Do not judge before the time, before the Lord comes, who
will bring to light the hidden things of darkness and disclose
the intentions of the heart." If it is wrong to judge actual vices,
how much worse must it be to condemn others for invented

vices, concocted for no other reason than to slander and wound them? There are other inducements now, too—ratings, politics, the gratification of an audience that wants to hear the worst, then, perhaps, share it over coffee cake. Perhaps a new vocabulary is needed for new variants of old sins. Perhaps not.

These days people can be heard wondering how we have come to this place of rancor and division, and how we can move beyond it. To effect change in a culture so vast and complex as this one would seem imponderably difficult. But there are a good many Christians among us, even if only the faction who consider themselves an embattled minority can claim to qualify. They, and all the rest of us who accept the authority of Scripture, can find many passages that describe the Christian life, which is, as it says in Titus 3:2, "to speak evil of no one, to avoid quarreling, to be gentle, and to show every courtesy to everyone." In Galatians, on the one hand Paul says, "The fruit of the Spirit is love, joy, peace, patience, kindness, generosity, faithfulness, gentleness, and self-control." And on the other hand, in the first chapter of Romans, he lists the sins of the worst pagans. Among other things, "they were filled with every kind of wickedness, evil, covetousness, malice. Full of envy, murder, strife, deceit, craftiness, they are gossips, slanderers, God-haters." The list is long. I quote from it to make the point that malicious speech ranks among the gravest transgressions. In the third chapter, again describing sinfulness, Paul quotes from Psalms and Isaiah: "There is no one who shows kindness, not even one." And, "Their throats are open graves; they use their tongues to deceive." And, "The venom of vipers is under their lips." And, "Their tongues are full of cursing and bitterness." He tells the Colossians that as Christians they must give up old sins. "You must get rid of all such things—anger, wrath, malice, slander, and abusive language from your mouth." To Timothy he says, "Avoid profane chatter, for it will lead people into more and more impiety, and their talk will spread like

310 WHAT ARE WE DOING HERE?

gangrene." Peter says, "Rid yourself . . . of all malice and all
guile, insincerity, envy, and all slander." Damaging speech, the
use of words to do harm, is clearly both a mark of sinfulness
and a major sin in its own right. Other kinds of evil actions
proceed from it. So Scripture tells us, so history tells us.

In the ordinary course of life we can evaluate what we hear
and apply standards of plausibility. People who seem to respect
the norms of courtesy and rectitude and abide by them are
probably not up to anything too outlandish, so we give them
the benefit of the doubt—unless we nurse a discreditable motive of our own for wanting to see them taken down a peg.
Only if some kind of evidence emerges or if we see something
with our own eyes are we inclined to consider a slander to reflect more discredit on the person who is its object than on the
bearer of opprobrium. Gossips are a type, often resentful, generally looking to establish a bond of friendship or intimacy at
the expense of someone's privacy or reputation. If we choose
to tolerate them, it is often because we can't avoid them. But we
know who they are, and this is another means we have of appraising what they say.

But when the objects of slander are not individuals but
groups, so that the departure of the generous, upright, intelligent individuals one actually knows from the characterizations
that damn the group as a whole are to the credit of those individuals only, and can be excluded from evidence that the characterization of the group is false, then people lose the stabilizing
tendency to consult experience in order to establish the limits
of probability. And when no source can be identified for whis-
pers and slurs, so that the source seems to be, or is, a consensus
among a population with which one identifies, they are granted
plausibility on these grounds. Historically one great consequence
of all this is what we now call polarization, by no means a new
phenomenon—Jews were ghettoized, African Americans were
ghettoized—and increasingly most of us isolate ourselves, mu-

tually in our case, as affinity groups or perhaps aversion groups, the division between us based not so much on origins or race or even faith as on our sources of information, or of what we credit as information. Even when we are not isolated from one another as, for example, urban and rural, even when, at holidays, we have dinner around the same table, many of us can no longer simply talk politics without igniting a battle of conflicting certitudes. A substrate of all this is religion—so, at least, many people say and believe. I acknowledge passion on the side that identifies itself as religious, but neither this passion nor the worldview that sustains it resembles religion as I understand the word. In any case, people who feel they are defending religion by looking at the world the way they do cannot, on principle, accept the legitimacy of another view of it.

My teaching and writing have given me an unusual perspective on all this. When I applied for a faculty position at the Iowa Writers' Workshop, the job description said that candidates should be able to teach the Bible as literature. People always seem to be surprised to hear this. I suppose writers are assumed to be raffish sorts with self-destructive habits and an ironic indifference to the sacred in all its forms. This notion must have set in at about the time that French painters became forever associated with berets and waxed mustaches. In my experience, writers are estimable people with an extraordinarily broad range of interests and sympathies. It is appropriate to teach Scripture in programs like ours because the Bible is so important to our literature that young writers are usually interested in it, if only because it helps them to understand earlier writers they admire. Many of them were uncomfortable at being seen carrying a Bible on campus because the groups who have been so successful at claiming Christianity as their own exclusive province have also been successful in associating it with intolerance, guns, and hostility to science, among other things. In the present environment, Christianity is not scorned or rejected because it is the Gospel of faith, hope, and love but because this Christianity of theirs, on whatever pretext, is determined to bring bad news to the poor and the stranger, and is even self-righteous about this. People who claim to care for the future of Christianity should listen to their critics rather than falling back on resentment and indulging the notion that they are embattled and abused by rampant secularism. They would learn that the faith they urge on the rest of us is precisely deficient in Christianity. If slander is a factor in all this, the first object of slander, the one traduced, is Jesus of Nazareth. And this is not the work of the atheists.

I write books that are straightforwardly Christian, and I write religious and theological essays. A question I am asked, almost always by Christians, is: Weren't you afraid? This question truly, deeply gives me the creeps. I have been confirmed again and again in the belief that I live in a free country. I write about what is on my mind. I love the scale and poetry of metaphysical theology. It has a beauty appropriate to its subject, like Bach's *St. Matthew Passion*. I am unusual in my interests, but I have suffered absolutely no negative consequences for my attention to them. I have been given extremely generous reviews by critics in this country and abroad, who often say they have no knowledge of or attraction to religion. When I am reminded that there is the possibility of a kind of fear that might have kept me from living out my own interests, the thought appalls me. When I think how many people there must be who suppress their interests, fundamentally misdirect their lives, out of groundless and uncharitable fear of other people, I am appalled all over again. The worst part of it is that they imagine they are coerced by other people when they are in fact trapped in their own fears, and they resent those imaginary others for posing this dreadful threat. They imagine the outside world as being attended with every undesirable trait they associate with secularism, having invented most of them or learned them from the like-minded. There is a parable about this. It was fear that made the servant bury his talent. Of course he did in fact have an alarming master to fear, and still he was shamed and impoverished for his failure to summon a necessary courage. This present brand of Christianism speaks of itself as threatened and embattled, and it approaches the rest of the country cowering and threatening and wagging its finger, then declares it is on account of its exceptional piety that so many people find it unattractive. Paul says in Galatians 5:1 that it was "for freedom Christ has set us free." We as a country claim to count ourselves fortunate in our forebears, who have, in a worldlier sense, made us free. And what is our freedom for? To be explored, lived out, enjoyed, enlarged. For freedom Washington and Lincoln made us free. The great surrender of meaningful freedom, the great cession of freedom, is the habit of fear. And we become a threat to the freedom of other people when, consciously or not, we shape our lives and our sense of the world around fearing them.

Of course there are those who are afraid that the larger world might make them depart from their faith, in the church or in a conversion experience—not intentionally, merely in the course of its own rambunctious life. The assurance of salvation is, in every form, conditional under scrutiny, so that assurance itself can be a source of fear and anxiety—of doubt, in fact, which is for some the thing most to be feared. From time to time I am asked by people at religious colleges if I was not uncomfortable teaching in a big, secular, public university. In fact I love the humane, heroic openness of my big, secular, public university, and the phenomenon of American public institutions of every kind. By my lights, a middle school that admits everyone and tries to teach everyone is more effectively Christian than a school that practices any kind of exclusion, even if no specifically religious word is ever spoken there. Many people now think in terms of a Manichaean struggle between secularism and all we hold dear. On these grounds they have launched an attack on American civil society, formerly a famous strength, which they see as secular because it is nonsectarian. It seems to be assumed that any cultural or intellectual jostling that results from a diverse population together in one place must be hostile and threatening. Lord have mercy. We are normalizing cowardice.

Nevertheless, there is the great problem of distinguishing slander from the normal give-and-take we talk about, perhaps too indulgently, and apart from the serious business of appraising the state of the country and the quality of its leadership. If we are to continue as a democracy, we must find a way to stabilize the language and temper of our debates and disputes. We can see now that intemperate speech can spiral off into fear and rage, that we are as vulnerable to incendiary language as any society ever has been, that we become loyal to our hostilities and reduce our words to weapons, a phenomenon not unrelated to the recent tendency of some to amass weapons. Any of us knows as experience the difference between evaluating the truth of an accusation and seizing on it to fuel our resentments. Always, but certainly in situations when great things are at stake, it behooves Christians to think and act like Christians. This would mean practicing self-restraint, curbing our speech, remembering that our adversaries are owed the respect due to the divine image, which no one can be redeemed enough to be excused from honoring. Dystopian media arose with this Christianity of the Right. It would lose a great part of its market share if Christian standards were applied to its product, and then the atmosphere of this dear country would change in a week. The truth about Obama's birthplace or Trump's relations with Russia will never be established to the satisfaction of everyone, but Christians know truth of another order, that human beings are created in the image of God. They are created equal, endowed with unalienable rights—that is, unalienable claims on our respect. This is the truth that has made us free.

Acknowledgments

I would like to thank my invaluable assistant, Margaret MacInnis, and my wonderful agent, Ellen Levine.